the
year-round
garden

the year-round garden

GEOFF STEBBINGS

First published in 2005 by Collins

an imprint of HarperCollinsPublishers

77–85 Fulham Palace Road, London, W6 8JB

www.collins.co.uk

© HarperCollinsPublishers

The majority of photographs in this book were taken by Tim Sandall, with contributions from the author. All other images: p172 (top), p215, p217 (top right), p227 (all images), p228 (top left & bttm), p233 (all images) – Harpur Garden Library; p217 (top left), p226 (top), p231 (both images), p232 (left), p234 (top) – Garden World Images; p216 (both images), p218 (bttm left & right), p220 (middle & bttm), p222 (bttm), p223 (top & bttm left), p229 (bttm), p230 (bttm right), p234 (bttm left & right) – The Garden Picture Library; p218 (bttm right), p221 (bttm left & right), p229 (top right), p230 (bttm left) – Photos Horticultural. Thanks also to David Austin Roses, Bowling Green Lane, Albrighton, Wolverhampton WV7 3HB.

Front cover photography by Alamy Images.

Back cover photography by Tim Sandall.

Design and editorial: Focus Publishing, Sevenoaks, Kent

Project editor: Guy Croton

Designer: David Etherington

For HarperCollins

Senior managing editor: Angela Newton

Art Director: Mark Thomson

Design Manager: Luke Griffin

Editor: Alastair Laing

Production: Chris Gurney

A CIP catalogue record for this book is available from the British Library.

ISBN 0-00-719310-6

Colour reproduction by Colourscan

Printed and bound in Italy by L.E.G.O.

Contents

Introduction

Everyone dreams of having a garden that is beautiful all year round, filled with colour and scent and interest. Yet we live in a climate with distinct seasons and few plants look the same in winter as they do in summer.

Rather than be defeated by the changing seasons, we should rejoice in the variety that they bring and make the most of the each time of the year. There are plants that look attractive all year round and most of these are evergreen; ideal for gardeners who do not want to spend much time in their gardens. These plants are especially important in winter, but a garden filled with these would be dull after a while, simply because they do not change enough to attract our attention.

So, despite their often fleeting displays, we like to grow seasonal flowers that brighten our spirits when they are at their peak. Snowdrops would hardly be noticed if they flowered in summer but, when little else is stirring in the garden, their delicate blooms tell us that, even if spring has not yet arrived, it is not far away.

Showy peony flowers and majestic lupins and irises may not be with us for long, but our gardens would be

"With so many wonderful plants to grow, there really is no reason why your garden should not be beautiful all year round."

all the poorer without them and bedding plants, often considered time-consuming and expensive because they are killed by frost, give bold splashes of colour when we are most often relaxing and entertaining in our gardens.

The key is to have a mix of plants, some of which give a good background for a long time, often grown primarily for their foliage, and other plants that deliver bold blasts of colour that entice us out of the house and into the open air.

Knowing your plants, the conditions that they prefer, how big they will become and when they will flower, is the key to a successful garden, but then you can have

"This is the joy of gardening; discovering through experience which plants you like and which plants like you."

some real fun as you let your imagination and artistry run riot. You can then combine plants for effect, grouping plants with complementary colours, diverse forms and shapes. As you grow your plants you will discover many things about them, such as if they need staking, when they bloom and whether they grow well in your garden. Every year is different and weather conditions and where you live will affect their growth and exact flowering time.

This is the joy of gardening, discovering through experience which plants you like and which plants like you. No book can replace this hands-on experience, but knowing the basics can help you avoid some mistakes.

Most plants can be moved if they are in the wrong place and you can divide and grow more of the plants you love. But grow a mixture if you want an interesting garden all year round; a garden filled with just poppies will be lovely for a month but dull the rest of the year. With so many wonderful plants to grow, there really is no reason why your garden should not be beautiful all year round.

spring

Ajuga reptans 'Catlin's Giant'

Ajuga reptans (bugle) is a wild plant of grassy banks and woodland edges and there are many variegated and coloured-leaf forms; all are attractive. But 'Catlin's Giant' is special because of its size. The leaves are 15cm (6in) long and the spikes of blue flowers can reach 20cm (8in) high. The foliage is deep purple in colour and increases the intensity of the blue flowers. It is evergreen and forms a thick, weed-suppressing carpet all year, but its real beauty is in spring when in flower. It is easy to grow and will survive almost anywhere but it is at its best in damp soil in light shade, where it will also be less prone to mildew. Bright sun, however, does bring out the best foliage colour.

Spring companion
Tulipa tarda

Autumn companion
Colchicum speciosum

Arabis caucasica 'Flore Pleno'

Along with aubrieta, Arabis is a common ingredient of rockery displays in spring, providing the white or pink shades. Most arabis are easily grown from seed but they also set seed, which reduces the duration of their display. *Arabis caucasica* 'Flore Pleno' has double flowers on spikes that look like miniature stocks, though without the fragrance. The blooms look almost like pure white roses and the whole plant, which forms mats of greyish foliage, is buried under the profuse flowers. Arabis prefers a sunny, well-drained spot and does not thrive in shade. To keep it compact, trim it hard after flowering and use some of the new shoots as cuttings.

Spring companion
Myosotis

Summer companion
Dianthus 'Doris'

Armeria maritima

Commonly called thrift, Armeria is a rather forgotten, old-fashioned plant. At first, it forms dense domes and then hummocks of narrow evergreen foliage. It is the perfect edging plant beside paths and is also useful for rockeries. It is a seaside plant and many cliffs are covered in colonies that are indistinguishable from the grass until late spring, when it becomes a tapestry of pink. Typically the flowers are bright pink, but white-flowered plants are also available and both are easy to grow from seed. The 'Joystick Series' is a cultivated strain that is easily grown from seed and is bigger than most, reaching 25cm (10in) high when in bloom. All prefer full sun and well-drained soil.

Spring companion
Muscari 'Valerie Finnis'

Winter companion
Sempervivum arachnoideum

Aubrieta 'Whitwell Gem'

Aubrieta is almost unseen for most of the year but dominates the spring scene when covered in its bright, four-petalled flowers. Aubrieta requires full sun and withstands drought and limey soils, so is often seen cascading over low walls and sprouting from cracks in paving. Most have purple or mauve flowers and 'Whitwell Gem' is a popular variety. Although aubrieta can be grown from seed, they are best propagated by cuttings. To prevent seeds being formed on your plants aubrieta needs a tight trim immediately after flowering. This prevents the plants from becoming straggly and increases their lifespan. Cuttings can be taken of the new shoots in early summer and they root easily.

Spring companion
Arabis caucasica 'Flore Pleno'

Summer companion
Campanula poscharskyana

Bergenia 'Perfect'

Everybody recognizes the thick, plasticky leaves of bergenias, but most people content themselves with pieces passed from friends. This is a mistake, because there are lots of lovely bergenias with superior foliage and flowers in shades of pink, white and magenta. 'Perfect' is a compact variety with deep pink flowers. The blooms are also white and a pretty contrast to the more common pink varieties. This is not the toughest bergenia and it deserves a place in good soil and light shade. 'Bressingham Ruby' is similar with rich red flowers.

Summer companion
Athyrium filix-femina

Winter companion
Helleborus foetidus

Brunnera macrophylla 'Jack Frost'

Everybody loves the delicate blue flowers of forget-me-nots and brunnera can be thought of as a giant forget-me-not but with the advantage of bold leaves. *Brunnera macrophylla* has large, heart-shaped leaves that expand as the airy sprays of pretty blue flowers, 45cm (1.5ft) high, are fading. However, 'Jack Frost', a recent introduction, has wonderful foliage that is silver with a thin green margin and green veins. Brunneras thrive in light shade and moist soil but are adaptable and resilient and will grow anywhere that is not baked dry in summer. They are

long-lived and trouble-free but if mildew appears in summer, just cut off the foliage and a new, healthy crop will appear.

Spring companion
Athyrium filix-femina

Summer companion
Alchemilla mollis

Caltha palustris

The common kingcup or marsh marigold is one of our prettiest wild flowers. The double-flowered form, 'Flore Pleno', is even more beautiful with clusters of large, green-eyed blooms of a startling brightness enhanced by the large, glossy, bright green foliage. As its name suggests, it is happiest by the edge of water and is a popular marginal pond plant, but it will grow happily in any damp soil in the border. Unfortunately, it is best in its youth and by summer the large leaves are often covered in mildew and are ugly. Surrounding it with plants such as iris will help to partially hide them after their spring glory has subsided, without covering the blooms in spring.

Summer companion
Iris sibirica

Autumn companion
Schizostylis coccinea

Convallaria majalis

If the flowers of lily-of-the-valley had no scent it would not have such a place close to our hearts. However, these stiffly nodding, pure white bells are made to be picked and brought into the home. Despite being grown in gardens for centuries, it is a wild thing at heart and unpredictable. It is a woodlander that prefers light shade and humus-rich soil but will grow in most soils. In some gardens it forms a dense clump but in others it runs around at speed, sending up its pairs of foliage at random across the border. It is best not to expect a dense

cover of foliage but to plant it under shrubs or among other plants and see what it wants to do. In autumn the foliage turns butter yellow and sometimes there are spikes of (poisonous) orange berries.

Spring companion
Omphalodes cappadocica 'Starry Eyes'

Summer companion
Geranium endressii

Corydalis solida

This tuberous perennial is usually planted as dry tubers, but because it does not withstand drought well should be planted early in autumn. It is a charming woodland plant that thrives in semi-shade or in sun, and it flowers early in spring, then disappears underground later in the season. The tubular, dusky pink flowers are carried in clusters above the feathery, grey-green leaves and create a misty, smoky effect about 15cm (6in) high. When left undisturbed it will self seed into large colonies, especially under shrubs. 'George Baker' (pictured) has flowers that are deep salmon pink but is much more expensive.

Spring companion
Epimedium grandiflorum 'Rose Queen'

Autumn companion
Caryopteris x clandonensis

Corydalis cheilanthifolia

The beautiful olive-green, finely divided foliage of this corydalis is reason enough to grow it but the flowers are beautiful, too. The leaves form a 30cm (12-inch) rosette of leaves that resemble carrot foliage but of an unusual colour and from the centre, 25cm (10in) spikes of deep yellow, tubular flowers are sent up for several months. These are followed by seedpods that ensure it spreads slowly through your borders.

Spring companion
Lamium galeobdolon 'Herman's Pride'

Autumn companion
Carex comans bronze

Doronicum orientale 'Magnificum'

Everybody loves daisy flowers and doronicums have bright golden blooms above fresh green leaves in spring. 'Magnificum' is taller than some and has several large blooms on 50cm (20in) stems. The leaves are bold and heart-shaped but have little to endear them once the flowers have finished, so it is worth planting something taller in front to disguise them in summer. 'Fruhlingspracht' is slightly shorter and has large, double, golden flowers. Doronicums prefer rich, moist soil and part shade, though they will grow almost anywhere. Drought, however, just accentuates their miserable appearance in late summer.

Spring companion
Brunnera macrophylla

Summer companion
Geranium 'Rozanne'

Epimedium grandiflorum 'Snow Queen'

Epimediums are beautiful plants for ground cover in part shade. Some creep slowly but this one forms neat clumps and the evergreen foliage is divided into heart-shaped leaflets. The young foliage is bronze and makes a wonderful foil for the clusters of pure white flowers. These are intricately shaped and have four spurs. It is one of the choosier epimediums and deserves a place in light shade with a rich, moist soil that has been improved with garden compost and mulched with leafmould or compost to retain moisture.

Spring companion
Anemone blanda

Autumn companion
Tricyrtis formosana

Epimedium x perralchicum 'Frohnleiten'

This is one of several epimediums that slowly creep to form dense clumps that smother weeds. It is not invasive, though, and is good ground cover for shade or partial sun. It is also more adaptable than most clump-forming species and will tolerate drier soils. The young foliage is bronze and very beautiful and the large, bright yellow flowers are carried on upright 40cm (1.3ft) spikes above the foliage. Though evergreen, it is best to shear off the old foliage in late winter so the new leaves and flowers can be fully appreciated.

Spring companion
Dryopteris erythrosora

Winter companion
Helleborus foetidus

Euphorbia polychroma

Few plants give a brighter show than this in spring. Almost as soon as the shoots emerge from the soil the dazzling acidic yellow bracts start to expand. They grow and get brighter as the shoots reach 30cm (12in) high. A lime yellow dome is produced that gradually turns to green as the bracts fade but it is always neat and tidy and ideal for the front of a border. It will grow in any soil in a sunny spot. 'Candy' has purple foliage that rather dilutes the acid yellow effect but is more interesting later in the season.

Spring companion
Brunnera macrophylla 'Jack Frost'

Summer companion
Anthemis tinctoria 'Sauce Hollandaise'

Lamium maculatum 'White Nancy'

Lamiums suffer from their common name of dead nettle which is hardly glamorous, but the finest are beautiful plants. Often recommended for ground cover in dry shade, *Lamium maculatum* can be a disappointment because it will wilt and get mildew in summer. So plant it in light shade and keep it watered for the best growth and if it looks untidy just shear off the growth and mulch the plant with 2cm (0.8in) of garden compost. Then water it thoroughly for a fresh new burst of growth. 'White Nancy' forms low carpets of silver leaves and has a flush of pure white flowers in spring and a few more throughout the year.

Spring companion
Hosta 'Halcyon'

Winter companion
Iris foetidissima

Lamium galeobdolon 'Hermann's Pride'

Lamium galeobdolon is a thug that will cover vast areas of soil in sun or shade with its marbled foliage on arching stems. It should be planted with care. 'Hermann's Pride', however, is a dwarfer plant with silvery leaves and lots of yellow flowers. It has better manners, though it will still spread to form a 45cm (18in) high carpet. It is best suited to semi-wild areas where the flowers will attract bumblebees and wildlife can ramble under its cover.

Spring companion
Euphorbia amygdaloides var. *robbiae*

Autumn companion
Cotoneaster horizontalis

Lamium orvala

This is a giant lamium that will impress your friends, who may well look at the flowers and think it is an orchid. It forms large clumps of stems with deeply veined, nettle-like leaves on stems. These stems reach 60cm (2ft) high and the large, exotic flowers are produced in clusters from the base to the top. The blooms are pale purple in colour and intriguingly streaked and spotted with white and purple. It is not a ground cover plant but thrives in light shade in most soils and is most suitable under shrubs in large areas. It is rather dull after flowering and is more a

quiet rather than a showy character. There is also an attractive, white-flowered form available.

Summer companion
Digitalis purpurea

Autumn companion
Persicaria campanulata

Lathyrus vernus 'Alboroseus'

Most lathyrus are climbers, but this is a charming, small herbaceous plant that can be fitted into any garden. The leaves appear in spring and are flushed with red. Almost before they are fully developed the bright pink and white pea flowers start to open, and as the plant grows, more flowers are produced until the plant is about 25cm (10in) high and studded in pink. Long seed pods develop but you should trim these off neatly to leave a

hummock of pleasant leaves for the rest of summer. It thrives in most soils in sun or partial shade and grows slowly into a dense clump.

Spring companion
Hosta 'Halcyon'

Summer companion
Iris innominata

Omphalodes cappadocica 'Starry Eyes'

Blue flowers are common in spring but few have the cheeky beauty of this easy herbaceous plant. It is deciduous and as the fresh green, heart-shaped leaves start to unfurl, short clusters of bright blue flowers, like forget-me-nots but in two shades of blue with a starry eye, start to open and continue for many weeks, forming a pastel carpet 20cm (8in) high. The foliage then covers the soil forming a mat of pleasant foliage. It creeps slowly but is never a nuisance and thrives in most soil in light shade.

Spring companion
Milium effusum 'Aureum'

Autumn companion
Liriope muscari 'John Burch'

Primula vulgaris

The wild primrose is such a pretty flower that it deserves a place in every garden, but grow it from seed or buy cultivated plants, never dig it up from the wild. The big hybrids that you can buy in spring are flashy but rarely last well in the garden, whereas the wild plant has a special charm and is one of the first flowers of spring. It is a plant of semi-shady places and thrives best in similar situations in the garden where it should then seed itself around. If you grow other coloured primroses or polyanthus in your garden it will hybridize and you will end up with all sorts of colours, but none are prettier than the real thing.

Spring companion
Pulmonaria 'Occupol'

Summer companion
Athyrium filix-femina

Primula veris

The wild cowslip flowers slightly later than the primrose and carries its fragrant, small, deep yellow flowers in nodding bunches above the leaves. It also likes slightly different conditions, preferring more sun and drier soils. It is easy to grow from seed and often seeds itself down sunny, grassy banks – plant it at the top and watch it seep down with gravity. If naturalized in grass, do not make the first cut until the seed pods have ripened and shed seeds. Also, leave the cut grass for a week before you rake it up so that the seed can be shed.

Spring companion
Erysimum 'Bowle's Mauve'

Summer companion
Euphorbia dulcis 'Chameleon'

Primula florindae

This Tibetan giant cowslip is one of the latest primulas to bloom. It has 60cm (2ft) stems of large, nodding yellow flowers above large, lush leaves, and the flowers carry a sweet perfume. It is one of the easiest of the large primulas to grow, loving boggy soil but coping with average soils, too, and even tolerating lime. Once established it will self-seed to form large clumps. There are coloured forms with amber and copper flowers.

Summer companion
Alchemilla mollis

Winter companion
Luzula sylvatica 'Aurea'

Primula denticulata

Commonly called the drumstick primula, this is a spectacular spring plant with round heads, packed with yellow-eyed flowers. They are typically lavender or mauve but there are also white, pink and magenta varieties that are all beautiful. A well-grown plant will produce dozens of 'drumsticks' 45cm (1.5ft) high, but young plants, such as you are likely to buy, are much more dainty. It is a bog plant that will grow in any moist soil, but if the soil is not wet, it should be given light shade. After flowering, like most other primulas, it is a dull plant and should be positioned beside something that will hide it.

Spring companion
Astilbe 'Cattleya'

Autumn companion
Persicaria affinis 'Superba'

Pulmonaria 'Occupol'

Pulmonarias are grown for their silver-marked foliage and their early flowers, usually in shades of blue and pink. Most open from pink buds and the blooms change to blue as the flowers age. Contrary to this, the 'Occupol' (Opal) has pale blue flowers. These open early and last for several months. The early flowers are on short stems but these reach as much as 30cm (12in) as the season progresses. As the flowers fade the silver-spotted foliage develops and is attractive all summer. Pulmonarias are prone to mildew and if the leaves become affected you can shear them off in summer and fresh new leaves will grow. 'Majeste' has leaves that are almost completely silver, bright blue and pink flowers.

Spring companion
Primula vulgaris

Autumn companion
Hakonechloa macra 'Alboaurea'

Pulmonaria rubra 'Redstart'

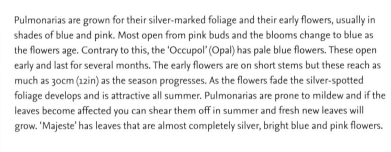

This is usually the earliest pulmonaria to flower, with bright, coral red flowers that show up well against the light green foliage. After flowering, the leaves form good ground cover but are plain, unspotted and not exciting. Like other pulmonarias, this thrives in light shade and moist soil and you should remove the dead flower stems to make the leaves look neater and to prevent seeding. They are all easy to divide in spring.

Spring companion
Lamium galeobdolon 'Hermann's Pride'

Winter companion
Ruscus aculeatus

Pulmonaria angustifolia 'Azurea'

This pulmonaria has flowers of the brightest gentian blue with only the merest hint of red, while the foliage is plain green. It only grows 20cm (8in) high and makes a perfect carpet under deciduous shrubs. Like all pulmonarias it is a useful early nectar source for bumble bees.

Spring companion
Doronicum x *excelsum* 'Harpur Crewe'

Autumn companion
Anemone x *hybrida* 'September Charm'

Pulsatilla vulgaris

Although this is a rare wild flower of chalk downland, this beautiful plant is quite common in gardens. Called the Pasque flower, it usually opens its rich purple flowers in time for Easter. The buds, that are coated in silvery hairs, emerge from the soil with very few leaves and are usually nodding with golden centres. As the season progresses, the grey, carroty foliage develops and the flowers are transformed into fluffy seedheads 20cm (8in) high. It must have well-drained soil and full sun and hates to be dug up and divided once established. Ideally, seed is the best way to propagate it. Plants with white and various shades of pink and red are available.

Spring companion
Erysimum 'Bowle's Mauve'

Autumn companion
Origanum laevigatum 'Herrenhausen'

Saxifraga x *urbium* 'Variegata'

London Pride is an evergreen ground cover plant that slowly spreads across the soil by forming rosettes of foliage into a dense cover. In this variegated plant the leaves are spotted with yellow throughout the year but it is in spring, when the slender spikes of tiny white and pink flowers form a froth over the plants that it is most beautiful. When these fade they should be sheared off to keep the plants neat. It grows in sun or semi-shade and is one of the best ground cover plants because it is not an aggressive spreader, needing little maintenance and being longlived.

Spring companion
Alchemilla mollis

Autumn companion
Euonymus fortunei 'Emerald 'n' Gold'

Tolmiea menziesii 'Taff's Gold'

This is a curious ground cover plant that is often called the pick-a-back plant because a young plantlet grows from the base of each mature leaf and these can be rooted and planted separately. The plain plant is rather dull with maple-like leaves and 60cm (2ft) spikes of odd, brown, whiskery flowers. Yet 'Taff's Gold' has leaves that are spattered with yellow and it is a bright and fun plant for ground cover in shade or partial sun. It will withstand almost all soil types but grows best in moist soil, wilting in dry conditions. It quickly recovers when watered but looks best when growing luxuriantly.

Spring companion
Epimedium x perralchicum 'Frohnleiten'

Autumn companion
Stipa arundinacea

Trillium grandiflorum

This is the most common of the North American wood lilies and one of the most beautiful. Growing from a sturdy rootstock, each upright stem has three leaves and if the plant is established, in the centre of these is a single, pure white flower with three large petals. This is a woodland plant and must have moist, acidic soil that is rich with humus such as garden compost or leaf mould. It will thrive in partial shade and will tolerate sun if the soil is moist at all times. It grows to about 40cm (1.5ft) high, and large plants may be 60cm (2ft) across. It grows painfully slowly, however. The double 'Flore Pleno' is even more beautiful but hideously expensive.

Spring companion
Pulmonaria angustifolia

Winter companion
Skimmia japonica 'Rubella'

Vinca minor 'Illumination'

The lesser periwinkle is the most common ground cover plant in garden centres. It will form a dense carpet of glossy evergreen leaves on a tangle of wiry stems, growing in sun or shade and in almost any soil. It can, however, become a nuisance, as the stems reach far and wide across the garden. Never accept just the common form because there are much better plants. 'Illumination' has the typical blue flowers and lovely leaves with a butter yellow splash in the centre. It is also much less invasive. 'Atropurpurea' has wine red flowers and 'Azurea Flore Pleno' has double blue blooms. It is worth

trimming vincas hard in late winter and mulching them with garden compost. This will expose the new shoots, which produce the most flowers and make sure that you see all their beauty. The mulch also keeps the plants young and vigorous.

Spring companion
Anemone nemorosa 'Allenii'

Summer companion
Dryopteris erythrosora

Vinca major 'Maculata'

The greater periwinkle is a giant version of *Vinca minor* with much larger leaves, bigger flowers and a much bigger spread. Plants will range far and wide, reaching 45cm (1.6ft) high unless the stems find a shrub to scramble through, when they can reach 2m (6.5ft). Although it can be a nuisance, its flowers are so lovely that, where there is room, it can be a beautiful and trouble-free ground cover. 'Maculata' has leaves that are prettily marked with yellow in the centre and, like the creamy edged 'Variegata', it is less vigorous so easier to manage and will brighten up dark spots in shade. It will grow almost anywhere.

Spring companion
Euphorbia amygdaloides var. *robbiae*

Autumn companion
Euonymus alatus

Vinca difformis 'Jenny Pim'

This vinca is rather better behaved than others and prefers a little more sun because it is a native of southern Europe. In addition to a flush of flowers in very early spring it also flowers in autumn and while it usually has blue or white flowers, 'Jenny Pim' has pink flowers with white centres, a colour that is unseen in others. The leaves are deep green and the flowers show up well against these. It grows to about 30cm (12in) high and will spread far and wide if unchecked. Like all vincas, 'Jenny Pim' spreads as the arching and trailing stems root where they touch the soil. However, it is very straightforward to cut off and move the new plantlets in autumn and spring if the plant starts to take over its surroundings.

Spring companion
Euphorbia characias subsp. *wulfenii*

Autumn companion
Euonymus fortunei 'Emerald 'n' Gold'

Acacia dealbata

In recent years gardeners have been pleasantly surprised at how well this Australian tree has performed in gardens. It is generally regarded as not totally hardy, but if you live in a town, city or by the coast it is worth taking a risk with this beautiful evergreen tree. It grows rapidly and may reach 15m (50ft), with finely divided foliage and large clusters of fragrant, fluffy yellow flowers in early spring. It does not cast much shade so is suitable for medium-sized gardens. It tolerates most soils except chalk and needs a sunny, sheltered position, flowering at an early age.

Spring companion
Corokia cotoneaster

Summer companion
Acanthus mollis Latifolius Group

Amelanchier lamarkii

Amelanchiers are small trees with several seasons of interest. In spring, *Amelanchier lamarkii* has young foliage that is bronze and shortly afterwards clusters of pure white flowers cover the tree. The foliage is green in summer but turns bright scarlet and purple in autumn as the small red berries ripen. These fruits are loved by birds. It is a spreading tree that does not cast too much shade and grows to about 6m (20ft) high and across. It can also be pruned regularly to keep it as a large shrub.

Spring companion
Muscari armeniacum 'Blue Spike'

Autumn companion
Rosa rugosa

Berberis darwinii

Many berberis are just spiny and dull, but this is one of the most spectacular of all spring shrubs. The arching branches are covered with tiny, holly-like leaves all year round and in spring they are covered with clusters of golden orange flowers. As summer progresses these are followed by deep purple berries, which pleases the birds. It is a tall, arching shrub at least 2m (6.5ft) high and will flower best in a sunny spot. It grows well on most soils.

Spring companion
Viburnum x burkwoodii

Summer companion
Physocarpus opulifolius 'Diabolo'

Berberis linearifolia 'Orange King'

This evergreen berberis has narrow leaves and vicious spines and, at about 2m (6.5ft) high, is suitable for most gardens. Though it is a useful evergreen it is the flowers that make it so special. In late spring the plants are almost buried under a mass of small bright orange flowers that make a pleasant change from the mass of yellow and white in spring. It will grow in light shade but flowers best in full sun. It will tolerate pruning, immediately after flowering, to keep it neat.

Spring companion
Photinia x fraseri 'Red Robin'

Autumn companion
Hydrangea paniculata 'Grandiflora'

Camellia x williamsii 'Donation'

Despite being rather particular about soil conditions, camellias are one of our favourite shrubs. They are hardy, evergreen and have beautiful flowers when most other plants are only beginning to think about stirring from their winter slumber. 'Donation' is one of the best because it flowers freely, and the old flowers drop off before they go brown so the plant always looks fresh and bright, unlike *Camellia japonica* varieties. It has semi-double, silvery pink flowers. Varieties of *Camellia x williamsii* grow at least 2m (6.5ft) high and, like other spring-flowering types, dislike lime in the soil. If your soil is not suitable they can be grown in pots of lime-free (ericaceous) soil. They prefer light shade and cool growing conditions and must be kept moist throughout summer or the developing flower buds will not develop properly. North- and west-facing sites are best. 'J. C. Williams' has single, pale pink flowers and *C. japonica* 'Elegans' has double pink blooms.

Spring companion
Pieris japonica 'Debutante'

Autumn companion
Rehmannia elata

Ceanothus 'Concha'

The Californian lilacs are immensely popular as wall shrubs because of their fast growth and brilliant blue flowers. They need a sunny, sheltered site and prefer well-drained soil. They will then flower profusely and in late spring their branches are weighed down with thousands of tiny, blue flowers. 'Concha' has deep blue flowers that open from red buds to give a rich, violet display on plants that can reach 3m (10ft) tall and wide. All spring-flowering ceanothus should be lightly pruned after flowering to keep the plants neat, requiring support on walls and fences to support them. Ceanothus are not longlived and anything over a decade, except in sheltered, dry sites, should be considered a bonus. 'Dark Star' is an alternative with deep green, small leaves and rich indigo flowers.

Spring companion
Berberis darwinii

Summer companion
Lavatera x clementii 'Bredon Springs'

Ceanothus arboreus 'Trewithen Blue'

This is a giant ceanothus with large leaves, up to 10cm (4in) long, and large clusters of pale blue flowers that are fragrant. It is a big plant, up to 6m (20ft) in height, and can be grown as a free-standing shrub in mild gardens, but it is less hardy than the smaller-leaved ceanothus, so is only suitable for urban and coastal gardens.

Summer companion
Robinia hispida

Autumn companion
Clematis 'Gravetye Beauty'

Cercis canadensis 'Forest Pansy'

This fine small tree, up to 8m (26ft) high, is valued for its glorious foliage, but in spring the bare branches carry clusters of small, deep pink flowers. When these drop the dark burgundy, heart-shaped leaves cover the branches and retain their colour all summer until autumn when scarlet and orange tints join the purple. It grows slowly and can be trimmed to keep it small.

Summer companion
Aquilegia vulgaris 'William Guinness'

Autumn companion
Anemone x hybrida 'Honorine Jobert'

Chaenomeles speciosa 'Nivalis'

Japanese quinces are tough and easy to grow, having many seasons of interest. They are often grown as wall shrubs but are just as suitable as garden shrubs and can even be used as hedges. Most have red flowers, but 'Nivalis' has pure white flowers, just as the bright green leaves start to emerge. It has a twiggy habit and can be grown as a shrub in the open garden but often looks its best against a brick wall or dark wooden fence to show off the pale flowers. The blooms are followed by small, edible, fragrant fruits and the leaves turn yellow in autumn. Full sun produces the best flower displays, but it will tolerate light shade and any soil, including clay, is suitable.

Spring companion
Epimedium x perralchicum 'Frohnleiten'

Autumn companion
Physalis alkekengi

Cornus mas

Among a group of plants that are largely grown for their coloured stems, this large shrub is too often forgotten although it is one of the finest and toughest, spring-flowering shrubs. It is a strong, spreading shrub that can reach 5m (16ft) high and across with small, glossy leaves that turn yellow and red in autumn. Sparkling among these are bright red fruits that attract birds. In spring the end of every shoot is crowded with a dome of tiny, yellow, starry flowers that create a golden cloud. Old plants have an attractive, gnarled character and it can easily be pruned into a small tree. It will tolerate most soils, including chalk, but flowers best in full sun.

Spring companion
Vinca major 'Maculata'

Winter companion
Mahonia aquifolium 'Apollo'

Corokia cotoneaster

The wire-netting bush is a useful plant for the border as well as for hedging but is usually grown as a wall shrub. The name refers to the twisted, silvery stems and tiny leaves, and it does not have thorns. It will grow in semi-shade but is best in sun and well-drained soils where it will flower profusely. Though the flowers are small and star shaped, they can smother the plant to create a billowing golden cloud because of the small, narrow leaves. In warm summers the flowers are followed by small, orange or red berries. Corokias can be pruned as hard as you like and will grow back rapidly. *Corokia x virgata* 'Red Wonder' and 'Yellow Wonder' have fragrant flowers and red or yellow fruits.

Spring companion
Euphorbia characias subsp. *wulfeni*

Winter companion
Helleborus argutifolius

Corylopsis pauciflora

Corylopsis are elegant shrubs with spreading branches and delicate, fragrant flowers in spring. *Corylopsis pauciflora* produces pale yellow, small flowers that hang in small clusters from the twigs just before the leaves appear. The leaves have a bronze flush when young but soon turn pale green. Corylopsis need moist conditions and prefer an acid soil. They must be planted in a sheltered position that is protected from strong winds or the foliage will become scorched. Semi-shade is preferable. In ideal conditions it will grow to 3m (10ft) high and across, but this takes many years.

Spring companion
Tolmeia menziesii 'Taff's Gold'

Summer companion
Lysimachia ciliata 'Firecracker'

Crataegus laevigata 'Rosea Flore Pleno'

Although the common hawthorn is a favourite hedgerow shrub, few would plant it in their gardens, except as a hedge. Yet hawthorn is hardy, tough, tolerant of most soils and will grow in windy spots and polluted air. Therefore, this double-flowered hawthorn with pink blooms is often seen as a street tree in cities and towns, though it is not as popular now as it was 30 years ago. In late spring, the branches are covered with thousands of deep pink flowers similar to miniature roses that make a wonderful spectacle.

Unfortunately, these turn brown and look unsightly as they die, and there is no other colourful display later in the year. But if you need a tough small tree for a cold or windy garden, this might be for you.

Spring companion
Photinia x *fraseri* 'Red Robin'

Summer companion
Potentilla 'Abbotswood'

Cytisus x praecox 'Warminster'

Brooms are fine shrubs for impatient gardeners, because they grow quickly and are spectacular in bloom. The mass of small, pea-shaped flowers is enhanced by the near leafless state of the green twigs so that every petal can be appreciated. 'Warminster' has masses of creamy white blooms and, like all brooms, thrives in poor, acid, sandy soil. In fact, they do not always grow well on clay or chalky soils. Brooms must never be pruned hard but should be lightly trimmed after flowering to remove all the dead flowers. This removes developing seed pods, that would exhaust the plant, and keeps it neat. It reaches 1.2m (4ft) high and C. x *praecox* 'Allgold' has deep gold flowers.

Spring companion
Poncirus trifoliata

Summer companion
Artemisia absinthium 'Lambrook Silver'

Daphne mezereum

Daphnes have a reputation for being difficult to grow, and indeed some are. But at least the mezereon is common and easy to replace if it does die. It is deciduous and in early spring four-petalled, bright pink flowers that are wonderfully fragrant appear from its leafless branches. In warm summers these are followed by bright orange, but poisonous, berries. The shrub has an upright habit and prefers full sun and well-drained soil, and tolerates chalky soils. Young plants usually grow well but they often have virus diseases, which appear as yellow streaks in the leaves.

Plants can live ten years or more and exceed 1m (3ft) in height but they can suddenly die for no obvious reason.

Spring companion
Pulsatilla vulgaris

Autumn companion
Physalis alkekengi

Daphne bholua

Most daphnes have beautiful, fragrant flowers, but this Himalayan species really excels. There are various forms that are either deciduous or semi-evergreen but all have an upright habit and will reach about 2m (6ft) high after four years. They require a semi-shaded spot out of cold winds but are not too fussy about soil as long as it is not too dry or waterlogged. The fragrant, pink flowers, which open from deeper pink buds, start to open as early as the New Year and can continue for three

months, scenting the surrounding air. Cutting odd shoots to enjoy indoors does not do any harm, though pruning daphnes is generally not advisable.

Spring companion
Omphalodes cappadocica 'Starry Eyes'

Summer companion
Dicentra 'Pearl Drops'

Erysimum 'Walberton Fragrant Sunshine'

Most wallflowers are biennials and are discarded once they have flowered, even though they have the potential to live for several years. However, there are several perennial wallflowers that flower for many months and can be expected to live for several years. Requiring a sunny, well-drained spot, they will steadily build into small, mounded shrubs. The best known is 'Bowles' Mauve' which, however, has no scent. 'Walberton Fragrant Sunshine' is a recent introduction that has large golden flowers with a strong scent and a long

flowering season, creating a mound of vivid colour in late spring and early summer. Light pruning after flowering will prolong the life of the plant.

Spring companion
Aubrieta 'Red Carpet'

Summer companion
Cedronella canariensis

Euphorbia amygdaloides var. *robbiae*

Euphorbias range from succulents and shrubs to herbaceous plants. This creeping, ground cover plant for shade has upright stems with evergreen, dark leaves. In spring each shoot has a spike of lime green bracts that reach about 45cm (18in). After these start to fade, the old stems should be cut off to make room for the new shoots to flower the following year. In time it can spread to form large clumps but it is rarely a nuisance and is useful for large areas. Although it is most vigorous in light shade and moist soil, it will also survive in dense shade under trees.

Spring companion
Leucojum aestivum

Winter companion
Mahonia x *wagneri* 'Pinnacle'

Euphorbia characias subsp. *wulfenii*

This shrubby euphorbia from southern Europe is a bold, architectural plant for a sunny spot that thrives in dry soil. The plants branch from the base and produce upright stems with long, narrow, grey leaves along their length. In winter, the tips curl over to protect them from the weather and in spring they turn up again to produce a column of lime green bracts. After several months, once these have faded, the stems should be cut out to allow a new set to take their place. The plant is attractive at all times and grows to about 1.2m (4ft) high when in bloom. Euphorbias have irritant sap, so wear gloves when pruning.

Spring companion
Allium 'Globemaster'

Summer companion
(bearded) *Iris* 'Edith Wolford'

Exochorda x *macrantha* 'The Bride'

Exochorda is a welcome addition to any garden, as flowering shrubs following the first flush of spring blossom are not common. The spreading branches almost disappear under the mass of white blossom that opens from round, white buds, and the show continues for several weeks, after which the foliage is neat, though unexceptional. Although a shrub, you can prune away the lower branches to form a small tree up to 3m (10ft) high. It will flourish on most soils, but the leaves may become yellow if planted on chalky soils.

Spring companion
Lamium maculatum 'White Nancy'

Summer companion
Athyrium filix-femina

Forsythia 'Courtalyn' (Weekend)

Forsythias may be rather dull in summer but the bright yellow flowers that cover their branches in spring are welcome. They are also easy to grow, because they thrive in most soils, including heavy clay and on chalk. Because they are so common it is worth planting something special such as the variegated 'Golden Times', with wonderful yellow edges to the leaves, or 'Coutalyn', which is especially free-flowering and has a neat habit. Forsythias can be used as hedging but avoid clipping them to the same size each year as this leads to a mass of dead, twiggy growth that flowers poorly after a few years. Prune out a few of the older stems each year to encourage new growth which will flower better than old stems.

Spring companion
Euphorbia amygdaloides var. *robbiae*

Autumn companion
Clematis 'Alba Luxuriens'

Kerria japonica 'Pleniflora'

The pale orange, double pompon blooms of Kerria have made it one of the most popular spring shrubs. It is tough, hardy and flowers reliably. Because it sends up new, suckering shoots from the base, it is also easy to propagate by simply chopping off a clump in winter and putting it in its new home. It is a tall, willowy plant, reaching 2m (6ft) in a few seasons and is usually grown as a wall shrub. Oddly, the single-flowered form and its variegated kind have a lower, bushier habit. They all have some autumn interest as the foliage turns yellow and the young stems are bright green in winter.

Spring companion
Doronicum x *excelsum* 'Harpur Crewe'

Autumn companion
Pyracantha 'Saphyr Orange'

Magnolia stellata

Though it lacks the flower size and great goblet shape of some of its relatives, this is one of the finest magnolias for small gardens because of its bushy habit. Throughout the years it forms a mound of tangled stems all the way down to the ground and as it ages you can remove the lowest stems to create a small tree-like shape. Another advantage is that the buds open over several weeks, so if late frosts destroy the floral display, there is a good chance that you will get a repeat display a week or so later. The blooms are fragrant and have many, narrow, white petals. 'Water lily' and the pink-tinged 'Royal Star' have larger flowers than most. This magnolia rarely gets taller than 3m (10ft) and is usually 2m (6ft 6in) or less.

Spring companion
Chionodoxa lucillae

Winter companion
Helleborus hybridus

Magnolia x soulangeana

This is the magnolia that most gardeners think of when buying one for their garden. It can be dramatic in spring when covered in its upright, pink-flushed, creamy white flowers. They deserve close inspection so you can appreciate the intricate internal structure along with the sweet perfume. It is among the easiest to grow but does not like cold, windy sites or very chalky soils, though clay is tolerated. You should also avoid frosty sites because late frosts can turn the sumptuous blooms into brown mush overnight. This is a large shrub or small tree, so make sure you have enough room for it to develop naturally. Pruning will not harm the plant but can result in an awkward shape and lack of flowers if it is done regularly. There are many varieties, such as deep rose 'Lennei' and large, late-flowering 'Brozzonii'.

Spring companion
Bergenia 'Ballawley Hybrids'

Summer companion
Paeonia lutea var. *ludlowii*

Magnolia 'Iolanthe'

Magnolias are loved for their blooms, which are the largest of all hardy shrubs. 'Iolanthe' is one of a series of vigorous New Zealand hybrids that have blooms that dwarf all others. The pink-flushed flowers are 25cm (10in) across and even small plants bloom well. Give this superb small tree ideal conditions in a sheltered spot in acid to neutral soil that does not dry out in summer, and it will attract gasps of admiration from all who see it.

Spring companion
Camellia x *williamsii* 'Donation'

Winter companion
Sarcococca hookeriana

Paulownia tomentosa

This Chinese tree might possibly be the most magnificent of all flowering trees, rivalling magnolias and surpassing them in the lavender purple of its trumpet-shaped flowers. It is often called the foxglove tree and is easy to grow in most soils but for one problem. The flower buds that form in autumn must remain on the bare branches over winter until they open in late spring, just before the leaves unfurl. All is well in mild winters, but cold and gales can damage the buds and lead to a poor spring display. However, if you have a sheltered, sunny spot, this large tree is worth the risk and will start to produce flowers when 3m (10ft) high. Plants grow quickly and flower at a young age, but they can look rather

gaunt during winter. It is often grown for its huge, furry leaves 60cm (2ft) across. To achieve this the plants are pruned back hard each spring, near to the ground, but no flowers will be produced with this treatment.

Spring companion
Chaenomeles speciosa 'Geisha Girl'

Summer companion
Kolkwitzia amabilis 'Pink Cloud'

Photinia x fraseri 'Red Robin'

Among the must-have plants for any garden, this must come close to the top. It is evergreen, easy to grow, free from major pests or problems and looks beautiful all year round. The new growth in spring is bright red and if pruned it will produce flushes of new growth. You can keep it to 1.5m (5ft) high with regular pruning or it can be left top reach 3m (10ft) high, when it will produce masses of pretty, white flowers in spring. As the leaves age they become a deep, lustrous green. Plant a row as a screen or to keep clipped as a hedge. Although it grows in sun or light shade, the best foliage colour is produced in sunny sites. It is a good alternative to Pieris on non-acid soils and can even exceed those showy shrubs with its spring display.

Spring companion
Berberis darwinii

Winter companion
Aucuba japonica 'Crotonifolia'

Pieris japonica 'Debutante'

Pieris are deservedly popular shrubs for spring interest, but they must have lime-free soil in order to thrive. They can be grown in large containers where garden soil is not suitable, though they must be watered well at all times. Pieris also suffer from late-spring frosts which burn the new shoots. Thus, they are best placed under the canopy of other shrubs which protect them from frost in spring and burning sun in summer. They are not ideal for pots on sunny patios. 'Debutante' is a low, compact plant from the Japanese island of Yakushima, the home of the dwarf *Rhododendron yakushimanum*. After the bright red spring growth, white flowers in upright clusters appear. 'Flamingo' has deep red buds and pink flowers, and *Pieris formosa* var. *forrestii* 'Wakehurst' is one of the most popular, with a vigorous habit and white flowers that contrast well with the bright red leaves.

Spring companion
Corydalis solida

Summer companion
Kalmia latifolia 'Freckles'

Poncirus trifoliata

While there are no hardy oranges or lemons, this Chinese shrub is a good alternative with large, 5cm (2in) white, fragrant flowers in spring that surpass the beauty of other citrus. These are carried on green stems with formidable spines that make this a good choice for an impenetrable, loose hedge. It is also worth planting as a shrub, and after a good summer the stems carry felty, small, pale orange fruits that look promising but are, however, inedible. It thrives in a sunny, dry spot and in autumn the foliage turns bright yellow before it falls. It is bushy and grows to about 2m (6ft) high, but can be trained as a small tree in the border, by pruning away lower branches so that plants can be grown under its light shade.

Spring companion
Epimedium x *perralchicum* 'Frohnleiten'

Autumn companion
Callicarpa bodinieri var. *giraldii* 'Profusion'

Prunus cerasifera 'Nigra'

The myrobalan, or cherry plum, sometimes causes excitement in late summer when it produces masses of red or yellow fruits that litter the ground under the trees and attract birds and wasps. Though small, this fruit is edible and tasty. Still, gardeners value the trees most for the foliage and flowers of the purple-leaved varieties such as 'Nigra' and 'Pissardii'. 'Nigra' is a small tree up to 5m (16ft) high, though it can also be trimmed as a hedge and has deep purple leaves and stems. In spring the branches are wreathed in pale pink flowers, earlier than most other cherries, and make a bright, if fleeting display before the richly coloured foliage expands.

Spring companion
Lamium maculatum 'White Nancy'

Winter companion
Helleborus hybridus

Prunus 'Kursar'

This is a beautiful small tree for spring and autumn colour. The flowers are not large but are vibrant pink and open in early spring, adding a splash of much-needed colour. The green, summer foliage is unexceptional but turns orange and red in autumn before it falls.

Spring companion
Pulmonaria angustifolia 'Azurea'

Summer companion
Digitalis purpurea 'Sutton's Apricot'

Prunus 'Kanzan'

Blousy, flowering cherries are not as popular as they once were, but 'Kanzan' will please those who need a cloud of pink blossom and a showy carpet of fallen petals. Upright in habit at first, it broadens with age to form a tree 4m (17ft) high, covered, in spring, with bright pink, slightly mauve, large, double flowers. It is not subtle, but there are few better sights in the spring garden. Like all cherries, it has surface roots that can dry out the soil and make planting difficult under the tree. They can also surface in lawns and then produce suckers.

Spring companion
Vinca minor 'Azurea Flore Pleno'

Autumn companion
Cotinus coggygria 'Royal Purple'

Rhododendron 'Pink Pearl'

Rhododendrons provide a welcome blast of colour in late spring, though they are only suitable for acid soil and prefer moist soil that is rich in organic matter. They vary from small to large shrubs and though they only flower for a few weeks, they are among the most desired of all shrubs. 'Pink Pearl' is one of the most popular and is a large shrub with masses of large, mid-pink flowers when at its best. 'President Roosevelt' has the bonus of a bold, gold splash in the centre of each leaf, making it beautiful all year round. 'Sappho' is a popular, large variety with white blooms, marked with a purple blotch, and 'Yellow Hammer' has pairs of bright yellow, bellshaped flowers in early spring, decidedly more delicate than most.

Spring companion
Pieris japonica 'Debutante'

Summer companion
Astilbe 'Cattleya'

Rhododendron 'Percy Wiseman'

The smaller rhododendrons are ideal for modern gardens and are also suitable for tubs and raised beds. There is no compromise in flower display just because these plants are small. 'Percy Wiseman' is one of numerous hybrids of the dwarf *R. yakushimanum*, all of which are superb, compact shrubs. It has pale pink flowers in domed clusters above the foliage. A bonus of these dwarf hybrids is that the leaves are covered, when young, with a white, felty coating so the new leaves contrast with the dark green older foliage. For something brighter, try 'Elizabeth', a low, spreading plant with vibrant red flowers.

Spring companion
Pulmonaria 'Occupol'

Winter companion
Erica carnea 'Springwood Pink'

Rhododendron – Japanese azalea

The evergreen, Japanese azaleas thrive in sun if the soil is moist but are best placed where they get some shade from the midday sun in summer. They are hard to resist in garden centres when in bloom and are usually covered in small flowers in late spring, in a dazzling array of flower colours and sizes. Most are neat and easily fitted into any garden with acid soil, reaching 1.2m (4ft) when mature. Their small, glossy leaves are attractive all year, even after the flowers are long gone. 'Hinode-giri' has large, vibrant pink flowers and 'Rose Bud' has double flowers in a pretty shade of deep rose pink. 'Vuyk's Rosyred' is one of the most popular of all and has dazzling pink flowers.

Spring companion
Primula denticulata

Summer companion
Athyrium nipponicum var. *pictum*

Rhododendron – deciduous azalea

The deciduous azaleas are upright when young but spreading when mature and give an exceptionally colourful, and often fragrant, display in late spring, just before the leaves unfurl. They thrive in sun or partial shade and must have acid soil. They tend not to be so dense in leaf as the evergreen rhododendrons and are easier to plant under. They combine well with primulas and hostas, which also like moist soil and light shade. In autumn they often have a bright leaf colour and most grow to about 1.5m (5ft) high. 'Homebush' has narrow, funnel-shaped flowers that are bright pink and semi-double. 'Irene Koster' has cream and orange flowers, suffused with pink and gold that are sweetly fragrant, and 'Spek's Orange' has large, dazzling orange flowers.

Spring companion
Epimedium grandiflorum 'Rose Queen'

Summer companion
Dicentra spectabilis 'Alba'

Ribes sanguineum 'Brocklebankii'

The flowering currant, *Ribes sanguineum* is a tough, reliable, hardy shrub with pink flowers in pendant clusters in spring. You can see it in every street even though it is dull and even smelly (often described as 'catty') in summer. The flowers are usually mid-pink but there are better forms, such as 'Red Pimpernel' with bright red flowers. 'Brocklebankii', however, is worth a place in any garden because the flowers are followed by, and open with, the bright yellow leaves which retain their colour all summer. It grows in any soil but the yellow foliage may be scorched in bright sun if the soil is dry in summer. It will reach about 1.5m (5ft), slightly less than other flowering currants. No pruning is necessary but you can cut the plant back after flowering to keep it neat.

Spring companion
Pulmonaria rubra 'Redstart'

Summer companion
Hypericum 'Hidcote'

Ribes x *gordonianum*

This pretty shrub is a hybrid of the common flowering currant and the buffalo currant (*R. odoratum*). It is a fast-growing plant with flowers that combine the colours of its two parents – yellow and pink. Strange though this may seem, the flowers are actually very attractive, revealing their yellow centre as the salmon buds open. It is a colour not common in spring and it is easy to grow. Later in the season it is not exceptional but the foliage is brighter and more attractive than *R. sanguineum*.

Spring companion
Sambucus nigra 'Black Beauty'

Autumn companion
Indigofera amblyantha

Rosmarinus officinalis

Rosemary is such a common herb that we forget it is also a beautiful shrub that will thrive in those difficult places that are hot and dry in summer. The pale blue flowers cover the branches in spring and there are smatterings of flower later in the year, too. It will reach about 1m (3.2ft) high and withstands pruning to keep it in check or to add flavour to your food. In addition to the common rosemary you find in herb sections there are low-growing and pink-flowered forms that are all as easy to grow in dry, sunny gardens and all are edible.

Spring companion
Ipheion uniflorum 'Froyle Mill'

Autumn companion
Origanum laevigatum 'Herrenhausen'

Spiraea prunifolia

This is usually seen as the double form, 'Plena', even if it is not labelled as such and is one of the prettiest spring flowers. The arching branches are wreathed in pure white, very doubled flowers that look like fairy roses. The plant is delicate yet vigorous, reaching about 1.5m (5ft) high in time. Regular pruning of the shoots and taking out a few of the oldest stems after flowering will help to keep it smaller. In autumn the small, narrow leaves turn orange and red. It will grow in almost any soil but flowers best in full sun. It is not a common plant and is larger than most spiraeas, but extremely beautiful when in bloom.

Spring companion
Leucojum aestivum

Autumn companion
Persicaria affinis 'Superba'

Stachyurus praecox

Impatient gardeners may be frustrated that the flower clusters of this handsome shrub form in autumn but do not open until spring. However, they are then rewarded with stiff, pendant clusters of small, creamy flowers that hang from the beetroot purple twigs. Although it is not often seen, it is hardy and will grow on most soils and in sun or light shade, forming a large shrub 2.5m (8ft) high and across.

Spring companion
Euphorbia amygdaloides 'Purpurea'

Summer companion
Itea ilicifolia

Syringa 'Michael Buchner'

Lilacs have a reputation of being dull and producing suckers, as though they have no merit in flower, but a lilac tree in flower is a treat for the eyes and nose. They are not exciting after flowering and can sucker, but this usually happens if they are pruned hard or if the soil around them is constantly dug. This damages the roots, so it is advisable to plant ground cover or shrubs to avoid this. They are easily pruned by cutting away the lower branches to form a beautiful small tree, but other pruning should be avoided, as flowering is almost always affected, though you can pick off the dead flowers to prevent seeding if you have time. 'Charles Joly' has dark, purple, double flowers and is later than most. 'Michael Buchner' is also exceptional and has double, pink flowers and 'Primrose' is a novelty with small, single, pale yellow flowers. *Syringa meyeri* 'Palibin' is a dwarf lilac for the border with pinkish flowers.

Spring companion
Convallaria majalis

Autumn companion
Cyclamen hederifoilum

Tamarix tetrandra

The common tamarix is a common sight at seaside gardens because it withstands cold winds and salt spray. Still, that is not a reason to ignore it for inland gardens. In late spring the plant is covered with a candyfloss froth of sugar pink, tiny blooms that have the same texture as the feathery foliage. Although a large shrub or small tree, it responds kindly to pruning, though this should be done after flowering to avoid loss of flowers the following year. It is easy to propagate and walking-stick length stems, stuck in the ground in winter, will usually root and grow.

Spring companion
Exochorda x macrantha 'The Bride'

Autumn companion
Liriope muscari

Viburnum x burkwoodii

Among more than 100 species of viburnum, this hybrid has become one of the most popular because it is semi-evergreen and has domed clusters of small, pure white flowers in spring. These have one of the most wonderful perfumes of the whole year and last about a month. In time it will reach about 2m (6ft) high. In autumn some of the leaves will fall after they have turned red and 'Mohawk' is noted for this trait as well as having red buds that give the flowers a pink tinge. This hardy shrub will grow well in any soil including on chalk, flowering best in sun. *Viburnum x carlcephalum* has similar flowers but is deciduous and 'Eskimo' is semi-evergreen.

Spring companion
Cytisus x praecox 'Albus'

Summer companion
Nicotiana sylvestris

Erysimum cheiri 'Fair Lady Mixed'

Wallflowers are an essential part of the spring garden and are now sold in pots in spring to tempt gardeners who forgot to plant them in autumn or sow them in summer. They are biennial and must be sown in early summer. They should be planted out in a sunny spot in late summer/early autumn and are discarded after flowering. Wallflowers are prone to clubroot disease, common in cabbages, to which they are related, and grow best in alkaline soils which help prevent this disease. They are not always successful in pots and are best grown in the border in a light, airy spot in full sun. Most wallflowers are available as mixtures and 'Fair Lady Mixed' is a pastel mixture of colours with the typical strong perfume.

Spring companion
Tulipa 'Apeldoorn'

Winter companion
Skimmia japonica 'Rubella'

Myosotis 'Blue Ball'

Myosotis, forget-me-nots, are best known for bringing pastel blues to the garden and are usually used as edging, mixed with polyanthus and pansies, along with tulips, in bedding displays. But they are also useful in herbaceous borders and among shrubs where they will self seed and spread over the years. Like other biennials, they are sown in summer and planted in autumn to bloom the following spring. After flowering they are pulled up and composted and if you do not want them to seed everywhere you should pull them up as soon as the last flowers fade. At this stage they usually succumb to mildew anyway and are best removed. In addition to the usual blue such as 'Blue Ball' there are white and pink varieties. Plants are sometimes sold in bloom in the spring, but these are not of good value because they are at the end of their life span.

Spring companion
Ajuga reptans 'Catlin's Giant'

Winter companion
Euonymus fortunei 'Emerald Gaiety'

Polyanthus and primrose

Polyanthus and primroses brighten spring with their early flowers in a wide range of colours. Most primroses sold in pots have huge flowers and are not adapted to use outside in the garden, though they can be used in containers in sheltered spots. However, most polyanthus have smaller flowers that can withstand rain and wind and will brighten up the garden in sun as well as partially shaded spots. Polyanthus differ from primroses only in that the flowers are carried in a bunch on a stem above the leaves and have all the colour range and charm of primroses. Buy them in autumn or grow your own from seed, sown in early summer on the surface of the compost and kept in a cool, shady place.

Spring companion
Tulipa 'Red Riding Hood'

Winter companion
Ilex crenata 'Golden Gem'

Viola

Winter-flowering pansies are now the most popular of all spring flowers, though they often do not flower well in winter, as the name might suggest. The large flowers are also prone to damage from wet and cold whereas the smaller-flowered violas, such as the tough and reliable 'Orange Duet', which is grown from seed, often fare better. Though the flowers are smaller they are produced in great numbers and are ideal for edging beds, containers and windowboxes. If you deadhead the plants to stop them producing seeds and keep them free from aphids, they will flower for many months.

Spring companion
Hyacinth 'Gipsy Queen'

Winter companion
Buxus sempervirens 'Marginata'

Clematis macropetala 'Markham's Pink'

The early, smaller-flowered clematis are often overlooked in favour of the big, blousy types that flower in summer, but they have several advantages, apart from their early display. They are easy to grow and they do not suffer from wilt and other problems so often associated with clematis. Though the flowers are small, they make a lavish display, and 'Markham's Pink' is one of the best, with nodding, double flowers of pale pink. It will reach about 3m (10ft) in height and is suitable for most positions. If pruning is necessary it should be done immediately after flowering. 'Pink Flamingo' has pretty pink blooms and *C. alpina* 'Frances Rivis' has deep blue and white flowers.

Spring companion
Ceanothus 'Concha'

Summer companion
Phlomis fruticosa

Clematis montana 'Elizabeth'

Clematis montana is among the easiest of all clematis to grow well but it is very vigorous and will quickly cover large wall or cover shrubs. Thus, it needs to be planted with thought. Fortunately, it can be pruned immediately after flowering to keep it under control and in this way it can be grown in association with other plants. 'Elizabeth' has large flowers of soft pink and like most, they are sweetly fragrant.

Spring companion
Prunus cerasifera 'Nigra'

Autumn companion
Euonymus alatus

Wisteria sinensis 'Prolific'

Wisteria is a popular climber and easy to grow, but it does not always flower well. It pays to buy a named variety such as 'Prolific', which flowers as a young plant. Cheap, small plants are always a risk because they may not flower for many years. Wisteria can be grown up a sunny wall or over pergolas but it must be planted in a sunny spot and given adequate support because a single plant will cover at least 10m (33ft) in all directions if not pruned. Pruning should be done in late summer, reducing the length of all stems not needed to make the plant bigger, to three or four leaves.

Spring companion
Exochorda x *macrantha* 'The Bride'

Summer companion
Lavatera x *clementii* 'Bredon Springs'

Allium cristophii

This is the most satisfactory of all alliums because it is inexpensive and the bold heads of starry flowers last many weeks while being large and impressive. The stems grow to about 45cm (18in) high and the heads can be 20cm (8in) across with hundreds of metallic mauve flowers. While other alliums lose their structure as they age, these retain their petals and are as pretty when straw-coloured in summer as they are when in full bloom. Like all alliums, the leaves are not ornamental, and they start to die as the flowers open. It thrives in well-drained soil in full sun.

Spring companion
Lamium maculatum 'White Nancy'

Summer companion
Nepeta grandiflora 'Dawn to Dusk'

Allium 'Globemaster'

This is the best of the taller alliums with larger heads and several weeks more colour than the commoner *Allium giganteum*. Neither are cheap, but 'Globemaster' is good value because of the large heads of purple flowers on 90cm (3ft) stems. On well-drained soil it will increase slowly, and three bulbs will make a good clump after several years. The foliage is broad and bright green, loved by snails, so some protection is advisable.

Spring companion
Euphorbia characias subsp. *wulfenii*

Winter companion
Carex comans bronze

Spring Bulbs

Anemone blanda

All the tuberous anemeones are inexpensive and readily available. They thrive in sun or partial shade and the flowers open almost as soon as the crooked shoots appear through the soil. The flowers open flat above the ferny foliage and, in time, will create a carpet 10cm (4in) high, studded with blooms. The common form has masses of soft blue flowers and a large clump is a beautiful sight in spring. 'Radar' is the most striking of all, with vibrant pink flowers with a white centre. Mixtures are available but these often hold a large proportion of the common blue and it is best to buy several varieties to mix yourself, soaking the tubers overnight before planting. 'Charmer' is pale pink, 'Violet Star' is lilac and 'White Splendour' will create a wonderful sheet of white.

Spring companion
Epimedium grandiflorum 'Rose Queen'

Summer companion
Berberis thunbergii 'Dart's Lady Red'

Anemone nemorosa

The native wood anemone is one of the prettiest of all spring flowers and will spread in suitable, moist soils as its rhizomes explore the space under shrubs. The flowers are usually white and 'Vestal' has double, white flowers of great beauty. 'Allennii' has beautiful blue flowers. Dried rhizomes in packs rarely thrive and you should buy growing plants in pots or fresh rhizomes in moist packing material.

Spring companion
Erythronium dens-canis

Summer companion
Prunella grandiflora 'Pagoda'

Chionodoxa lucillae

Chionodoxas are aptly called glory-of-the-snow because they flower early in spring. The bright blue, white-eyed flowers are carried on 10cm (4in) stems above the narrow leaves and the bulb flourishes in sunny spots. It will self-seed in gravel and under shrubs. As it is inexpensive, it is ideal for borders or for adding to winter baskets or windowboxes to give some extra colour. 'Pink Giant' has large, pale pink flowers with a white centre and C. *sardensis* has smaller flowers that are a particularly bright shade of blue.

Spring companion
Aubrieta 'Red Carpet'

Summer companion
Hakonechloa macra 'Alboaurea'

Crocus vernus 'Remembrance'

The common Dutch crocus, with their large, glossy flowers that open in the sun to reveal the bright orange stigmas, are ideal for borders or for naturalizing in grass. The colour range is rather limited and comprises various shades of purple, white and purple striped with white as well as bright yellow but they are sturdy and reliable. 'Remembrance' has large flowers of a pale purple with a silvery tint. 'Peter Pan' is probably the finest white, with a bright orange centre, and 'Yellow Mammoth' is the standard and just yellow. Only the yellow crocus tend to be attacked by sparrows in most gardens.

Spring companion
Stachyurus praecox 'Magpie'

Summer companion
Tradescantia 'Concorde Grape'

Crocus tommasinianus

In addition to the common Dutch crocus, there are many other types that are just as easy to grow but bring new colours, though most have smaller blooms. *Crocus tommasinianus* is possibly the earliest crocus to bloom, and the flowers open from thin, pale lilac buds. It is the easiest of all to grow and will self seed to form large expanses of starry flowers. *C. sieberi* 'Hubert Edelstein' is rather special and has dumpy blooms that are deep violet in bud and open to flowers that are yellow at the base with a white zone. The many varieties of *C. chrysanthus* include all shades of yellow as well as patterned flowers that are all scented with honey. 'Ladykiller' is one of the prettiest and has flowers of pure white and purple.

Spring companion
Pulmonaria angustifolia 'Azurea'

Summer companion
Leycesteria formosa 'Golden Lanterns'

Erythronium 'Pagoda'

Erythroniums, the dog's tooth violets, are named after the shape of their strange, fleshy roots. In fact, the flowers are not much like violets. 'Pagoda' is one of the finest and has stems with several pendant, bright yellow flowers similar to elegant, small lilies but many months before we could hope to have lilies in the garden. The stems are about 25cm (10cm) high, holding the flowers above the spreading foliage that is broad and marbled with bronze.

Spring companion
Lamium 'Golden Anniversary'

Winter companion
Asplenium scolopendrium

Fritillaria imperialis 'Maxima Lutea'

The crown imperial is the most dramatic of spring flowering bulbs, growing with astonishing speed. The shoots are thick, and they rapidly unfurl their leaves as the stems reach heights of 1m (3ft) or so, crowned with a ring of pendant flowers under a leafy tuft. These flowers are in shades of burnt orange or yellow and have large drops of nectar at the base of each petal. 'Maxima Lutea' is the best known yellow and is a wonderful, bright plant when in flower. Crown imperials thrive best in rich soil in a sunny spot and disappear as quickly as they appeared, leaving the ground bare by early summer. The flowers are not scented but the whole plant has a strange, musky odour. *Fritillaria persica* 'Adiyaman' has grey leaves and spires of small, deep purple flowers, preferring a sunny, dry site.

Spring companion
Euphorbia characias subsp. *wulfenii*

Summer companion
Lavendula angustifolia 'Imperial Gem'

Hyacinth 'Blue Jacket'

Hyacinths are usually planted in containers or formal beds, but they are just as suitable for borders, where they will flower for many years if they are given rich soil and full sun. Loved for their fragrance, the flowers are available in a wide range of colours including deep purple, yellow and orange. 'Fondant' is one of the finest pinks, 'Blue Jacket' is deep blue and 'Gipsy Queen' is salmon orange.

Spring companion
Omphalodes cappadocica 'Starry Eyes'

Winter companion
Ophiopogon planiscapus 'Nigrescens'

Ipheion uniflorum 'Froyle Mill'

Most spring bulbs have a fairly short season of bloom, but this one seems to produce a never-ending succession of starry, pale blue flowers in spring. The grassy foliage appears in late winter and is unremarkable at first. Soon, though, the first flowers appear and they continue for several months. Each flower is held on a stem about 10cm (4in) high and is sweetly scented, although the plant actually has an onion scent. It thrives in dry, sunny sites and is ideal for edging, though it disappears by late spring.

Spring companion
Pulsatilla vulgaris

Summer companion
Convolvulus cneorum

Leucojum vernum

Leucojum vernum is the spring snowflake that flowers in early spring, along with late snowdrops and crocus. The white flowers have green or yellow spots at the tips of each petal and hang singly or in pairs from the 15cm (6in) stems before the bright green leaves appear. It grows best in sun or shade in moist soil. The summer snowflake (*L. aestivum*) is a much bigger plant, 60cm (2ft) high with smaller flowers. It actually flowers in late spring and is more robust, ideal for wild gardens or for naturalizing in grass or under shrubs.

Spring companion
Primula denticulata

Summer companion
Mimulus guttatus

Muscari armeniacum 'Valerie Finnis'

The grape hyacinths are hated by some gardeners because *Muscari armeniacum* can seed widely, thus producing a 'lawn' of green foliage that appears in autumn and dominates the blue flowers. However, many grape hyacinths are far less invasive though most start to produce their foliage in autumn. 'Valerie Finnis' is a demure grape hyacinth and never a nuisance. It has pale blue flowers that are very delicate in colour and a welcome change from the norm. 'Blue Spike' is a tamer, double variety of *M. armeniacum* that does not seed as freely and is valuable for its intense blue flowers, thriving in sun or partial shade. It is easy to grow and good for cutting for posies in spring. *Muscari*

latifolium is even more beautiful, with broad leaves and spikes of blooms in two shades of blue, dark at the base and pale at the top of the stems.

Spring companion
Magnolia stellata

Winter companion
Erica carnea 'Springwod Pink'

Narcissus 'Ice Follies'

Daffodils can be found in virtually every garden, yet there is always room for a few more. Though golden trumpet daffodils are most common, there are varieties in all shades of yellow as well as orange, white and pink. 'Ice Follies' is one of the best for garden display, with flat cups that open cream but fade to white, the same colour as the surrounding petals. It is a strong grower and can be used in borders or for naturalizing in grass. For best results, leave the foliage for six weeks after the flowers fade before trimming it back to allow the leaves to feed the bulbs for next season – never tie the leaves in knots. 'Geranium' is also popular and has clusters of white flowers with orange centres which are strongly scented. 'Ambergate' is rather unusual, having orange petals and a small cup, but is best in shade to prevent the colour from fading.

Spring companion
Doronicum x excelsum 'Harpur Crewe'

Summer companion
Paeonia 'Krinkled White'

Narcissus – dwarf 'Pipit'

The smaller daffodils are gaining in popularity because they are so useful for pots and containers. Also, they are better suited to small gardens and windy sites where they are less likely to be damaged by spring gales. 'Pipit' is a real miniature with small, pale yellow flowers on 20cm (8in) stems, while 'Bell Song' is one of the last to bloom and has one or two white flowers with pale pink cups on 30cm (1ft) stems. 'Jetfire' is slightly bigger and has a long, orange trumpet and flared, yellow petals. Growing to about 40cm (16in) high, it is big enough for large-scale planting under shrubs as well as being neat enough for windowboxes. It is a strong and healthy plant and increases well.

Spring companion
Chaenomeles 'Lemon and Lime'

Winter companion
Euonymus fortunei 'Emerald 'n' Gold'

Ranunculus ficaria var. *aurantiacus*

Celandines can be weeds, and difficult to eradicate, but there are many interesting varieties and these can be used to bring colour and interest to the garden in spring. They are easy to grow and will thrive in sun or shade, forming carpets of colourful flowers. They also die down rapidly after flowering to make room for other plants and are ideal under deciduous shrubs. *Ranunculus ficaria* var. *aurantiacus* has green leaves, but the flowers are bright orange, an unusual colour in the spring garden. To increase plants, lift, divide and replant them as they start to die down.

Spring companion
Ajuga reptans 'Catlin's Giant'

Summer companion
Potentilla 'Abbotswood'

Scilla sibirica 'Spring Beauty'

This is one of the most beautiful of all small spring bulbs and is inexpensive and easy to grow. The flowers open as soon as the stems appear above the soil and each bulb produces several stems, which lengthen to about 10cm (4in) as the flowers mature. The blooms are bright, cobalt blue and are bell-shaped. It is ideal for hanging baskets and spring containers and also for open borders, where it will seed to form large carpets of bright colour in sun or partial shade.

Spring companion
Lamium maculatum 'White Nancy'

Summer companion
Fuchsia magellanica var. *molinae*

Tulipa 'Apeldoorn'

Tulips are essential in the spring garden, and there is a bewildering variety of shapes and colours. For something traditional, with bright, cheery blooms, try 'Apeldoorn', the most popular bright red tulip. The parrot tulips are the most luxurious of all with their frilled and curled petals as well as dazzling colours. 'Blue Parrot' is among the most sophisticated, carrying lilac flowers with gently frilled petals and a bright blue base. 'Carnival de Nice' is a tall, double tulip with white flowers that are striped with red. All tulips grow best in full sun and can be left for several years without being lifted if planted 15cm (6in) deep so as not to get damaged by later plantings. But they are usually bedded out and lifted after flowering. They should be stored dry, the largest bulbs being selected for replanting.

Spring companion
Erysimum cheri 'Cloth of Gold'

Autumn companion
Sedum 'Herbstfreude'

Tulipa – short T. tarda

Short tulips are ideal for containers as well as borders and although their stems are short, their flowers are still showy, and many have unusual qualities lacking in the taller types. *Tulipa tarda* is sometimes confused with a crocus because each bulb produces a cluster of starry, almost stemless blooms of bright yellow, edged with white. *Tulipa praestans* 'Unicum' is a gem with several bright red flowers on 25cm (10in) stems. But it is the leaves that are so special, being grey-green with broad edges of creamy yellow, providing interest before and long after the flowers. 'Red Riding Hood' is the most popular dwarf tulip with bright red, large flowers on 20cm (8in) stems above the purple-striped leaves. All dwarf tulips grow best in full sun and most can be left in the ground for several years without attention.

Spring companion
Viola 'Tiger Eye'

Winter companion
Sempervivum tectorum

summer

Acanthus mollis Latifolius

The plant that inspired classical architecture can add drama and beauty to your garden, too, with its bold, deeply cut, arching foliage and majestic flower spikes. It is a tough, long-lived perennial with spiky stems of white and purple flowers, but can suffer from mildew in poor, dry soil. It is important to find the right position for the plant from the start, as it roots deeply. If you ever try to move the plant, those deep roots that are left in the soil will resprout. It is a large, bold plant not meant for cramped borders and can grow to be 1m (3ft) high, spread 1m (3ft) across.

Summer companion
Gypsophila paniculata 'Bristol Fairy'

Autumn companion
Eupatorium rugosum 'Chocolate'

Acaena microphylla 'Kupferteppich'

Acaenas are low-growing relatives of roses, though you would hardly guess from the spherical heads of tiny flowers that mature into spiny seed heads of the type that might be used by sadistic fairies. But the leaves are rose-like and form spreading mats of foliage, bronze-green in this variety, and make interesting ground cover in dry or poor soils in the sun.

Summer companion
Geranium cinereum 'Ballerina'

Spring companion
Scilla sibirica 'Spring Beauty'

Achillea 'Red Velvet'

Achilleas have their faults – they get mildew and can seed too freely if not deadheaded – but their good points, such as tolerating any soil and drought, as well as providing great cut flowers, make them invaluable border plants. Their feathery foliage is pleasant and the flat heads of small flowers, on 70cm (28in) stems, are available in a range of bright, as well as pastel colours. After the main flush of flowers in mid-summer, deadhead them for more, later flowers. 'Red Velvet' is exceptional, with green foliage, instead of the usual grey, and bright red flowers that do not fade. Others to try are pink 'Marie

Anne', salmon 'Lachsschoenheit' and orange 'Terracotta'.

Summer companion
Coreopsis grandiflora 'Early Sunrise'

Autumn companion
Physalis alkekengi

Agastache foeniculum 'Golden Jubilee'

Agastache are mint-like perennials with woody bases that bring fragrance and colour to sunny borders. They thrive in warm, dry beds, and smaller types are useful for pots, as well. The biggest species can reach 1m (3ft) or more, with coarse leaves and terminal heads of small, blue or white flowers in summer. 'Golden Jubilee' is of this type but has bright yellow foliage as the foil for its blue flowers. 'Apricot Sprite' is a smaller plant with narrow, grey-green foliage and tubular orange blooms. All have aromatic foliage and flowers that attract bees.

Summer companion
Achillea 'Terracotta'

Autumn companion
Rudbeckia fulgida var. *sullivantii* 'Goldsturm'

Agapanthus praecox

Agapanthus have large umbels of (usually) blue, trumpet-shaped flowers in mid- to late summer. They have a reputation for being tender and for taking several seasons to flower. However, buying an established plant in a pot of a named variety will usually ensure success. Plant in a sunny spot in good soil or grow them in large pots of John Innes no 3 compost. They are slightly tender so need a sheltered spot. Plants in containers can be moved to a frost-free greenhouse in winter. *Agapanthus praecox* is evergreen and has broad green leaves and large clusters of bright blue flowers. It is less hardy than the following but is worth growing in a large tub. 'Loch Hope' is one of the most spectacular, with 1.5m (5ft) stems with dark blue flowers. 'Liliput' is a dwarf plant with stems just 40cm (16in) high. Headbourne hybrids are among the hardiest and have many, small heads of blue flowers and narrow leaves.

Summer companion
Iris – bearded 'English Cottage'

Spring companion
Euphorbia characias subsp. *wulfenii*

Alchemilla mollis

It is not easy for plants to become clichés, but alchemilla is so popular and such a useful plant that it hardly seems necessary to say how effective it can be in paving, at the front of borders or under roses. This tough, herbaceous plant spends winter as tight brown crowns and crumpled, immature leaves. With the warmth of spring, though, it bounds into luxurious growth, creating soft mounds of rounded leaves, covered with velvet hairs that catch dewdrops. In summer these are joined by plumes of tiny, lime green flowers which last for months and are useful for padding out bunches of roses and sweet peas. It thrives in most soils, light or clay, and in sun or part shade, reaching 60cm (2ft) high and rather more across. It does self-seed, but seedlings are rarely unwelcome.

Summer companion
Hosta 'August Moon'

Spring companion
Erythronium 'Pagoda'

Alstroemeria

The 'Princess' series of alstroemerias are from the same stable as the wonderful cut-flower varieties and include tall and short varieties in a wide range of colours. They are an improvement on old alstroemerias because they flower all summer, but they must be planted in sheltered, well-drained soil because winter wet will kill them. Alstroemerias hate root disturbance, so only buy potted plants. Plant them in a slight hollow, filling in the soil during the first season so the crown is 5–10cm (2–4in) below soil level, to give frost protection. *Alstroemeria aurea* 'Orange King' has a flush of bright orange flowers on 1m (3ft) stems in early summer but can spread alarmingly. 'Ligtu Hybrids' (pictured), in gold, pink and orange, are easily raised from seed and flower in their second year, flowering on stems 60cm (2ft) high.

Summer companion
Cerinthe major 'Purpurascens'

Spring companion
Tulipa 'Blue Parrot'

Alcea rosea

Hollyhocks conjure images of quaint cottages and country gardens, chocolate boxes and Victorian prints. However, hollyhocks have developed somewhat in the past century and are not all 2m (6ft) high perennials. You can now grow annuals that are just half that height. Annual hollyhocks, which flower the first year but often survive the winter and act as perennials, are especially useful because, if you do not have hollyhocks in the garden in winter and clear away the old plants in autumn, you reduce the

chance of rust, their biggest problem. 'Chater's Double Mixed' and 'Giant Single' are tall and perennial. Plants often selfseed and most of these plants are attractive.

Summer companion
Lilium – trumpet 'Pink Perfection'

Autumn companion
Persicaria affinis 'Superba'

Anthemis tinctoria 'Sauce Hollandaise'

Anthemis are old-fashioned, reliable perennials that thrive in average soil in sun or partial shade. Reduced to tight clumps of feathery green leaves in winter, they erupt into 60cm (2ft) clouds of 5cm (2in) daisy flowers in early summer. Plants are straggly after flowering so trim them back to keep them tidy, and divide clumps every other year in spring to maintain vigour. 'Sauce Hollandaise' has beautiful, pale yellow flowers and 'Grallach Gold' is deep, brazen yellow.

Summer companion
Santolina chamaecyparissus

Spring companion
Lamium galeobdolon 'Hermann's Pride'

Anthemis punctata subsp. *cupaniana*

Unlike its taller cousins, this dwarf sub-shrub is ideal for the front of the border, for rock gardens and for planting in paving and gravel. The woody stems support a dense carpet of metallic silver, finely divided foliage that is the perfect foil for the comparatively large, yellow-eyed, white daisies in early summer. It is at its best in year two or three and is most successful in poor, dry soil.

Summer companion
Thymus x citriodorus 'Silver Queen'

Spring companion
Chionodoxa luciliae

Aquilegia vulgaris

The common columbine is a short-lived perennial that adds colour and grace to borders in early summer. Plants should be grown from seed and are at their best in their second and third year. Different varieties hybridize freely, but most plants have attractive flowers in shades from white, through pink and red to deepest purple above the lobed foliage. Plant them in sun or partial shade in any soil. 'William Guinness' has interesting, spurred flowers in white and blackcurrant and is best planted with quiet colours to show off its subtlety. *Aquilegia vulgaris* var. *stellata* is the clematis-flowered columbine, with pretty, flat, spurless flowers in various shades. Try to avoid this crossing with other types because intermediate forms are ugly. The 'Songbird series' has huge flowers with long spurs on compact, 40cm (16in) plants, in a wide range of colours. It is more exotic than *A. vulgaris*.

Summer companion
Polemonium caeruleum

Spring companion
Muscari armeniacum 'Blue Spike'

Artemisia absinthium 'Lambrook Silver'

Artemisias include *A. dracunculus* – tarragon – but there are many ornamentals too, most with aromatic foliage. They all thrive in dry, well drained soil and full sun. 'Lambrook Silver' has beautiful, feathery silver leaves that quickly grow, from a hard spring prune, into a frothy mound 1m (3ft) high with loose clusters of grey flowers in summer, which can be trimmed off. It has a woody base but needs annual pruning to prevent it becoming straggly. 'Powys Castle' has even finer foliage and is lower in height. *Artemisia stelleriana* 'Boughton Silver' is a spreading plant with lobed leaves of dazzling silver that grows just 15cm (6in) high. However, it spreads to form a brilliant carpet of foliage. All are unlikely to thrive in wet, clay soils.

Summer companion
Eremurus 'Cleopatra'

Autumn companion
P. x rectus 'African Queen'

Aster thomsonii 'Nanus'

Most perennial asters are large, late-flowering plants that are ignored in summer, but this small plant is a notable, if undeservedly ignored, exception. Slowly building into a neat clump of narrow leaves, it starts to produce its yellow-eyed, lavender flowers in summer, and they continue for several months, making this one of the longest-flowering of all garden perennials. Reaching only 20cm (8in) high, it is ideal for rock gardens where the soil is not too dry, in paving, and the front of borders.

Summer companion
Brachyscome 'Strawberry Mousse'

Autumn companion
Rehmannia elata

Aruncus dioicus

Where the soil is too heavy or dry for astilbes to thrive, aruncus is a good alternative and is even more majestic and dramatic. Large, bold, heavily divided foliage makes a mound almost 1m high and is then topped with pyramidal, feathery heads of cream, fluffy flowers reaching 1.5m (5ft) or more. Trouble-free and easy to grow, it establishes slowly to produce a long-lived clump that never disappoints. Unfortunately, the cream-coloured flower is the only existing colour. If you do not have room for this, try the smaller 'Kneiffii', which has elegantly and coarsely cut foliage.

Summer companion
Campanula lactiflora 'Loddon Anna'

Autumn companion
Aconitum x cammarum 'Bicolor'

Astilbe 'Venus'

Astilbes are without equal for early summer colour. Their branched plumes of tiny flowers create a candyfloss effect in shades of white, red and pink above attractive, ferny foliage. But they can be difficult to please in the garden unless you have soil that is constantly moist. They flower best in full sun, but they must also have plenty of water or they will look miserable and gradually fade away. 'Venus' is typical of the best varieties with conical spires of fluffy, pale pink flowers rising to 1m above a dense clumps of attractive foliage. 'Cattleya' has deep pink flowers on dark stems, 'Diamant' is cool, greenish white and 'Hyazinth' is lavender pink. The most popular of all is 'Fanal', which is an intense, deep red and is just 60cm (2ft) high.

Summer companion
Hosta 'Krossa Regal'

Spring companion
Leucojum vernum

Astilbe chinensis var. *pumila*

This dwarf plant is much easier to grow than its taller relatives, and it creeps through the soil in sun or shade to create dense ground cover in moist or average soil. Growing just 25cm (10in) high, it produces dense, branched spires of deep pink flowers in late summer.

Summer companion
Filipendula ulmaria 'Aurea'

Autumn companion
Anemone hupehensis var. *japonica* 'Bressingham Glow'

Astrantia major 'Ruby Wedding'

Astrantias are useful summer plants that are vigorous but not invasive and will survive in most soils and positions. Their deeply cut leaves make weed-suppressing clumps and their flowers, in shades of pink and white, are pretty and ideal for cutting. Each flower is really a cluster of tiny blooms surrounded by bracts which give the plant its real beauty. They last for many weeks, but the stems can become too heavy and flop, especially when grown in shade. 'Ruby Wedding' has dark red flowers throughout summer on stems 50cm (2ft) high. 'Shaggy' is a pale pink and green with large bracts on taller stems, while 'Sunningdale Variegated' has pale pink flowers above boldly variegated leaves, which are at their best in spring.

Summer companion	**Autumn companion**
Chelone obliqua	*Geranium* 'Jolly Bee'

Athyrium nipponicum var. *pictum*

Most ferns are grown for their fresh green, finely divided fronds, but this Japanese fern has wonderfully colourful foliage in shades of grey and burgundy. It thrives in moist soil in partial shade and associates well with rhododendrons, hostas and other woodland plants, making clumps up to 45cm (18in) high and looking beautiful all spring and summer.

Summer companion
Hosta 'Halcyon'

Spring companion
Erythronium 'Pagoda'

Athyrium filix-femina

Some ferns are slow to establish or sensitive to drought, needing moist, shady conditions. However, the lady fern *Athyrium filix-femina* is much tougher than its delicate foliage would suggest. Creating a cone of fine foliage 60cm (2ft) high, it brings a light touch to plantings in shade, contrasting with hostas and bergenias and it will disguise the dying foliage of daffodils and other early bulbs. The leaves turn yellow and brown in autumn. There is a plethora of unusual forms with narrow, twisted or crested fronds, all just as easy to grow. Plant in light shade in moist soil, though dry conditions and dense shade are tolerated when established.

Summer companion
Iris Siberian 'Butter and Sugar'

Winter companion
Iris foetidissima

Campanula carpatica

Dwarf, rockery campanulas look delicate but are usually easy to grow and some are rampant, suited more to paving and gravel gardens than rock gardens. Their flowers also vary, though most are blue, from nodding bells to open, starry flowers. *Campanula carpatica* forms 30cm (12in) clumps covered in bowl-shaped blue or white flowers for several months. The most common form is 'Weisse Clips' ('White Clips) with white flowers. *Campanula poscharskyana* runs around, covering wide areas with its white, underground stems, but it can be forgiven its enthusiastic habit when its long stems

of starry, pale blue flowers open in early summer. *Campanula cochlearifolia* is another runner but does not spread far and has 8cm (3in) wiry stems with several nodding, bell-shaped flowers of pale blue. It is exceptionally beautiful and will fill gaps in crazy paving.

Summer companion
Scabiosa 'Butterfly Blue'

Winter companion
Sedum spathulifolium 'Cape Blanco'

Campanula lactiflora 'Loddon Anna'

Mid-summer gardens are always improved by this large, leafy plant that becomes covered in lilac pink flowers in mid-summer. The stems can reach 1.5m (5ft) high and plants are about the same width, but if you pinch out the growing tips when about 60cm (2ft) high, the plants will be shorter and less likely to need staking.

Summer companion
Lilium 'Pink Perfection'

Spring companion
Brunnera macrophylla

Campanula glomerata 'Superba'

This, the clustered bellflower, is available in most garden centres. It slowly creeps through the soil to form wide clumps with upright, 45cm (18in) stems, with a tight head of purple-blue flowers in early summer. If cut down after flowering, you will prevent seeding and encourage a second flush of flowers. 'Superba' is the most common variety and grows strongly and flowers freely.

Summer companion
Sidalcea 'Elsie Heugh'

Spring companion
Allium albopilosum

Campanula 'Kent Belle'

One of the best new introductions of recent years, this vigorous perennial forms wide clumps of low, heart-shaped leaves. Large, dark blue tubular bells, which nod gracefully, grow from the upright stems that reach a height of 60cm (2ft). After the main flush of flowers, many later stems are produced to continue the display throughout the summer.

Summer companion
Symphytum 'Goldsmith'

Spring companion
Muscari armeniacum 'Blue Spike'

Carex elata 'Aurea'

Sedges are usually lumped in with grasses, to which they bear a close resemblance, but they obviously differ in having their leaves in three rows which give the base of the shoots a triangular cross-section. This is one of the most common sedges and also one of the brightest, with yellow leaves that form beautiful, arching clumps about 60cm (2ft) high. Like most European sedges, it prefers moist soil, but it will grow in any soil that is not too dry in summer. It is deciduous and should be cut back to ground level in late autumn to allow the fresh new growth to be shown at its best advantage.

Summer companion
Prunella grandiflora 'Pagoda'

Winter companion
Ophiopogon planiscapus 'Nigrescens'

Carex comans bronze

This beautiful sedge from New Zealand will thrive in average soil in a sunny spot, forming flowing tufts of narrow, grassy leaves of toffee brown. These are about 45cm (18in) high and across and mix well with most plants in the garden, especially orange and red tulips in spring. It is easily grown from seed or clumps can be split in spring.

Summer companion
Convolvulus cneorum

Winter companion
Luzula sylvatica 'Aurea'

Catananche caerulea

When not in flower, catananche or, 'Cupid's Dart', is not particularly attractive, forming rather scruffy clumps of narrow, grey green leaves. But in mid-summer, a profusion of stiff stems erupts from the foliage, each with a beautiful, pale, silvery blue or white flower 5cm (2in) across. These last well and are also good for cutting and drying. The blooms are even pretty as buds because of the silvery scales that surround the flowers. It grows to about 75cm (30in) high and is suitable for sunny, dry borders, looking especially good with grasses.

Summer companion
Stipa arundinacea

Spring companion
Erysimum cheri 'Cloth of Gold'

Cedronella canariensis

Although this aromatic plant is native of the Canary Isles, it is usually hardy in our gardens if grown in full sun in well drained soil. It will thrive in dry soils where other plants struggle to survive. It has a woody base and will reach 1m (3ft) high, and it is best to prune it hard each spring to keep it tidy. It can also be trimmed in summer to reduce its size. The foliage is divided into three leaflets and is strongly aromatic. In summer, it produces masses of small pink flowers in tight heads at the end of the shoots. It is easy to grow from seed and can be grown as an annual in cold areas. It is also easy to grow from cuttings.

Summer companion
Osteospermum 'Nairobi Purple'

Autumn companion
Nerine bowdenii

Centaurea montana 'Gold Bullion'

Centaurea montana is a giant cornflower with beautiful flowers 7cm (3in) across in blue with a purple centre. It creeps slowly, and the plain green form makes large clumps with stems up to 45cm (18in) high that tend to flop. The leaves are grey green but tend to get mildew in summer, especially if the plants are grown in full sun and in dry soil. If the foliage is cut back and the plants watered, fresh foliage will be produced. 'Gold Bullion' has the usual blue flowers but the foliage is bright gold, a wonderful contrast to the flowers. However, it needs careful placing because the leaves will scorch if the plant is grown in full sun and deprived of water.

Summer companion
Gaillardia 'Dazzler'

Spring companion
Anemone blanda 'Violet Star'

Centranthus ruber

This is a plant that you rarely have to plant twice, so readily does it spread by seed. Its bright clusters of tiny pink flowers are followed by seeds with parachutes that are carried great distances and will germinate in a variety of places, including walls and in paving. The three colours, a dusky pink, bright red, and white, are all attractive to bees and butterflies. All flower for many months, reaching 1m (3ft) high in good soil. They are smaller in poor, dry soil, though. Young growths in spring are commonly attacked by aphids.

Summer companion
Geranium endressii

Spring companion
Narcissus 'Ice Follies'

Chelone obliqua

The North American turtlehead, named for the shape of the flowers, has never become very popular, despite being easy to grow and able to cope with any weather our summers throw at them. They will thrive in most soils, including those that are poorly drained, and have erect stems with long, dark green leaves. At the top of the 60cm (2ft) stems, compact heads of deep pink or white flowers open in late summer. Chelone is a useful plant for late summer and autumn colour, contrasting with the mass of daisy-type flowers that are so abundant during those seasons.

Summer companion
Fuchsia magellanica var. *gracilis* 'Tricolor'

Spring companion
Euphorbia amygdaloides 'Purpurea'

Coreopsis verticillata

Coreopsis include annuals and perennials, but it is the perennials that are the most popular in gardens, partly because some will flower from seed during the first year, giving great value. They are all neat plants with bright, daisy- like flowers in shades of yellow, and most bloom for several months in a sunny spot. *Coreopsis verticillata* is easily grown in a sunny border and forms clumps of finely divided leaves covered in lots of golden flowers. 'Moonbeam' is identical but has pale yellow flowers on 45cm (18in) clumps. *Coreopsis grandiflora* is easily grown from seed and 'Early Sunrise' can be treated as an annual. Plants form a low clump of bright green leaves with masses of semi-double golden flowers.

Summer companion
Oenothera fruticosa 'Fyrverkeri'

Spring companion
Chaenomeles speciosa 'Geisha Girl'

Delphinium 'Magic Fountains'

Old-fashioned herbaceous borders always include delphiniums, their height and blue shades providing a contrast to lower plants in early summer. They are not difficult to grow and they thrive in alkaline soils, but slugs and snails can devour the shoots in spring, and mildew can be a nuisance in summer. In addition to named varieties that are propagated by cuttings, delphiniums can be grown from seed and new, dwarf hybrids such as 'Magic Fountains' may even flower the first year from an early sowing. Even though shorter than the more traditional varieties, they may need to be staked in wet and windy weather. 'Pink Sensation' is completely different, with tall stems of salmon pink flowers, though it tends to be shortlived. All delphiniums can be propagated by basal cuttings in spring.

Summer companion
Artemisia absinthium 'Lambrook Silver'

Autumn companion
Echinacea purpurea 'White Lustre'

Dianthus

Dianthus is a huge group of plants that includes 300 wild species and hundreds of cultivated plants, including carnations and garden pinks. Old-fashioned garden pinks have just one, glorious burst of bloom but modern pinks produce flowers throughout summer. 'Doris' has become one of the most popular of all. Neat and evergreen, the grey foliage of pinks is always attractive and 'Doris' has fragrant, salmon pink flowers on 30cm (12in) stems, which are excellent for cutting. Dianthus love alkaline soil and prefer a sunny, well-drained soil. They are at their best in their second or third year,

though they then deteriorate and become bare in the centre. Cuttings can be taken in summer to replace old plants. Annual pinks (pictured) are easy to grow and give a colourful display from a spring sowing.

Summer companion
Scabiosa 'Butterfly Blue'

Autumn companion
Origanum laevigatum 'Herrenhausen'

Diascia 'Lilac Belle'

Every year sees the introduction of new diascias, plants that were almost unknown a few decades ago. These South African plants are neat and low-growing, flowering throughout summer and producing small blooms in shades of pink with two horns at the back. They thus create two dark eyes in the face of the cheeky flowers. They are hardy in most gardens if the soil is not waterlogged but they are usually grown as bedding plants and put in borders in late spring. Their habit varies a little and some trail.

Summer companion
Festuca glauca 'Blaufuchs'

Autumn companion
Yucca filamentosa 'Bright Edge'

Dicentra spectabilis

This is the most familiar of all dicentras and is readily available in spring because the luscious, ferny foliage and bright pink and white flowers are impossible to resist. However, it is not the easiest to grow in the garden and needs a deep, rich, moist soil and light shade to thrive. The arching stems, which reach as much as 1m (3ft) in good conditions, but are normally considerably less, carry pendent flowers that are heart-shaped and deep pink with a white mark at the base. Often called Dutchman's breeches because of the shape, you need some imagination to see why it is also called lady-in-the-bath. When you pick and upturn a flower and then pull the two pink petals apart slightly, you can see the likeness. Lovely though this plant is, the pure white 'Alba' is far superior and also more vigorous. The yellow-leaved 'Goldheart' should be avoided if only because the golden foliage burns horribly in sun and drought.

Summer companion
Tradescantia 'Concorde Grape'

Spring companion
Lathyrus vernus 'Alboroseus'

Dicentra 'Pearl Drops'

This long-lived perennial has creeping rhizomes that form a dense clump with ferny foliage about 20cm (8in) high of steely grey. In summer, many glassy stems carry creamy white flowers that hang elegantly just above the foliage. It is easy to grow in sun or partial shade. 'Stuart Boothman' is similar but has deep pink flowers.

Summer companion
Hosta 'Patriot'

Autumn companion
Euonymus alatus

Dierama pulcherrimum

Dieramas are supremely elegant plants with slender, grass-like foliage up to 1m (3ft) long. Their strong, wiry stems arch over them and carry many bellshaped flowers in shades of pink, crimson and red. Although often seen next to ponds, where they look at their best, they do not need wet soil and actually thrive in dry soils. They can be propagated by seed or division but usually take several years to settle down after planting and start flowering, so patience is required. They flower for many weeks in summer and always attract attention. 'Blackbird' is compact and has deep pinkish purple flowers.

Summer companion
Penstemon 'Andenken an Friedrich Hahn'

Autumn companion
Phygelius x *rectus* 'African Queen'

Digitalis purpurea

Digitalis (foxgloves) are shortlived perennials that sometimes die after their first flower spikes and are grown from seed. Always buy them as young plants or sow seed and do not be tempted by flowering plants in pots which will almost certainly die after blooming. Foxgloves thrive in sun or partial shade and although *D. purpurea* is often considered a woodland plant, it usually grows at the edge of woodlands, not in deep shade. When sowing seed, sow in summer and do not cover the seeds, which require light to germinate, and ensure they do not dry

out by covering the pots with polythene. 'Sutton's Apricot' has soft apricot flowers on stems 1.5m (5ft) high, and *D. x mertonensis* is a dwarf plant, just 90cm (1m) high with large flowers the colour of crushed strawberries.

Summer companion
Polemonium caeruleum

Spring companion
Doronicum x excelsum 'Harpur Crewe'

Dryopteris erythrosora

Some ferns are particular in their requirements and demand moist soil, but most dryopteris are easy to accommodate, as they tolerate some dryness at the roots. *Dryopteris erythrosora* is one of the most beautiful and useful because it is partially evergreen in sheltered sites and has bold, deep green leaves about 60cm (2ft) high. The young foliage is especially attractive because it is copper coloured and contrasts well with the older fronds and with other spring foliage. For something more frilly, choose *Dryopteris affinis* 'Cristata', which has arching fronds up to

75cm (30in) long with crested tips. The common *D. filix-mas* is the toughest of all, but it still makes an attractive clump of delicate foliage, up to 1.2m (4ft) high in moist soil.

Summer companion
Fuchsia magellanica var. *molinae*

Winter companion
Iris lazica

Echinops ritro

Echinops are tough, reliable, bold plants with spiny, large, divided leaves that slowly rise into substantial clumps of dark green. Added interest is provided by the undersides of the leaves which are usually white or silvery, a good contrast to the deep green upper surface. They are not plants for small borders because the plants usually reach 1.2m (4ft) high and at least 60cm (2ft) across. In summer the leafy flowering stems appear above the clumps and carry globular heads of starry, prickly flowers in shades of grey or blue. *Echinops ritro* is exceptional because it is more compact than most. Grow echinops in full sun in any soil, including clay, but they are best in dry soil and dislike winter wet.

Summer companion
Ricinus communis 'Carmencita'

Spring companion
Tulipa 'Blue Parrot'

Eryngium

Eryngiums are valued for their spiny flowerheads, which comprise a cone of tiny flowers surrounded by longlasting, tough, prickly bracts that are usually in shades of grey or blue. They are mostly perennials that grow best in well-drained soil in full sun. The best known is *E. maritimum*, the sea holly, but this is not the best for gardens because it can be difficult to keep in any but dry soils. *Eryngium giganteum* is one of the most beautiful but is biennial. In the first year the plants produce rosettes of shiny, green leaves but in the second these erupt into 80cm (2ft 8in), branched stems with silvery white flowewr heads that are viciously spiny. It often seeds around the garden. Among the perennial species *Eryngium planum* forms clumps of soft, green leaves and produces tall, slender stems up to 90cm (3ft) high with small heads of blue flowers on branched stems. It is not the most dramatic but has a long season of blooms and is good for cutting, though it often needs staking. *Eryngium alpinum* is the most beautiful, with large flowerheads with frilly bracts, and *E. bourgatii* (pictured) is useful because it is dwarf, just 30cm (12in) high, with silver-veined, spiny leaves. All attract bees and are good for drying.

Summer companion
Santolina chamaecyparissus

Autumn companion
Caryopteris x clandonensis

Euphorbia griffithii 'Dixter'

Many euphorbias are worth a place in the garden, valued for their yellow-green bracts around the small flowers. *Euphorbia griffithii* is exceptional because the thick, purple-tinted shoots that emerge in spring are immediately intriguing, and the bracts are so keen to open that they start to show brilliant orange colour almost before the leaves are developed. 'Dixter' is more compact than most, reaching 75cm (30in) high. This plant can run through the soil but is least likely to be a nuisance on moist soil, though it will survive almost anywhere.

Summer companion
Eremurus 'Cleopatra'

Spring companion
Tulipa 'Apricot Beauty'

Euphorbia dulcis 'Chameleon'

Euphorbia dulcis is a small, neat plant that spreads slowly by rhizomatous stems but also seeds freely. In summer it produces yellowish bracts on stems about 30cm (12in) high, and in autumn the foliage turns brilliant shades of scarlet and gold. 'Chameleon' is more popular than the plain green species and has rich purple leaves. The bracts are a similar colour, with yellow centres. It spreads slowly, seedlings breeding true, and it mixes well with other plants, popping up here and there, though never becoming a nuisance.

Summer companion
Tagetes erecta 'Crackerjack'

Spring companion
Narcissus 'Jetfire'

Festuca glauca

This is the most popular of all ornamental grasses because it is neat, does not spread and is such a useful colour in the garden. A clump-forming grass, it makes a tussock of upright leaves of bright blue-grey, 20cm (8in) high. In summer, it produces dull flower stems, which should be trimmed off to prevent seed being produced. Plants can be divided in spring, and clumps make for pleasant edging in sunny spots, also as a contrast to heathers. The colour of the foliage varies, and 'Blaufuchs' is one of the brightest and best.

Summer companion
Gazania Kiss series

Winter companion
Sempervivum arachnoideum

Filipendula ulmaria 'Aurea'

The wild meadowsweet is not often grown in gardens, but this plant, with bright yellow foliage, is valued for its foliage. The leaves are vivid yellow in spring, fading slightly in summer when the fragrant, fluffy, cream flowers open on 75cm (30in) stems. If these are removed before they open, the foliage will retain its beauty longer. In any case, the flower stems should be cut off as soon as the flowers fade. In light shade the foliage will be lime green. It must have moist soil or the leaves will scorch and become brown around the edges. If the flowers are removed, the foliage will be about 20cm (8in) high.

Summer companion
Aquilegia vulgaris 'William Guinness'

Spring companion
Muscari 'Valerie Finnis'

Gaillardia 'Kobold'

Gaillardias have cheerful, daisy flowers in shades of yellow and red, often with zones of colour, throughout summer. They are short-lived perennials but are easy to grow from seed, and they often flower in their first year from seed. They should be planted in full sun in average to poor soil because they dislike damp and shady positions and do not survive the winter well on wet clay. The plants are roughly hairy and have branched stems with flowers up to 15cm (6in) across. The most popular is 'Kobold' ('Goblin') which only grows to 30cm high but has large, rich red flowers edged with gold. 'Dazzler' has similar, deep red flowers edged in bright yellow on stems 75cm (30in) high. It is a good plant for cut flowers, blooming over a long period.

Summer companion
Potentilla 'William Rollison'

Autumn companion
Phygelius aequalis 'Yellow Trumpet'

Geranium endressii

Hardy geraniums are some of the most useful garden plants. They are generally easy to grow, thriving in sun or part shade, and they flower for many months. Some are spectacular, while others assume a background role, covering the ground and providing a long season of gentle colour. *Geranium endressii* is a spreading plant, about 45cm (18in) high and slightly wider, with lobed leaves. It is partially evergreen, spending winter as a tight clump of light green leaves. The upward-facing, bright pink, five-petalled flowers have a silvery sheen and are produced throughout summer. If plants get scruffy by late summer, simply shear them over and new growth and a fresh flush of flowers will be produced. It thrives in most soils, apart from very dry, sunny borders.

Summer companion
Phalaris arundinacea var. *picta* 'Picta'

Autumn companion
Pennisetum alopecuroides 'Hameln'

Geranium macrorrhizum

Geranium macrorrhizum is a useful, evergreen plant that will survive in deep shade and even under trees. In autumn, some of the leaves turn brilliant scarlet and the flowers, which open in one flush in early summer, are deep pink or white in 'Album'. The foliage is also aromatic and forms a carpet about 20cm (8in) high with the flower stems reaching 30cm (12in) or more.

Summer companion
Weigela 'Florida Variegata'

Autumn companion
Stipa arundinacea

Geranium x oxonianum 'Spring fling'

This is one of the best hardy geraniums where you need to cover the ground, because the stems seem to grow throughout summer, smothering small weeds and providing a tapestry of colour in shades of pink, on plants about 60cm (2ft) high and more in width. It will grow almost anywhere but, like others, benefits from a trim in summer if it gets untidy. Although a spreading plant, stems will clamber through low shrubs and create interesting and unplanned combinations. 'Spring Fling' stands out from the rest because the foliage is bright yellow and marked with pink in spring, but it then becomes green with pink flowers like the rest, in the summer.

Summer companion
Matteuccia struthiopteris

Spring companion
Vinca minor 'Atropurpurea'

Geranium 'Rozanne'

This superb hardy geranium has spreading stems with attractively lobed leaves and large blue flowers with a pale centre. It has larger flowers than most others and flowers continuously throughout summer. It is the best of the many blue geraniums. 'Jolly Bee' is very similar.

Summer companion
Physostegia virginiana 'Summer Snow'

Spring companion
Chaenomeles x superba 'Lemon and Lime'

Geum 'Lady Stratheden'

Geums are grown for their bright red, yellow or orange flowers on bristly stems above deeply lobed and veined rich green leaves. They are strong, robust plants that should be mixed with other plants so their flowers pop up among other flowers and foliage. They are easily grown from seed and thrive in sun or part shade in rich, moist soil. 'Lady Stratheden' has bright yellow, semi-double flowers about 5cm (2in) across in loose clusters on 60cm (2ft) stems throughout summer. *Geum coccineum* ('Borisii') has deep orange or scarlet flowers with prominent yellow stamens on 30cm (12in) stems above luxuriant, lobed leaves.

Summer companion
Dahlia 'Tally Ho'

Autumn companion
Rudbeckia hirta 'Rustic Dwarfs'

Gypsophila paniculata 'Bristol Fairy'

Frequently called baby's breath, do not let the idea of the stale aroma of sour milk put you off growing this classic perennial. From a large taproot, numerous stems branch to create a tangle of rather brittle stems with small grey leaves, and eventually these coalesce to create a cloud of small white flowers that, in 'Bristol Fairy', are larger than normal, 1.5cm (½in) across and double. It is less vigorous than the single-flowered species and must be grown in full sun and well-drained soil. It will reach up to 1m (3ft) high and as much across. Gypsophilas relish chalky, dry soils and must not be planted in borders that are wet in winter or they will rot. Young shoots benefit from staking and protection against snails. Where conditions do not suit the perennials, sow annual *G. elegans* 'Monarch White' instead.

Summer companion
Verbena bonariensis

Autumn companion
Pennisetum setaceum 'Rubrum'

Hakonechloa macra 'Aureola'

This fine grass, made famous by Adrian Bloom of Bloom's Nursery, who showed it as a container plant, should be included in every garden. The foliage is carried on arching stems, forming a neat central clump to create a fountain of yellow-striped foliage 30cm (12in) high and about 45cm (18in) across. It increases in size and beauty throughout summer until the fine, feathery but insignificant flowers appear in late summer. Then the foliage turns to orange shades in autumn, before dying in the frosts when it should be cut down. It is suitable for containers if grown in loam-based compost. Its only defect is that it is rather slow to establish and never looks like much in the first season. Plant in sun or part shade in any moist soil.

Summer companion
Meconopsis cambrica

Spring companion
Hyacinth 'Blue Jacket'

Hemerocallis

Daylilies are robust, easy going perennials with arching, linear leaves that make attractive clumps even before the flowers appear. Some are evergreen but most lose all their leaves in winter. They flower best in full sun but will grow in part shade and are at their best in moist, rich soil. They also tolerate clay soils. In summer they produce leafless stems (scapes) that are usually taller than the foliage, with clusters of lilylike flowers. Each bloom only lasts a day but because of the number of buds, a clump will be colourful for many weeks. 'Corky' has rather small flowers, 6cm (2 ½in) across, yellow with a brown reverse, but they are freely produced on 75cm (30in) stems. Others with more spectacular individual blooms include 'Joan Senior' with 15cm (6in) white flowers, red zoned, apricot 'Siloam Virginia Henson' and unusual, lavender 'Prairie Blue Eyes'.

Summer companion
Hosta 'August Moon'

Spring companion
Narcissus 'Geranium'

Heuchera 'Chocolate Ruffles'

Heucheras have become popular in recent years, thanks to an influx of exciting varieties with colourful leaves from America. Heucheras are evergreen and form clumps of foliage that is at its best in summer. Tall stems of small flowers, usually in pale shades but sometimes in bright shades of pink, are produced in early summer. They should be cut off before they set seed, though. Heucheras can be grown in borders in sun or partial shade but are best in moist, rich soil. They are also suitable for containers but here they may suffer from vine weevils that feed on the roots. They are ideal companions for hostas and ferns.

Summer companion
Diascia 'Blackthorn Apricot'

Spring companion
Tolmeia menziesii 'Taff's Gold'

Hosta – yellow

Hostas can be used in so many places in the garden and are beautiful from the moment their leaves first unfurl in spring to when they turn yellow and copper in autumn. There are hostas for every part of the garden, but most need shade for at least part of the day, preferring moist soil. Varying in size from just 5cm (2in) high to 1m (3ft) or more, they can be used for edging or as bold specimen plants, and most have beautiful white or lilac purple flowers that are also useful for cutting. The yellow-leaved hostas prefer a site with sun for at least part of the day, to bring out their bright colouring. 'August Moon' is a good

medium-sized hosta with leaves that get brighter as summer progresses and grows to about 75cm (30in) high. 'Gold Edger' is smaller with lilac flowers, reaching 30cm (12in). 'Sum and Substance' (pictured) is one of the biggest of all, with huge, lime green to gold, plastic-textured foliage.

Summer companion
Tagetes patula 'Juliette'

Spring companion
Lamium maculatum 'Golden Anniversary'

Hosta 'Halcyon'

Blue hostas have foliage that varies from steely grey to soft shades of pale blue, and most have lavender flowers. They all thrive best in moist soil and in sites where they rarely get touched by direct sunlight. Bright sun burns the edges of their leaves and also reduces the blueness of their leaves. 'Halcyon' has beautiful, narrow, heart-shaped leaves that are bright, grey-blue and attractive lavender, bell-shaped flowers on stems 45cm (18in) high. 'Krossa Regal' is one of the most beautiful and should be planted so that its vase-like habit, with rather upright leaves, can be appreciated. The leaves reach about 60cm

(2ft) high, and the flowers stand well clear of these on 1.2m (4ft) stems. 'Blue Angel' is larger and very elegant with grey, wavy-edged leaves and white flowers on 1m (3ft) stems.

Summer companion
Polygonatum x *hybridum*

Winter companion
Polystichum aculeatum

Hosta 'June'

Variegated hostas offer a bewildering range of foliage patterns, which can be used to brighten shady areas of the garden and are, perhaps, at their best when planted with plants with contrasting leaf shapes and sizes. These include ferns, bergenias, or green hostas. 'June' is a variegated mutation of 'Halcyon', with grey-blue leaves and a central splash of gold, growing about 45cm (18in) high. 'Patriot' has deep green leaves with a

bright white edge and lavender flowers on stems 75cm (30in) high. 'Frances Williams' is one of the largest and most popular.

Summer companion
Dryopteris filix-mas

Autumn companion
Liriope muscari

Iris – Siberian

Siberian iris are easy to grow and do not need regular attention and division, so they are perfect for easy-care borders. They have attractive, grassy foliage that may be rather erect or may splay out to create a waterfall effect. The leaves are usually deep green, but may also be flushed with purple at the base. In autumn the leaves turn rusty brown and should then be trimmed off. The flowers are produced in early summer, after the bearded iris have reached their peak, and the stiffly upright stems carry several blooms that open over several weeks. Siberian iris flourish in moist and heavy soils in sun or partial shade, though you will get most flowers if they are in a sunny

spot. Colours range from white through yellow to pink, wine purple and all shades of blue. 'Butter and Sugar' has yellow and white flowers, 'Shirley Pope' is inky purple and 'Silver Edge' is deep blue with a white rim to the petals. All grow to about 75cm (30in) high. They can be lifted and divided in spring, but this is only necessary after four or five years.

Summer companion
Hosta 'Krossa Regal'

Autumn companion
Eupatorium rugosum 'Chocolate'

Iris – bearded

Bearded iris are the most flamboyant of all early summer flowers, and their large, sumptuous flowers combine virtually every colour you can imagine. They get their name from the furry beard on each of the three lower petals (falls). They need a sunny spot and prefer light, well-drained soils, happy on alkaline soils. Their fans of grey foliage grow from thick, creeping rhizomes, and these must be allowed to see the sun. You should therefore not allow other plants to crowd them or they may rot. There is a bewildering range of varieties, and heights vary from 20cm (8in) to 1m (3ft) when in bloom.

Summer companion
Gypsophila paniculata 'Bristol Fairy'

Spring companion
Crocus tommasinianus

Iris innominata

Pacific coast iris are attractive, small iris that are long-lived and make neat clumps of deep green, grassy foliage, covered in rather flat, intricately marked blooms in early summer. They dislike being divided and disturbed and can be left to grow for many years. They prefer lime-free soil and light shade and are perfect for planting around rhododendrons and azaleas in soil that does not dry out too much in summer. *Iris innominata* is one of the easiest, producing pale yellow, apricot or lavender blue flowers on 25cm (10in) stems. 'High Trees' has pale yellow flowers, 'Goring Butterfly' has purple flowers flashed with gold, and 'Banbury Gem' has rust and yellow flowers.

Summer companion
Trollius x *cultorum* 'Orange Princess'

Spring companion
Primula denticulata

Knautia macedonica

This is one of the easiest of all perennials to grow. Seed, sown in spring, will produce flowering plants after just a few months. Looking like a purple scabious, it forms a rosette of toothed, greyish leaves at first and then sends up tall, branching stems that produce flowers for many months. Because it is rather spindly it should be grown through other plants. It thrives in most soils, including alkaline soils, and it thrives in dry sites in full sun, often selfseeding freely. It is a good companion for taller grasses and may naturalize in meadows. Plants reach about 1m (3ft) when in flower. 'Melton Pastels' is a seed-raised mixture that includes the usual deep beetroot purple and various pinks.

Summer companion
Sambucus nigra 'Black Beauty'

Spring companion
Spiraea arguta

Kniphofia 'Bressingham Comet'

Kniphofias bring dazzling, exotic colour to the border at various times in summer. They produce stiff stems with heads of subtle or bright, narrow flowers in dense heads. Most have grassy, partially evergreen foliage that builds into dense clumps, providing a popular home for snails. Although some are rather frost-tender, most will survive the winter unscathed if planted in full sun in well-drained soil. They also mix well with ornamental grasses. Those with fine, narrow foliage that flower in late summer are most susceptible to wet soil – those with broader, coarser leaves are generally tougher. 'Bressingham Comet' has fine foliage, prefers light soil and is deciduous. The yellow and orange flowers in late summer are dazzling, reaching just 45cm (18in) high. 'Timothy' is tougher and taller, with soft orange blooms, whereas 'Percy's Pride' has 1.2m (4ft) stems with green and yellow flowers.

Summer companion
Achillea 'Terracotta'

Autumn companion
Anemone x *hybrida* 'Honorine Jobert'

Leucanthemum x superbum

Commonly called Shasta daisies, these strong, easily grown plants were made famous by the Read family in Norfolk, England, who bred many fine varieties, including 'Esther Read'. They thrive in rich, moist soil in full sun but also tolerate far from ideal conditions, growing well in clay, for instance. Plants form broad mats of deep green foliage and in spring start to send up stems about 1m (3ft) high with large, daisy-like flowers up to 12cm (5in) across. Typically these are white with a yellow centre, but there are many doubles, and 'Aglaia' has fringed, semi-double flowers. 'Sonnenschein' is notable because the flowers are pale yellow. They make excellent cut flowers but often need to be staked to support the flowers.

Summer companion
Lychnis chalcedonica

Autumn companion
Deschampsia caespitosa 'Goldschleier'

Liatris spicata

The gayfeather is commonly seen as a cut flower, the long stems carrying a spear of fluffy, purple flowers that have the odd habit of opening from the top down. It is also a good garden plant with narrow basal foliage and lots of colourful flower spikes in summer. It is best in an open position in fertile soil and looks especially good with grasses and echinaceas. Plants are best bought as growing plants, though bare roots are also very cheaply available in spring. However, care should be taken to make sure they have not dried out completely. Several varieties are available, including 'Floristan', which grows to 90cm (3ft), and the shorter 'Kobold'.

Summer companion
Malva moschata f. *alba*

Autumn companion
Aster novi-belgii 'Apple Blossom'

Ligularia dentata 'Britt-Marie Crawford'

Ligularias are big, bold plants with attractive foliage and spikes or clusters of yellow or gold flowers. They need plenty of space, and most demand a rich, fertile soil that is constantly moist. In dry weather they wilt in the sun and look miserable. They are also attacked by any snails that may be foraging in the garden and seem to be preferred even to hostas! *Ligularia dentata* has large, round leaves and forms clumps 1m (3ft) high and across, and the large, orange daisy flowers open on stems up to 1.5m (5ft) high in August. 'Desdemona' is the most common, with purple-flushed leaves, but 'Britt-Marie Crawford' is a superior plant, with darker leaves and a more compact habit, reaching 1m (3ft) high when in bloom.

Summer companion
Crocosmia 'Lucifer'

Autumn companion
Persicaria amplexicaulis

Lobelia siphilitica

Lobelias are still regarded principally as bedding plants even though this genus of nearly 400 species comprises a huge range of plants. *Lobelia siphilitica* is one of the easiest to grow and will thrive in sun or partial shade making a clump of long, pale green leaves. It then sends up stems about 1m (3ft) high, packed with pretty blue flowers. It is not fussy about soil and will grow in the average border and in clay soils and is hardy. Unfortunately, some of the other tall and more spectacular lobelias are less hardy. Furthermore, they need constant moisture in the soil to grow really well. But when happy, 'Queen Victoria' can be the highlight of your garden with beetroot red leaves and masses of flowers of searing scarlet. 'Russian Princess' also has purple leaves but this time the flowers are shocking pink. Both should be protected from frost in winter with a loose mulch of straw, while also protected from snails and slugs.

Summer companion
Dryopteris affinis 'Cristata'

Autumn companion
Solidago 'Goldenmosa'

Lupinus 'Band of Nobles Series'

Herbaceous lupins are essential components of the summer herbaceous border, but they do not thrive in all soils. They grow best in light, sandy soils and not grow in clay. They also hate chalky soils. Young plants are best, and it is easy to grow plants from seed, sowing them in late spring or summer and planting them out in late summer or autumn to flower the following year. Good varieties are then propagated by basal cuttings taken in spring. Plant them in full sun for the best flowers and to reduce the need for staking. Most mixtures provide a good range of colours.

Summer companion
Monarda 'Mohawk'

Spring companion
Doronicum 'Fruhlingspracht'

Lupinus arboreus

Though strictly a shrub, the tree lupin is easily grown from seed and is a superb plant for hot, dry soils where little else will grow. It flowers in its second year, and you should plant small specimens rather than leggy, potbound plants. The flowers are usually pale yellow, though some are lavender, and these are set off against the silvery, fine foliage on bushes about 1.2m (4ft) high. Like herbaceous lupins, these are attacked by their own, special, giant aphids which, if left unchecked, can kill the flower buds.

Summer companion
Papaver rhoeas 'Angel's Choir'

Spring companion
Anemone blanda 'Radar'

Lychnis coronaria

Magenta flowers can be difficult to place in the garden, but when they are combined with grey foliage the effect is softened. *Lychnis coronaria* is welcomed in all but the most carefully coordinated pastel garden. It is a shortlived perennial that is best grown from seed, seeding freely in sunny parts of the garden. Surviving dry and poor soils, it will grow in clay and rich soils, too, forming clumps of oval grey leaves that then erupt into branching grey stems with innumerable, 3cm (1in) wide, five-petalled flowers in vibrant pink. Stems reach 75cm (30in) when in bloom, and there are white and pink-eyed white strains available which are less racy.

Summer companion
Papaver somniferum var. *paeoniflorum* 'Black Peony'

Spring companion
Chionodoxa lucillae

Lychnis chalcedonica

Red and green are opposite each other on the colour wheel and among the brightest of garden contrasts, especially when the green is vivid and the red is deep scarlet. *Lychnis chalcedonica*, the 'Jerusalem Cross', provides just these colours on tall stems 1m (3ft) high. Flourishing in most soils in full sun, it can be difficult to combine because of the uncompromising colour of the flowers, so use it with yellow foliage or white flowers to be safe. Staking is usually necessary to prevent the stems from collapsing when in full bloom. It is easily grown from seed.

Summer companion
Rosa 'Margaret Merril'

Autumn companion
Physalis alkekengi

Lysimachia punctata 'Alexander'

The common *Lysimachia punctata*, sometimes called canary weed, is a rather invasive plant that forms large clumps of upright stems clothed with rather dull green leaves. But it can be forgiven when the masses of starry yellow flowers open up the top of the stems. 'Alexander' has the added attraction of variegated foliage that is tinged with pink when young. It will reach 1m (3ft) high and will grow in any soil, in sun or part shade.

Summer companion
Physocarpus opulifolius 'Diabolo'

Spring companion
Narcissus 'Geranium'

Lysimachia nummularia

This plant is also rather invasive, but its stems creep along the soil, rooting as they grow. The common form has green leaves which, to be honest, show off the yellow flowers better than 'Aurea' with its yellow foliage. It will grow almost anywhere, but the leaves scorch in bright sun if the soil is dry. In shade the foliage turns lime green. it is most commonly seen as a bedding plant for hanging baskets, but it can be used as groundcover under hostas and around ponds and waterfalls.

Summer companion
Diascia 'Redstart'

Spring companion
Ranunculus ficaria var. *aurantiacus*

Lysimachia ciliata

This fine plant has starry, yellow flowers, but in the variety 'Firecracker' these are set off by deep purple foliage on stems about 75cm (30in) high. It is beautiful even when not in flower and spreads slowly to form large clumps in sun or light shade.

Summer companion
Heuchera 'Chocolate Ruffles'

Autumn companion
Rudbeckia fulgida var. *sullivantii* 'Goldsturm'

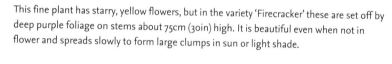

Lythrum salicaria 'Feuerkerze'

This selected form of the native purple loosestrife has upright stems to 90cm (3ft) tall from a woody rootstock. The upper parts of the stems are crowded with bright, rosy red flowers with strappy petals in summer and, if you cut off the faded flowers, sideshoots will grow and prolong the display. It must have moist soil to grow well and is popular as a poolside plant.

Summer companion
Monarda 'Croftway Pink'

Spring companion
Leucojum aestivum

Macleaya microcarpa 'Kelway's Coral Plume'

It is easy to fall for the charms of macleaya. The silvery shoots are beautiful as soon as they appear through the soil in spring and the large, round leaves are beautifully scalloped and are grey-green above and silver beneath. The stems reach 2.2m (7ft) by summer and create a mass of tiny flowers that form a cloud of cream and pink. But it is a thug and will send up shoots some distance away from where it was planted. Should you lose your nerve as it invades yet another border, it will take some effort to get rid of. It will grow in most soils and seems to run most rapidly in light soil.

Summer companion
Echinops sphaerocephalus

Spring companion
Euphorbia amygdaloides
var. *robbiae*

Malva moschata f. *alba*

This beautiful plant is neat and easy to grow, forming bushy clumps of upright stems. At first the leaves are heart-shaped, but as the stems grow they become finely divided and create a ferny effect before the masses of beautiful, five-petalled, mallow flowers open. Typically they are soft pink, but in f. *alba* they are pristine white. Plants grow to about 75cm (30in) high and flower for several months.

Summer companion
Catananche caerulea

Spring companion
Lamium maculatum 'White Nancy'

Matteuccia struthiopteris

The shuttlecock fern is a superb plant with feathery foliage that, in moist, rich soil, can reach 1.5m (5ft), but it is usually smaller. It grows best in damp conditions in light shade and prefers acid soil. Mature plants produce fertile, brown fronds in the centre of each rosette. *Matteuccia struthiopteris* spreads by underground stems that produce new plants.

Summer companion
Campanula persicifolia

Winter companion
Arum italicum

Meconopsis cambrica

The Welsh poppy may not have the fascination of its Himalayan relatives, but it is a fine plant for shade, where it will selfseed between rocks and paving, intermingling with ferns and other ground cover plants. It forms neat hummocks of coarsely cut leaves about 30cm (12in) high and above these, throughout early summer, the yellow, orange or scarlet flowers are produced, sometimes lasting through to autumn. It is perennial and will grow in most soils.

Summer companion
Dryopteris erythrosora

Winter companion
Euonymus fortunei 'Emerald Gaiety'

Meconopsis betonicifolia

This fabled blue poppy from Tibet is one of several with blue flowers, but it is the most common. It forms clumps of rather upright, greyish leaves and sends up stems to 1m (3ft) or more with many sky-blue flowers. It is grown from seed, and unfortunately, young plants often die after flowering. It is usually advised that the first flower spike is removed to allow the plants to bulk up – more easily said than done when the flowers are so beautiful. It is grown from seed which should be sown in summer, as soon as it is ripe – stored seed can be difficult to germinate. It needs moist, acid soil and light shade and is never longlived but, in favourable situations, will selfseed.

Summer companion
Malva moschata f. *alba*

Spring companion
Magnolia stellata

Mentha suaveolens 'Variegata'

Mints are invasive, herbaceous plants, but the variegated apple mint has furry leaves, broadly edged with white and can be allowed to roam through borders. It grows best in sun or light shade in moist soil. The stems rarely grow more than 30cm (12in) high and in summer the lilac flowers attract bees.

Summer companion
Polemonium yezoense 'Purple Rain'

Spring companion
Euphorbia polychroma

Mimulus cardinalis

Most mimulus (musk) require moist soil and are shortlived or not hardy, but this tall, brightly coloured species is tall and easy to grow in moist or average garden soil. It flowers best and is less floppy in a sunny spot, where it will form clumps of upright stems to 90cm (3ft) high with downy, pale green leaves and a long succession of bright scarlet flowers.

Summer companion
Filipendula ulmaris 'Aurea'

Spring companion
Primula florindae

Mirabilis jalapa

Often called the marvel of Peru or wonder flower, this is sometimes sold as dried roots, although it is easy to grow from seed. It is only hardy in mild areas and in well-drained soil, but it usually selfseeds and plants flower in their first year. It forms dome-shaped bushes 60cm (2ft) high with bright green, heart-shaped leaves. All summer the trumpet-shaped, small, fragrant flowers open all over the surface of the foliage and are followed by large, black seeds. The flowers may be white, red, pink or yellow, some combining two shades in intriguing striped patterns. The flowers open late in the afternoon, making it ideal for the gardens of people who work and giving it another common name, the four o'clock plant.

Summer companion
Paeonia 'Krinkled White'

Spring companion
Brunnera macrophylla 'Hadspen Cream'

Monarda 'Beauty of Cobham'

Monardas have fragrant leaves and bunches of tubular flowers in clusters at the top of the stems for many weeks in late summer. They creep slowly to form large clumps and are best divided every two or three years to retain their vigour and to help reduce mildew, the biggest problem with these colourful plants. They grow to about 1m (3ft) high and prefer a site in full sun and moist, rich soil, though they will also thrive in clay soils. Three varieties dominate sales; pale pink-flowered 'Beauty of Cobham', deeper pink 'Croftway Pink' and bright red 'Cambridge Scarlet', but look out for others in different colours such as white and purple. All are vigorous and will need support when in flower.

Summer companion
Nepeta grandiflora 'Dawn to Dusk'

Spring companion
Lamium maculatum 'White Nancy'

Nepeta grandiflora 'Six Hills Giant'

Nepetas include *N. cataria*, the true catmint with small white flowers, though all are commonly called catmint and most receive the attention of felines, which sometimes chew off the shoots as soon as they appear in spring. They are bushy plants with fragrant, greyish-green leaves, and most flop when in flower to make effective ground cover in summer. The masses of mostly blue flowers attract bees and create a hazy, summer shimmer of colour. 'Six Hills Giant' is the most popular of all, with lavender blue flowers on plants up to 75cm (30in) high and as much across

while 'Dawn to Dusk' is unusual for its lilac pink flowers. Nepeta prefer a sunny site and thrive in dry soils, but are also good planted under roses.

Summer companion
Rosa 'Iceberg'

Autumn companion
Aster amellus 'Sonia'

Oenothera fruticosa 'Fyrverkeri'

Oenotheras or evening primroses include annuals, alpines, biennials and large perennials, but most have yellow flowers with four showy petals, and many open in the evening and wilt by breakfast time, sometimes changing colour as they die, to orange or apricot. *Oenothera fruticosa* 'Fyrverkeri' ('Fireworks') is a perennial with a woody base and erect stems. Its narrow leaves are flushed with purple. Throughout summer, the red buds open to bright yellow flowers that create a bright and longlasting display. Plants grow to about 60cm (2ft) high and thrive in light soils in a sunny spot.

Summer companion
Spiraea japonica 'Goldflame'

Autumn companion
Echinacea purpurea 'White Lustre'

Oenothera speciosa 'Siskiyou'

While most oenotheras have yellow flowers, this superb, day-flowering species has bright pink blooms with pink veins, on a white background, and with yellow centres. It makes a mound of narrow foliage and is covered with the large, fragrant flowers for most of summer. It grows to about 45cm (18in) high and thrives in light soils in a sunny border. It can spread by underground stems but does not overwinter well on heavy, wet soils.

Summer companion
Teucrium hircanicum

Spring companion
Euphorbia amygdaloides 'Purpurea'

Paeonia – single 'Bowl of Beauty'

Single peonies have all the beauty of the wild kinds, with lustrous petals and a central golden boss of stamens. Peonies are longlived plants that can survive for decades if planted in the right spot. They flourish in rich, moist soil but can survive neglect, and though they flower most prolifically in full sun, the flowers last longest if they are in partial shade. They have a reputation for being difficult to transplant, but they will not miss a season's flowering if you take care to plant them so the crown of the plant is no more than 2.5cm (1in) below the soil surface. Peonies benefit from an application of rose fertilizer every spring and they may need staking to prevent the stems from being weighed down when in flower. However, doubles are more likely to need support than the singles. Peonies grow well in clay soils.

Summer companion
Geranium 'Jolly Bee'

Spring companion
Narcissus 'Bell Song'

Paeonia – double

Double peonies, with their mass of petals, create sumptuous, old-fashioned blooms and are essential in any cottage garden. The flowers collect water after summer showers so must be staked, but the blooms usually last much longer than the single peonies. They make excellent cut flowers, most having a pleasant scent. 'Felix Crousse' has dark red flowers touched with silver around the edge, 'Festiva Maxima' has fragrant, white flowers with crimson flecks, and 'Sarah Bernhardt' has large, fragrant, soft pink flowers on tall stems.

Summer companion
Hemerocallis 'Corky'

Autumn companion
Rudbeckia fulgida var. *sullivantii* 'Goldsturm'

Papaver orientale 'Patty's Plum'

Oriental poppies give us some of the biggest flowers in the garden, the huge, four-petalled flowers often more than 15cm (6in) across. They are usually vivid scarlet with their distinctive pepperpot seedhead in the centre, surrounded by black stamens that shed their pollen on foraging bees. Though their flowers are spectacular and the coarse, bristly foliage is pleasant in spring, the plants look dreadful after the flowers have faded. They should be cut down to remove the old stems and encourage more foliage. Plant them in full sun in moist, rich soil. Most grow to about 90cm (3ft) high when in flower, but the stems often flop under the weight of the blooms. 'Patty's Plum' has unusual greyish purple flowers.

Summer companion
Gypsophila paniculata 'Bristol Fairy'

Autumn companion
Ceratostigma willmottianum

Papaver nudicaule (P. croceum)

Iceland poppies are shortlived perennials that are usually grown as biennials. They are easily grown from seed and form low clumps of coarsely divided leaves. In early summer they produce a long succession of leafless stems with single flowers in citrus shades of white, yellow and orange. They prefer an open site in full sun and a fertile, well-drained soil. Modern strains include unusual and beautiful colours, including pastel pinks and bicolours. 'Champagne Bubbles' has pastel colours and grows to 45cm (18in), while most, such as 'Summer Breeze' in the basic colours, are 30cm (12in) high.

Summer companion
Diascia 'Blackthorn Apricot'

Spring companion
Allium moly

Penstemon 'Pershore Pink Necklace'

Penstemons are evergreen shrubs, but because they usually need pruning in spring to remove winter damage, they are treated much as herbaceous plants. They are not completely hardy and require a sunny spot and well-drained soil, but they are easy to propagate from cuttings in summer. These young plants can be kept in a greenhouse or coldframe to replace any winter losses. Throughout summer they produce a succession of upright stems 60cm (2ft) or more high, with masses of pretty, tubular flowers. 'Pershore Pink Necklace' has bright pink, trumpet-shaped flowers with white throats and a dotted ring of pink around the mouth of the blooms. 'Andenken an Friedrich Hahn' is among the most hardy and reliable, with deep red flowers, and 'Evelyn' is very bushy and compact with narrow foliage and masses of small, tubular, bright pink flowers.

Summer companion
Lilium 'Stargazer'

Spring companion
Anemone blanda 'Radar'

Phalaris arundinacea var. picta 'Picta'

Until recently, grasses were not popular plants because they had a reputation for being invasive, and this easily grown but spectacular plant was at least partly responsible for this common opinion. Its upright stems are clothed with narrow leaves that are brightly striped with white and green, and a clump lightens any border. But it can be invasive, especially on light soils, so should be planted with care and not near delicate plants that may be overwhelmed. It will grow in most soils and in sun or part shade and is seen at its best in front of dark-leaved shrubs.

Summer companion
Crocosmia 'Lucifer'

Autumn companion
Vernonia crinata

Phlox 'Harlequin'

Along with poppies and peonies, phlox complete the great trinity of Ps in the summer herbaceous border. There are only about 70 species of phlox, but they vary from annuals to small shrubs and perennials of various forms, all but one from North America. *Phlox paniculata* is the most important in gardens and is a tall, leafy plant up to 1.2m (4ft) high, with foliage in four rows up the stems. The round, five-petalled flowers with a long tube are produced in domed heads and are showy and fragrant. Though pink is the most common colour, the range is extensive, including salmon, orange, white, mauve and blue. 'Harlequin' has purple blooms and striking foliage variegated with cream. 'Red Feelings' is one of a new range with masses of tiny flowers comprising mostly of bracts that last for many months. *Phlox maculata* has smaller flowers in more cylindrical clusters, but it too is fragrant and beautiful. 'Omega' has white flowers with red eyes. Phlox prefer a rich soil in full sun and may suffer from mildew in dry soil. Stem eelworm can be a problem but is cured by propagating plants by root cuttings.

Summer companion
Liatris spicata

Autumn companion
Veronicastrum virginicum

Physostegia virginiana 'Summer Snow'

Physostegia is called the obedient plant because the small, snapdragon-like flowers, set in four rows up the narrow stems, can be pushed out of line and will stay where they are put. This party trick aside, it is a useful and beautiful plant for the border, flowering over a long period. The plants form slowly creeping clumps that send up square stems up to 1.2m (4ft) tall with narrow leaves. These branch near the top to create candelabra, with masses of mauve-pink flowers in summer, often with a second flush in autumn. 'Summer Snow' has beautiful white flowers, and *P. virginiana* var. *speciosa* 'Variegata' has pink flowers and spritely, variegated leaves. 'Vivid' has bright pink flowers. Plants grow best in full sun but are not fussy about soil.

Summer companion
Nigella damascena

Autumn companion
Pennisetum setaceum 'Rubrum'

Platycodon grandiflorum

Platycodon is the balloon flower, an Asian relative of campanulas, with bell-shaped flowers that open from large buds that 'pop' open. It has rather sprawling stems with oval, rather waxy, grey foliage and grows to about 60cm (2ft) high with clusters of blooms at the ends of the shoots. The flowers are 5–8cm (2–3in) across and usually deep, lilac blue, but there are also pink and white and double strains. Plants dislike root disturbance and are usually grown from seed. They thrive in well-drained, light soil in sun or part shade but are tolerant of many conditions except winter wet. 'Apopyama' is deep violet and only 30cm (12in) high.

Summer companion
Verbena 'Quartz Waterfall'

Spring companion
Lamium maculatum 'White Nancy'

Pleioblastus viridistriatus

Like many bamboos, this one has its name changed now and then and may be seen as P. auricomus. It is a short bamboo that is not an elegant accent plant but more like vigorous and tall ground cover. It varies in height and may reach 1.5m (5ft) in moist soil but is more often 1m (3ft) high, where it forms a thick clump of upright stems clothed in evergreen leaves that are striped in bright green and butter yellow. It should be planted in sun or part shade in any soil and is useful on banks and in light woodland but its invasive potential should be considered when planting.

Summer companion
Leycesteria formosa 'Golden Lanterns'

Spring companion
Vinca minor 'Illumination'

Polemonium caeruleum

Polemoniums are attractive plants with prettily divided foliage that makes ferny clumps when plants are not in bloom. These produce tall, upright stems that carry clusters of five-petalled, saucer-shaped flowers that are mid blue in *P. caeruleum*. It is rather variable in height, reaching 75cm (30in) in rich moist soil, though it will survive in most soils in sun or partial shade and will naturalize in grass if allowed to set seed. Seed is the best method of propagation and plants flower well in their

second year. The recent introduction, *P. yezoense* 'Purple Rain', has blue flowers above attractive, purple foliage.

Summer companion
Hebe x *franciscana* 'Variegata'

Spring companion
Chionodoxa 'Pink Giant'

Polygonatum x hybridum

Commonly known as Solomon's seal, this deciduous perennial has arching stems with oval leaves set at right angles along the length. Its creamy white, bell-shaped flowers hang in the leaf axils. An elegant foliage plant, it thrives in moist, rich soil in semi-shade but is easy to grow in any but the driest sites. It spreads slowly by creeping rhizomes, and division of these provides the easiest method of propagation. Its main pest is a sawfly that strips the foliage back to its main veins in a matter of days, though this rarely kills the plant.

Summer companion
Philadelphus microphyllus

Spring companion
Viola Sorbet series

Potentilla herbaceous 'William Rollison'

The herbaceous potentillas are useful background plants that start spring as tight clumps of three- or five-lobed leaves, looking rather like strawberries, then sending out straggly stems set with a long succession of petalled flowers. These have five petals that betray their relation to roses. They are usually red or yellow but there are many pastel shades including pinks. Planted in isolation they can be disappointing because of their gangly habit, but if allowed to sprawl though their neighbours they will be seen to be both beautiful and useful. They thrive in any well-drained soil in an open, sunny spot and most grow to about 45cm (18in) high. 'William Rollison' has larger flowers than most, which are semi-double and orange-red. *Potentilla* x *hopwoodiana* has apricot flowers marked with red, and 'Miss Willmott' has deep pink blooms.

Summer companion
Stachys monieri 'Hummelo'

Autumn companion
Sedum telephium 'Matrona'

Prunella grandiflora 'Pagoda'

This may be familiar as a close relative of the lawn weed, self-heal. But it is also a superb border plant for rough areas under shrubs, for naturalizing and for the front of borders. It will grow almost anywhere, though it tends to suffer from mildew in very dry sites. Forming a carpet of oval foliage, it is covered in 15cm (6in) spikes of hooded flowers in shades of pink and blue in summer. These will set seed if allowed and it is best to trim these off when they have faded and to give plants a dressing of fertilizer to encourage new foliage growth. It is easily grown from seed, cuttings or by dividing the clumps that extend as the creeping stems root where they touch the soil.

Summer companion
Artemisia ludoviciana 'Silver Queen'

Autumn companion
Aster x *frikartii* 'Moench'

Ranunculus aconitifolius

There are many attractive buttercups that merit a place in the garden, though some can be invasive. This is a clump-forming species with five-lobed, deep green leaves. From this background, branching stems of white flowers are produced in early summer, lasting for many weeks. It is a tough plant that flourishes in sun or part shade in average to moist soil and can be propagated by division.

Summer companion
Campanula glomerata

Autumn companion
Persicaria campanulata

Rhodohypoxis baurii

Rhodohypoxis are difficult plants to place in the garden and are often best grown in shallow troughs, where their precise requirements can be met. But they can be expected to grow well in some parts of the garden, particularly on rock gardens with moist, acid soils. Rhodohypoxis are dwarf plants with fleshy rootstocks and narrow leaves from which a long succession of small, starry flowers in shades of white and pink appear. These flowers and leaves rarely exceed 8cm (3in) above the soil but can create broad clumps of colour. This plant needs full sun and an acid soil, rich in organic matter, that never dries out in

summer. But, because the plant is not totally frost hardy, it needs some protection from cold in winter. A cloche, to keep cold and excess water off the plants, is the best way to make sure it will survive the winter.

Summer companion
Brachyscome 'Strawberry Mousse'

Autumn companion
Gentiana sino-ornata

Rodgersia pinnata 'Superba'

Rodgersias are big, bold foliage plants from Asia that also have spectacular heads of small flowers that will add interest to shrub borders and bog gardens, reaching their best when many plants in the garden look tired. They spread slowly by creeping rhizomes to form large clumps, and all grow best in moist, rich soil in sun or partial shade. They are hardy but often start into growth early in spring, and these precocious growths may be damaged by late frosts. *Rodgersia pinnata* has leaves rather like horse chestnut, on stems to 1m (3ft) high and stout stems of cream, fluffy flowers in late summer. 'Superba' has bronze leaves and pink flowers. *Rodgersia aesculifolia* is similar but taller, up to 2m (6ft) high, producing cream flowers in looser clusters.

Summer companion
Astilbe 'Cattleya'

Winter companion
Cornus sanguinea 'Midwinter Fire'

Romneya coulteri

It is impossible not to be seduced by the huge blooms of this poppy relative. Reaching almost 15cm (6in) across, each bloom has six, crumpled petals of pure white and a rich golden centre made up of numerous stamens. These open for many weeks in late summer above the coarsely divided, metallic grey foliage on upright or flopping stems. These stems can be anything from 1–2m (3–6ft) high and they will appear some distance away from the original plant because this Californian native is a free spirit and is difficult to restrain – few plants sucker as widely and as vigorously. It needs full sun and well-drained soil because it is not totally hardy. In cold areas it should be planted against a sunny wall. Ironically, it can be difficult and slow to establish.

Summer companion
Phlomis fruticosa

Spring companion
Allium 'Globemaster'

Scabiosa 'Butterfly Blue'

Scabiosa grow wild in Britain in dry grassland, often on chalky soils, and 'Butterfly Blue' is a useful plant for well-drained soil and full sun. It forms hummocks of divided, greyish foliage above low, woody stems and the lavender flowers open above this on 30cm (12in) stems, for many months throughout the summer. These blooms attract bees and butterflies and also make long-lasting cut flowers.

Summer companion
Dianthus 'Doris'

Spring companion
Ipheion uniflorum 'Froyle Mill'

Scabiosa atropurpurea

Scabiosa atropurpurea is sometimes grown as an annual but is really a short-lived perennial with lobed basal leaves and finely divided upper leaves. It is an upright plant, but large plants often collapse under the weight of the branches and flowers so support is required. The flowers are typically domed and scabious-like, and in 'Chilli Sauce' they are an unusual shade of red, while in 'Chile Black' they are as dark as most flowers get. It will only overwinter successfully in light, well-drained soils in full sun and if protected from slugs and snails.

Summer companion
Agastache 'Apricot Sprite'

Autumn companion
Stipa tenuissima

Sedum spathulifolium

This neat, hardy plant is usually planted on rock gardens, though it can also be used for edging and planting between paving. It has creeping stems and rosettes of fleshy leaves covered in white, mealy powder, creating a carpet of silvery foliage. In summer it produces 10cm (4in) stems with clusters of yellow, starry flowers. It is useful for sunny, dry soils but also survives in light shade. 'Cape Blanco' is heavily coated to create a more silvered effect, and 'Purpureum' has leaves that are heavily suffused with purple.

It is easy to propagate by detaching and rooting rosettes with short stems but is rarely invasive.

Summer companion
Acaena microphylla 'Kupferteppich'

Autumn companion
Sternbergia lutea

Senecio cineraria 'Silver Dust'

Although this small, shrubby plant is usually grown as a bedding plant, where its ferny, silver foliage makes a bright contrast to red and purple flowers, it will survive the winter in most areas to form a larger mound in its second year, 60cm (2ft) high and wide. It will then produce its bright yellow flowers, which some gardeners prune off to encourage a neater habit and more leaves. It thrives in dry soils in full sun and although it will grow in clay soil it is unlikely to survive the winter if the soil is damp. It is easily grown from seed though it can also be propagated by cuttings.

Summer companion
Petunia 'Purple Wave'

Autumn companion
Perovskia atriplicifolia 'Blue Spire'

Senecio viravira

This silver-leaved plant has finely divided foliage and sprawls through shrubs and other plants, often reaching 2m (6ft) in height. It is not completely hardy but grows well in dry soil in sunny positions and is often seen at its best when growing through wall shrubs such as ceanothus, on sunny walls. It is propagated by summer cuttings, and young plants can be added to bedding displays in the border and in large containers. The small, cream flowers have no great beauty.

Summer companion
Teucrium fruticans

Spring companion
Fritillaria persica 'Adiyaman'

Sidalcea 'Elsie Heugh'

Sidalceas are compact plants with glossy foliage and upright stems packed with 5cm (2in) mallow flowers, looking rather like miniature hollyhocks. The flowers are bright and have a silky texture. They can be grown in almost any soil, but they dislike winter wet and flower best in sunny borders. They bloom over a long period in summer and are free from problems. Rust may affect them though they are less prone to this problem than many other mallow relatives such as malvas and hollyhocks themselves. Most grow to about 75cm (30in) high and they rarely need support. 'Elsie Heugh' has deep pink flowers with fringed petals. 'Little Princess' is more compact and has pale pink blooms. 'Brilliant' has deep red flowers and *S. candida* has white flowers above finely cut foliage.

Summer companion
Polemonium yezoense 'Purple Rain'

Spring companion
Anemone blanda 'Violet Star'

Sisyrinchium striatum 'Aunt May'

With grey, narrow foliage rather like a slender bearded iris, *Sisyrinchium striatum* is a popular accent plant with tall spires of pale yellow, starry flowers in summer. It is a good choice for a sunny border in dry soils, and its height varies from 45cm (18in) in poor soils, to 90cm (3ft) in better, moister conditions. It self seeds freely if the faded flowers are not removed and can be a nuisance on sandy soils. 'Aunt May' is a superior and less vigorous plant with leaves that have irregular creamy white stripes along their edges. Plants may suffer from winter wet on clay soils.

Summer companion
Helianthemum 'Rhodanthe Carneum'

Autumn companion
Coprosma 'Rainbow Surprise'

Stachys macrantha

Stachys include many valuable border plants that are generally vigorous and leafy with spikes of tubular flowers in shades of pink. They have square stems and opposite leaves and are easy to grow in sun or light shade in most soils. *Stachys macrantha* forms mounds of dark green, deeply veined, oval leaves, and throughout summer it produces 60cm (2ft) stems crowned with pinkish purple flowers. *Stachys officinalis* 'Rosea Superba' is similar and has rose pink flowers. *Stachys monieri* 'Hummelo' has narrower spikes of purple flowers. All are recommended as reliable, easy-going fillers for the borders and are easy to increase by dividing clumps in spring.

Summer companion
Potentilla 'Princess'

Autumn companion
Hydrangea 'Pia'

Stokesia laevis

The cornflower-like blooms of Stokesia often exceed 10cm (4in) across and are produced throughout summer and autumn on stiff, 60cm (2ft) stems above the large, lance-shaped leaves. This is a plant for full sun and light soils, and if planted on clay soils it may rot in winter, though it is tolerant of winter cold. It is best combined with other drought-resistant plants such as echinaceas and grasses, which provide support for the flowers without causing too much shade. It is enjoying popularity as a component of prairie plantings. The flowers are usually pale blue or lavender but white and pink varieties are available. In rich soil in an open border the stems, though stiff, may bend at the base and support may be necessary.

Summer companion
Spiraea japonica 'Anthony Waterer'

Autumn companion
Rehmannia elata

Symphytum 'Goldsmith'

Symphytum (comfrey) are lusty, large perennials that will survive in most soils, including heavy clay, forming deep roots that search out water and make their removal difficult. Any thick roots left in the soil will sprout new plants. However, although they create large clumps, they are not invasive if the faded flowers are removed to prevent self seeding. Their large, rough leaves make effective ground cover and the tubular flowers, produced in long-flowering clusters, attract bees. The most popular have variegated leaves, and 'Goldsmith' has yellow-edged foliage and flowers in shades of red, white and blue in late spring. It grows 30cm (12in) high. 'Hidcote Pink' has pink flowers and green leaves and forms mounds 45cm (18in) high. Symphytum x uplandicum 'Variegatum' is a taller plant with lilac flowers on stems 1m (3ft) high throughout summer and leaves 30cm (12in) long with broad, cream margins.

Summer companion
Weigela 'Briant Rubidor'

Spring companion
Hyacinth 'Blue Jacket'

Thalictrum delavayi 'Hewitt's Double'

Thalictrums are beautiful plants for moist, rich soil, usually preferring light shade, though they will also grow in full sun if the soil is moist. They are valued as much for their delicate foliage, which can resemble maidenhair fern, as for their flowers. The blooms are produced in airy clusters, and much of the colour is produced by the numerous stamens, though some also have petal-like sepals. Thalictrum delavayi grows to 1.5m (5ft) and has delicate mauve flowers 2.5cm (1in) across with showy sepals. However, 'Hewitt's Double', with purple pompon flowers made up of numerous sepals, is the most common. It is not always easy to grow because it requires rich, moist soil, but it can be astonishingly beautiful with its clouds of flowers. It is far easier to grow T. flavum subsp. glaucum, which has coarser, grey foliage and fluffy yellow flowers. It thrives, even in clay, and grows to about 1.2m (4ft) high.

Summer companion
Lilium 'Pink Perfection'

Spring companion
Pulmonaria 'Majeste'

Tradescantia 'Concorde Grape'

Hardy tradescantias are reliable, tough perennials that begin the year as clusters of narrow, succulent leaves. Soon the flower stems appear and the small, three-petalled flowers are surrounded by long leaves. They will grow in sun or shade, but in dry soils the leaves become brown at the tips and look unsightly. As summer progresses the plants become rather scruffy, but they do produce a long display of intriguing, short-lived flowers with furry stamens. 'Concorde Grape' is especially attractive because of the grey-green foliage and purple flowers.

'Osprey' has pale pink flowers, whereas 'Blue and Gold' has blue flowers and yellow foliage, a striking combination. Most grow to about 60cm (2ft) high and will grow in sun or part shade.

Summer companion
Aquilegia 'Songbird Series'

Spring companion
Brunnera macrophylla 'Jack Frost'

Trollius x cultorum 'Orange Globe'

Trollius are called globe flowers because of their beautiful blooms that are like yellow or orange balls at first, then opening into wide bowls with showy, narrow, upright petals and stamens in the centre. They are related to buttercups, the flowers sharing their satin sheen. The flowers are carried above deeply cut, bright green leaves, opening in early summer. Trollius prefer a sunny site but must have moist, rich soil to thrive and are ideal for bog gardens or moist beds beside ponds. They look especially attractive with ferns. 'Orange Globe' and 'Orange Princess' have bright flowers and grow to about 60cm (2ft) high.

Summer companion
Carex elata 'Aurea'

Spring companion
Primula japonica

Verbascum bombyciferum

Verbascums are dual-purpose plants with attractive, silvery foliage and tall stems of bright flowers. Some are biennial and these are the most spectacular, because of the contrast between the growths in the first and second years. Verbascum bombyciferum is a large plant that forms a huge rosette of felted, silver leaves in the first year, sometimes more than 60cm (2ft) across. In the second year it then produces a stem up to 2.4m (8ft) high that carries a long succession of pale yellow, flat flowers with furry stamens in the centre.

It grows best in full sun in well-drained soil and dislikes wet clay soils.

Summer companion
Catananche caerulea

Spring companion
Cytisus x praecox 'Albus'

Verbascum 'Helen Johnson'

The perennial verbascums offer the gardeners some intriguing flower colours, but they are not long-lived and must be grown in an open, sunny site and in well-drained soils. 'Helen Johnson' has dense spikes of terracotta-coloured flowers and grey leaves and is among the most popular though it is not long-lived and may die if the soil is wet in winter. 'Cotswold Queen' has basal rosettes of wrinkled, grey foliage and 1.2m (4ft) stems of bright yellow flowers with maroon centres. 'Pink Domino' has deep pink flowers. Perennial verbascums can be propagated by root cuttings or by seed though they will not breed true.

Summer companion
Lavendula angustifolia 'Imperial Gem'

Autumn companion
Gaura lindheimeri 'Siskiyou Pink'

Veronica spicata

Veronica spicata is a variable species with upright stems, long green leaves and many narrow spikes of small, usually blue, flowers throughout summer. It is easy to grow from seed and is a good, easy perennial to bring some vertical accents and vibrant colour to the garden. It thrives in most soils and in sun or part shade, and the flowers are good for cutting and tend to attract bees. *Veronica spicata* subsp. *incana* 'Silver Carpet' has silvery leaves and blue flowers and only grows to about 20cm (8in) high. 'Rotfuchs' (pictured) is more typical and grows to 30cm (12in) high but has bright, deep pink flowers.

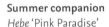

Summer companion
Hebe 'Pink Paradise'

Spring companion
Anemone blanda 'White Splendour'

Zantedeschia aethiopica

The arum lily is a bold specimen plant that has a reputation for being tender, but if the crowns are planted deep so as to be protected from frost it will thrive in most gardens. It prefers moist, rich soil in sun or part shade and the bold, fleshy, arrowhead leaves are impressive even without flowers. The blooms open in early summer and comprise a white spathe curled around the upright yellow spadix. They make excellent cut flowers, some of which are fragrant. 'Kiwi Blush' has flowers flushed with pink at the base and 'Green Goddess' has large blooms edged with green. Zantedeschia also makes a fine plant for a large container if supplied with copious water and fertilizer and can also be grown in a pond if the crown is covered by at least 8cm (3in) of water to prevent it being frosted.

Summer companion
Mimulus guttatus

Spring companion
Polyanthus

Abutilon x *suntense* 'Jermyns'

Most abutilons are frost tender but A. *vitifolium* and its hybrid A. x *suntense* are hardy in mild areas, frequently grown against sunny walls. They are fast-growing shrubs with soft, maple-like leaves, rapidly reaching 4m (13ft) in height. In early summer it produces clusters of saucer-shaped violet flowers 6cm (2¼in) across, creating a bright display for many weeks. If plants get too large, they can be pruned after flowering, but the scales on the foliage may cause irritation. Plant in sunny sites in well-drained soil, though plants will survive on clay soils if it is not wet in winter.

Summer companion
Kolkwitzia amabilis 'Pink Cloud'

Autumn companion
Clematis 'Alba Luxuriens'

Acer negundo 'Kelly's Gold'

The box elder is a medium-sized tree with unusual foliage for a maple, being divided into leaflets rather like an ash tree. Though the flowers are insignificant, it is an attractive foliage tree. 'Kelly's Gold' is the best golden-leaved form and has bright yellow foliage all summer. Like the pink and cream-splashed 'Flamingo', it can be allowed to grow as a tree or can be kept as a smaller bush, by pruning, when it will have its most dramatic foliage. If the plant is pruned hard each spring it can be kept at about 2m (6ft) high by the end of each summer. Otherwise, it will reach about 10m (35ft). *Acer negundo* will grow on most soils in sun or partial shade.

Summer companion
Clematis 'Alionushka'

Spring companion
Viburnum x *burkwoodii*

Berberis thunbergii 'Helmond Pillar'

Berberis thunbergii is a deciduous shrub with small leaves, creamy yellow flowers and brilliant autumn colour in scarlet and red with small, bright red berries. It will survive in most soils and sites and the thorny stems make it a good hedging plant. It usually has green summer leaves and will grow to about 1m (3ft) high. 'Helmond Pillar' has deep purple foliage and an upright habit, making a bold accent in the border. 'Dart's Red Lady' has deep purple foliage in summer and a scarlet autumn colour and a rounder habit. 'Aurea' has bright golden foliage and is one of the most beautiful yellow-leaved shrubs, but it must be placed in partial shade because strong sun scorches the foliage. All can be pruned without causing harm.

Summer companion
Potentilla 'Abbotswood'

Autumn companion
Clematis 'Gravetye Beauty'

Brachyglottis 'Sunshine'

This fast-growing shrub makes a loose mound of oval foliage that is grey-green above and bright silver underneath. It will reach 1m (3ft) high with a wider spread and when mature is covered with golden daisy flowers in summer. However, if hard pruned in spring to keep the plant neat, the flowers are less freely produced. It is a cheap and easy shrub for sunny, dry soils. 'Walberton's Silver Dormouse' is similar but more compact.

Summer companion
Nerium oleander

Autumn companion
Perovskia atriplicifolia 'Blue Spire'

Buddleia davidii 'Nanho Blue'

Buddleia davidii is such a common plant that it is simply known as the butterfly bush. Its long cones of tubular, fragrant flowers in shades of purple, pink and white tend to attract clouds of butterflies in late summer. It grows rapidly into bushes that can reach 3m (10ft) high and as much across but if pruned hard in spring, it will remain smaller and produce large clusters of flowers. 'Nanho Blue' is more compact than most with attractive grey leaves and pale lilac flowers. These buddleias flower in summer and if the old flowers are cut off, as they fade, they will produce a second flush of smaller flower spikes. They thrive in dry, sunny sites in most soils including chalky ground.

Summer companion
Cistus x *purpureus*

Autumn companion
Hydrangea quercifolia 'Snowflake'

Buddleia alternifolia

This is an early-summer-flowering buddleia with arching growth and masses of lilac, sweetly scented flowers. It is a very different shrub to the common *B. davidii* and should be trained up a stake so its weeping branches create a waterfall of colour. If pruned, this should be done after flowering. It is an ideal lawn specimen and succeeds in any soil in a sunny spot.

Summer companion
Lavatera x *clementii* 'Bredon Springs'

Spring companion
Muscari armeniacum 'Blue Spike'

Buddleia x weyeriana 'Sungold'

This buddleia is a hybrid between the early-summer-flowering *B. globosa*, which has round clusters of orange flowers, and the common *B. davidii*. It has long cones of flowers in late summer in an attractive shade of gold. It can be pruned in spring and forms a large shrub, appealing to gardeners and to butterflies.

Summer companion
Euphorbia griffithii 'Dixter'

Spring companion
Kerria japonica 'Picta'

95

Callistemon citrinus

The bottlebrush plant is a loosely branched, evergreen shrub with stiff, linear leaves and clusters of flowers along short sections of the new growth in early summer. The flowers have no petals and their colour is provided by the long stamens. It is not completely frost-hardy and is best planted in light soils in a sunny spot, preferably against a sunny wall where it can reach 2m (6ft) or more. However, it dislikes dry soil and should be

kept moist. It can also be grown in a pot in cold areas.

Summer companion
Alstroemeria aurea 'Orange King'

Spring companion
Corokia cotoneaster

Calluna vulgaris 'Silver Knight'

The Scottish heather or ling is a small, evergreen shrub with tiny, scale-like leaves and a spreading habit of growth, blooming in late summer. The upper parts of the shoots carry large numbers of tiny flowers, usually in shades of pink or white, in late summer, and they are very attractive to bees. Calluna requires a bright, sunny spot and a lime-free soil. Most grow to about 30cm (12in) high but spread considerably more. They should be trimmed over after flowering or in spring to keep the plants neat and preventing them from developing bare centres. 'Silver Knight' has attractive, silvery grey foliage that complements the pink flowers and the foliage is suffused with purple in winter. 'Firefly' has mauve flowers and the leaves are orange in summer and red in winter. 'Darkness' has crimson flowers and 'Silver Knight' has profuse mauve flowers and silver-grey foliage.

Summer companion
Carex hachijoensis 'Evergold'

Spring companion
Rhododendron 'Blue Diamond'

Cistus 'Silver Pink'

Cistus are Mediterranean evergreen shrubs with grey or deep green leaves and beautiful, five-petalled flowers in white or pink, often with maroon or yellow blotches at the base of the petals. The flowers open in early summer and only last a few hours, opening at dawn and dropping their petals by midday in warm weather. They are very useful for dry, sunny borders because they tolerate drought, and they usually thrive in alkaline soils. They should not be planted in heavy, wet soils. They can be pruned lightly in spring to be kept neat and tidy and to remove any growth that has been damaged by winter frosts. 'Silver Pink' has light pink flowers 8cm (3in) across and grows to about 75cm (30in) high.

Summer companion
Artemisia ludoviciana 'Silver Queen'

Autumn companion
Aster amellus 'King George'

Convolvulus cneorum

Of all the grey and silver-leaved shrubs, this is the brightest, and it is not until it opens its funnel-shaped white flowers that you would guess that it is related to bindweed. It is a domed, small shrub with intensely silver, narrow leaves, usually growing to about 60cm (2ft) high, making it ideal for the front of borders. It grows best in dry soil in a sunny spot and will not tolerate soils that are wet in winter. The pretty flowers open in early summer, but it is most valued as a foliage plant.

Summer companion
Myrtus communis 'Variegata'

Winter companion
Helleborus argutifolius

Convolvulus althaeoides

This relative of bindweed has lobed, silvery leaves and pretty, pink flowers, a pot full being the perfect addition to a rock garden. But the stems trail and wind through other plants and it spreads, once established, over wide areas so must never be planted with other, delicate plants. However, where it can be allowed to ramble, the long succession of delicate flowers will brighten your garden if you can find a well-drained, sunny spot for it.

Summer companion
Lavandula stoechas 'Willow Vale'

Autumn companion
Coprosma 'Coppershine'

Convolvulus sabatius

This creeping plant has beautiful, soft blue flowers throughout summer on its trailing stems. Though usually grown as a basket plant, it can survive the winter in a well-drained spot in full sun and is not likely to become invasive, even if planted in a rock garden.

Summer companion
Brachyglottis monroi

Autumn companion
Nerine bowdenii

Cordyline australis

The cabbage palm or Torbay palm is the most common 'palm' in gardens, even though it is not really a palm at all. However, its head of narrow foliage, eventually held aloft on a bare stem, create an exotic look. It is not always hardy in cold gardens and it achieves its greatest dimensions in mild and coastal areas, often making branched trunks and achieving 6m (20ft) or more. The leaves are usually green and the plants are easily grown from seed or bought as young plants but do not develop a full head of foliage until they are two years old. *Cordyline australis* grows best in rich, moist soil in a sunny spot but will tolerate semi-shade and can be grown in a pot. 'Albertii' (pictured) has bright foliage with cream and red stripes and 'Torbay Red' has deep red foliage, though there are many other decorative varieties, none of which are as hardy as the plain green.

Summer companion
Osteospermum 'Silver Sparkler'

Winter companion
Choisya 'Goldfingers'

Deutzia 'Mont Rose'

Deutzias are useful, deciduous shrubs that flower in early summer, after most others have finished. They produce masses of starry, five-petalled flowers in shades of pink and white. Although their foliage is rather dull, some have attractive, peeling bark in winter. They can be planted in all but the driest soils and thrive in clay, and although they flower best when planted in full sun, they tolerate light shade. 'Mont Rose' has pale, lilac pink flowers and grows to 1.2m (4ft) high. *D. x elegantissima* 'Rosealind' has deep pink and white

flowers and is the same height. The tallest is *D. scabra*, which reaches 3m (10ft) and has white flowers. Prune deutzias by cutting out a few of the oldest shoots, near the base, after flowering.

Summer companion
Astrantia major 'Ruby Wedding'

Autumn companion
Clematis 'Venosa Violacea'

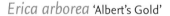

Erica arborea 'Albert's Gold'

This tree heather has bright gold young growth and tiny white flowers in early summer. It has an upright habit and requires lime-free soil. It is useful to plant with other heathers to create a contrasting plant shape as well as bright foliage colour. Pruning is not necessary but, after time, it may be necessary to stake the main stems.

Summer companion
Hakonechloa macra 'Alboaurea'

Autumn companion
Hydrangea 'Pia'

Erica vagans 'Mrs D. F. Maxwell'

This is the Cornish heath, which has showy, small flowers that form cylindrical spires on the new shoots in late summer. Unlike most summer heathers, it will tolerate alkaline soil if it is improved with organic matter and kept moist. 'Mrs D. F. Maxwell' has bright, dark pink flowers and grows up to 30cm (12in) high.

Summer companion
Veronica spicata 'Rotfuchs'

Winter companion
Euonymus fortunei 'Emerald Gaiety'

Erica cinerea

Sometimes called the bell heather because of the large flowers, this is a low shrub with dark green, needle-like leaves. It requires lime-free soil and a sunny spot, and although the flowers may be red or pink, 'Hookstone White' has white flowers, 'C. D. Eason' has magenta flowers and 'Pink Ice' has pink flowers and green foliage that is bronze in winter.

Summer companion
Genista pilosa 'Porlock'

Spring companion
Narcissus 'Jetfire'

Escallonia laevis 'Pride of Donard'

Escallonias are popular garden plants, particularly in coastal areas where they are used as hedges. They are easy to grow in most soils but are not hardy in cold, inland areas so should be given a sheltered, sunny spot. All flower profusely in summer and though the flowers are not large, they are carried in small clusters so make a pretty show. Their glossy leaves are attractive and often aromatic. 'Pride of Donard' has clusters of deep pink flowers in late spring and early summer and dark green leaves, reaching 1.5m (5ft) high. 'Peach Blossom' has bright pink flowers, 'Iveyi' has white flowers in late summer and 'Red Elf' has dark red flowers. Despite its' name it will reach 2m (6ft) high, no smaller than most others.

Summer companion
Crocosmia 'Dusky Maiden'

Winter companion
Euonymus japonicus 'Ovatus Aureus'

Fuchsia magellanica var. molinae

Fuchsia flowers combine delicacy of form with bright or subtle colours and are easy to grow. They prefer light shade and a cool spot and do not always succeed in hot, dry gardens. Millions of fuchsias are planted into summer gardens and most are discarded at the end of the season, but some are hardy and can be left in the ground all year. In cold areas they may get killed to ground level but will sprout from the base, though it depends greatly on the climate of your area and the severity of the winter. You should plant your fuchsias so that the original soil level in the pot is a few centimetres below soil level. It is worth experimenting even with fuchsias that are listed as tender. *Fuchsia* *magellanica* var. *molinae* has green leaves and elegant, small blooms of palest pink, making a bush up to 3m (10ft) high. *Fuchsia magellanica* var. *gracilis* 'Tricolor' has typical, small, red and violet flowers and variegated foliage. 'Mrs Popple' is one of the best large-flowered, hardy fuchsias, producing an abundance of purple and red flowers all summer.

Summer companion
Dahlia 'Fascination'

Winter companion
Lonicera pileata 'Silver Lining'

Genista aetnensis

This, the Mount Etna broom, is a large shrub or small tree, up to 3m (10ft) or more, actually a fine choice for a small garden. It grows rapidly and the almost leafless, green branches cause little shade so you can plant right up to the trunk. In summer it is covered in small, bright yellow, pea-like flowers. Either grow this shrub from seed or buy young plants – large specimens do not establish well and tend not to form good roots. Like most genistas, it thrives in sun and in dry soils.

Summer companion
Brachyglottis 'Sunshine'

Spring companion
Fritillaria imperialis

Genista tinctoria 'Royal Gold'

This low-growing shrub is deciduous and has bright green leaves in summer that are the perfect background to the golden yellow flowers that are held in small clusters in early summer. It will reach 1m (3ft) high and across.

Summer companion
Campanula poscharskyana

Spring companion
Tulipa 'Red Riding Hood'

Hebe x *franciscana* 'Variegata'

Hebes are pretty, evergreen shrubs with spikes of small, tubular, four-petalled flowers from early summer till autumn, depending on the variety. They vary in height from just a few centimetres to 2m (6ft) or so but most reach 60–100cm (2–3ft). They prefer a moist soil that is not too dry and in a sunny spot in summer, and some are not fully hardy. As a general rule, those with small leaves, less than 8cm (3in) long, are the most hardy. They tolerate wind and coastal areas where frosts tend to be less severe. *Hebe* x *franciscana* 'Variegata' is commonly available in autumn and has neat, round leaves edged with cream and squat clusters of violet flowers. It is moderately hardy and forms a 60cm (2ft) high mound.

Summer companion
Agastache foeniculum 'Golden Jubilee'

Winter companion
Phormium 'Yellow Wave'

Hebe 'Pink Paradise'

This is one of many modern hebes that have small leaves, are tough, and make good groundcover or edging for the border in a sunny spot. It has rather sprawling stems with tiny, olive green leaves and masses of small, deep pink flowers in early summer, with odd flowers later in the season.

Summer companion
Dianthus 'Laced Monarch'

Spring companion
Muscari armeniacum 'Blue Spike'

Hebe pinguifolia 'Pagei'

This dwarf hebe forms dense, low clumps of rounded, grey leaves, arranged, as is typical, in four rows along the stems. In early summer plants are smothered in clusters of small, white flowers. Like all hebes, it benefits from light pruning in spring to remove any shoots that have been damaged by winter frosts.

Summer companion
Iris 'Sarah Taylor'

Winter companion
Ophiopogon jaburan 'Vittatus'

Helianthemum

Helianthemums are dwarf shrubs, closely related to cistus. Their five-petalled flowers are similar but smaller and also drop their petals at midday, but there is a greater range of flower colours and forms. Most grow to about 30cm (12in) high and 60cm (2ft) wide and have green or grey leaves, and they flower in early to mid-summer. They benefit from a light trim after flowering to keep plants neat. Thriving in a hot, sunny border, they are drought-resistant. 'Fire Dragon' (left) has grey leaves and scarlet flowers 2.5cm (1in) across. 'Raspberry Ripple' has single, pink flowers with large white splashes across much of the petals and 'Rhodanthe Carneum' has silver leaves and pale, bright pink flowers.

Summer companion
Cistus salvifolius

Spring companion
Tulipa tarda

Hypericum 'Hidcote'

This is a reliable, tough, long-flowering shrub that is more or less evergreen and has bright yellow flowers 6cm (2⅓in) across. The leaves are narrow and dark green, forming a neat mound that is studded with flowers throughout most of summer. The flowers have five golden petals and a puff of yellow stamens in the centre. Plant it in sun or part shade in any soil except those that are wet in winter. It will reach 1.2m (4ft) high and can be pruned lightly in spring without affecting flowering.

Summer companion
Clematis x durandii

Spring companion
Fritillaria imperialis

Kalmia latifolia 'Pink Charm'

Kalmias are related to rhododendrons and, like them, dislike alkaline soils. They have clusters of flowers above evergreen leaves, but there the similarities stop, because these North American shrubs are sun lovers. They grow slowly and their lack of popularity is probably due to the cost of small plants and the fact that they are usually planted in shade, where they gradually decline. Plant them in a sunny spot in soil that does not dry out in summer – no mean feat. They are also suitable for pot cultivation. The saucer-shaped flowers open from delicate, intricately formed buds that are often deeper in shade than the open blooms. 'Pink Charm' has deep pink buds that open to pink flowers banded with maroon. 'Freckles' has pale pink flowers with a ring of deeper pink spots and 'Ostbo Red' has pale flowers and red buds. All grow to about 2m (6ft) high, but this takes several decades.

Summer companion
Calluna vulgaris 'Firefly'

Spring companion
Chionodoxa 'Pink Giant'

Kolkwitzia amabilis 'Pink Cloud'

Kolkwitzia is often called the beauty bush. It is a large plant that is covered in foxglove-like, pink flowers and is indeed a wonderful sight. It is an easy, deciduous shrub that will grow on light and heavy soil and will survive in sun or part shade, though flowering will be best in full sun. It is a rather large shrub, easily reaching 2.5m (8ft), with arching branches. The flowers are pale pink, marked with gold in the throat and are produced in great profusion in early summer. 'Pink Cloud' has deeper pink flowers.

Summer companion
Lilium 'Pink Perfection'

Autumn companion
Colchicum speciosum

Laburnum x watereri 'Vossii'

Laburnums are among the most beautiful of all early summer-flowering shrubs, blooming with the lilacs and producing great waterfalls of bright yellow. They are less popular than they were because the seeds are poisonous and their pods are interesting to children. However, *Laburnum x watereri* 'Vossii' not only has some of the most prolific flowers of all, it also sets no seed, reducing the danger to children but also the habit of not flowering well the year after a good crop of seed has set, a common problem with seed-bearing laburnums. It will reach 8m

(25ft) high with flower clusters 60cm (24in) long and will grow on most soils. It is hardy and quick to establish.

Summer companion
Escallonia laevis 'Gold Brian'

Spring companion
Allium 'Globemaster'

Laurus nobilis

The common laurel is not only a useful cooking herb, it is an easily grown evergreen that is usually bought either as inexpensive windowsill plants or expensive plants trained as topiary standards. They may not survive the winter in cold areas or after a cold winter, except in mild areas, but established plants usually sprout from the base if the top growth is killed so spring pruning is often necessary. Topiary specimens will tolerate drought, pollution and strong sun but they will grow far better, and be less likely to succumb to scale insects, if they are watered and fed well. Topiary plants should have their

shoot tips pinched out regularly to keep them neat. 'Aureus' is attractive because it has bright yellow foliage throughout the year, a good contrast to the dark green of the usual plant.

Summer companion
Crocosmia 'Lucifer'

Autumn companion
Euonymus alatus

Lavandula angustifolia 'Sawyers'

Lavenders are evergreen shrubs with grey leaves and fragrant foliage and flowers. They are Mediterranean plants and relish a hot, dry spot in the garden. They will flourish on acid or alkaline soils but dislike soils that are wet, especially in winter. They make good small hedges in formal situations but you must take care that plants bought for this purpose have been propagated by cuttings and not by seed. These will result in similar but not identical plants that will create an unsatisfactory result. Plants should be

trimmed lightly in spring and/or after flowering but hard pruning, cutting them into leafless stems, may kill the plants. 'Sawyers' has exceptionally silvery foliage and long spikes of deep purple flowers.

Summer companion
Helichrysum petiolare

Spring companion
Crocus vernus 'Remembrance'

Lavandula stoechas

This is French Lavender, which requires a sheltered, sunny spot in well-drained soil because it is less hardy than most other lavenders. Its chief attraction is the tuft of purple bracts at the top of the flower heads, though the leaves are rather dull compared to most others. 'Willow Vale' is one of many selections with larger bracts or tougher constitutions.

Summer companion
Fuchsia 'Mrs Popple'

Autumn companion
Sternbergia lutea

Lavatera x clementii 'Bredon Springs'

Shrubby lavateras are the ideal companion to buddleias in the border. They, too, are fast-growing shrubs, like dry soils and full sun and bloom for long periods. 'Rosea', which has pink flowers, usually represents lavateras as do 'Barnsley', with white flowers marked by a red eye. If planted in early summer, both will rapidly reach 2m (6ft) high by the end of the summer. In rich soil they almost grow too fast and may suffer wind damage in winter unless cut back by half in autumn before their annual prune in spring. They have flowers about 8cm (3in) across and greyish, heart-shaped leaves. 'Bredon Springs' is more compact than most with deep pink flowers and overlapping petals. 'Ice Cool' is also compact and has pure white flowers.

Summer companion
Verbena hastata 'Rosea'

Autumn companion
Callicarpa bodinieri var. *giraldii* 'Profusion'

Leptospermum scoparium 'Red Damask'

In most areas, leptospermums (tea tree) can only be grown in a frost-free conservatory or greenhouse but with a succession of mild winters, there is a good chance that plants may develop into attractive specimens against warm walls in favoured areas. Leptospermums are evergreen with tiny leaves and profuse, rose-like flowers in shades of pink, white and crimson in early summer. Plants can exceed 3m (10ft) in mild areas but they are also easily shaped through pruning and are popular for bonsai. Plants are often sold without variety names but this does not matter because all are pretty. 'Red Damask' is one of the most beautiful and has long-lasting, deep red, double flowers. It was bred from 'Nicholsii' which has purple foliage and crimson flowers. 'Kiwi' has similar colouring but is dwarf.

Summer companion
Gladiolus communis subsp. byzantinus

Autumn companion
Coprosma 'Rainbow Surprise'

Leycesteria formosa

Leycesteria, often called the nutmeg bush or Himalayan honeysuckle, is a large, leafy shrub that sometimes pops up unexpectedly in gardens, the result of birds eating the deep purple berries. The berries follow the small, tubular, white flowers that open in dangling clusters, surrounded by maroon bracts through summer. The plant has an upright habit with attractive green, hollow stems that arch at the tips. It is not brilliant in flower, being leafy and dense, but is interesting and will grow almost anywhere, in sun or part shade. Eventually reaching 2m (6ft) high and as much across, you can reduce its size by cutting out a few of the oldest stems near the base, each spring. 'Golden Lanterns' is a new, far more beautiful plant with yellow foliage that is bronzed when young.

Summer companion
Anthemis tinctoria 'Grallach Gold'

Winter companion
Phormium 'Dazzler'

Magnolia grandiflora

Most magnolias flower in spring, but this evergreen magnolia from the southern states of North America blooms throughout late summer and is beautiful even when not in flower. The leaves reach 20cm (8in) long and are thick and waxy, and the flowers, that can be 25cm (10in) across, are cream in colour with thick petals and a glorious, lemony fragrance. It is usually grown against a sunny wall because it is not completely hardy and the reflected heat from the wall encourages the flowers to form. It can reach 10m (33ft) so needs plenty of space.

Summer companion
Alstroemeria aurea 'Orange King'

Spring companion
Erysimum cheiri 'Fair Lady Mixed'

Myrtus communis

The common myrtle is a Mediterranean, evergreen shrub with small, dark green leaves, building up into a billowing mound, covered, in late summer, with 2cm (¾in) white flowers that have fluffy white centres. It requires a sunny, sheltered spot and, in cold areas, can be grown in a pot of John Innes compost. Although it can reach 2m (6ft) high, it is usually much smaller and is a good choice for the base of a sunny wall, where it will grow with other sun lovers such as lavender and bay. 'Variegata' has leaves prettily edged with white, though these do not show the flowers as well as the plain green sort.

Summer companion
Cistus 'Silver Pink'

Autumn companion
Phygelius 'New Sensation'

Olearia macrodonta

Olearias are daisy bushes and are generally fast-growing evergreen shrubs that need a sunny, sheltered spot, only suitable for mild areas. They tolerate wind and are ideal for coastal gardens. Most have white, daisy-like flowers in huge numbers and are spectacular when in flower. *Olearia macrodonta* is only suitable for the mildest gardens, but is exceptionally lovely because of the attractive, large, holly-like leaves and clusters of greyish white, 1cm (½in) daisies in summer. *Olearia stellulata* and *O. phlogopappa* are similar and reach about 2m (6ft) in height with greyish, woolly leaves that are buried under masses of small, white daisies in early summer. 'Comber's Blue' has blue flowers. The hardiest olearia is *O. x haastii*, but this is a dull, small shrub with small greyish flowers, and is hardly worth planting.

Summer companion
Hebe 'Great Orme'

Autumn companion
Sedum 'Pink Chablis'

Paeonia – tree *Paeonia suffruticosa* 'Rock's Variety'

Tree peonies (moutan) are among the most beautiful of all shrubs with huge flowers, 20cm (8in) across, in early summer. Their foliage is deeply cut and also beautiful, though the rather gaunt stems are somewhat ugly in winter. They are hardy, but the new growth in spring starts to grow early and may be caught by late spring frosts, so plant them either in sheltered places, perhaps against a wall, or in a shady place where they are not encouraged to make an early start. They prefer a rich, moist soil and a spot in partial shade, although they also succeed in shady spots. However, they may not flower as freely as in brighter places. *Paeonia suffruticosa* 'Rock's Variety' is possibly the most beautiful, with huge, white flowers marked with deep purple blotches.

Summer companion
Iris 'Silver Edge'

Autumn companion
Tricyrtis formosana 'Samurai'

Paeonia lutea var. ludlowii

This tree peony is a wild species that has smaller flowers than the hybrids and is easier to grow, even self-seeding in some gardens. The bold, deeply cut leaves are pale green and the bright yellow, cupped flowers nestle among these in early summer. It will grow almost anywhere, in sun or shade. In autumn the leaves tend to remain on the plants after they die and, if you have time, it is worth cutting them away to prevent the plants looking awful through winter.

Summer companion
Physocarpus opulifolius 'Dart's Gold'

Spring companion
Euphorbia polychroma

Philadelphus 'Belle Etoile'

Philadelphus or mock orange are popular because of their exquisitely fragrant, white, four-petalled flowers in early summer. Some of the most common are far too big for modern gardens and not easy to keep small without reducing the display of flowers. They should be pruned by cutting out a few of the oldest stems, near the base, after flowering, to leave room for younger stems to spread. Philadelphus will grow in any soil, including clay and in sun or part shade. The leaves are rather dull after flowering. 'Belle Etoile' is one of the most popular and has masses of white flowers, flushed with maroon in the centre. 'Manteau d'Hermine' is a superb plant with double, creamy white flowers, growing to 1m (3ft) high and across. Always choose these rather than the huge 'Virginal' unless you have plenty of room.

Summer companion
Clematis heracleifolia

Autumn companion
Aconitum carmichaelii 'Arendsii'

Philadelphus microphyllus

This beautiful shrub has orange-brown stems and small leaves that are silver underneath. It has an arching habit and reaches 1.2m (4ft) high and across with the arching habit. In early summer it is covered with small, single white flowers with a wonderful fragrance that hints at pineapple. It prefers a place in full sun.

Summer companion
Spiraea japonica 'Anthony Waterer'

Spring companion
Erysimum 'Bowles' Mauve'

Philadelphus coronarius 'Aureus'

This philadelphus is popular as a foliage plant because the leaves are bright yellow. However, the white, fragrant flowers are a valuable bonus, giving the plant a useful extra dimension. It can be difficult to grow well because, if planted in sun in dry soil, the leaves become scorched and brown.

But in shade the foliage stays lime green and lacks its potential brilliance. When grown well it is spectacular. Moist or heavy soils are better than light soils, which can dry out in summer. It can exceed 2m (6ft), but can be pruned if you do not mind losing some flowers.

Summer companion
Campanula persicifolia

Autumn companion
Aster 'Climax'

Phlomis fruticosa

Phlomis, sometimes called Jerusalem sage, is a Mediterranean plant with thick, woolly, grey leaves, adapted to hot, dry climates. It appreciates these conditions in your garden and will rapidly form a mound of long, furry leaves on square stems. In early summer the curious, hooded flowers are produced in clusters at each leaf, joint along the upper parts of the stems. These are mustard yellow and leave attractive seed pods when they fall, which can be cut and dried. This shrub grows quickly and should be pruned hard in spring to prevent it becoming lax and untidy. Plant it in sun in well-drained soil. It is not always hardy in wet soils in cold areas but thrives at the coast, reaching 1m (3ft) high in just a year or so.

Summer companion
Artemisia 'Powys Castle'

Spring companion
Erysimum cheri 'Cloth of Gold'

Physocarpus opulifolius 'Diabolo'

The plain green Physocarpus is hardly a thing of beauty with deeply veined, lobed leaves and small domed clusters of white flowers in early summer. But there are two selections with coloured foliage that deserve a place in any garden. The best is 'Diabolo', which has deep purple foliage with a brown undertone that makes a wonderful background for brighter flowers. The blooms are flushed with pink and the seedpods ripen to deep cherry red. It has an upright habit at first and will grow, in any soil, to 2m (6ft) or more but is easily pruned. The best foliage colour develops when it is planted in full sun. 'Dart's Gold' has bright yellow foliage that ages to lime green and white flowers. It is best in part shade to prevent the leaves getting scorched by hot sun.

Summer companion
Eremurus 'Cleopatra'

Spring companion
Lamium orvala

Potentilla shrubby 'Abbotswood'

The shrubby potentillas are tough, deciduous plants that thrive in full sun or part shade. They have thin, twiggy growth and prettily divided, small leaves that may be green or grey. The flowers are about 3cm (1in) across and have five petals, like tiny roses. Most have flowers in shades of yellow or white but there are also pink and red varieties. Heights vary, but yellow and white-flowered potentillas are the most vigorous and may reach 75cm (30in) while the pinks and reds are usually about 45cm (18in) high. They flower for many months in summer. In winter they are rather dull, with mounds of greyish or brown twigs. They will grow in any soil that is not waterlogged and can be pruned in spring without affecting the flowering much, though annual pruning is not necessary. 'Abbotswood' has blue-grey leaves and white flowers and 'Elizabeth' has bright yellow blooms. 'Princess' has pale pink flowers and 'Red Ace' has scarlet flowers in cool weather – they turn orange or yellow in hot, dry conditions.

Summer companion
Achillea 'Marie Anne'

Spring companion
Bergenia 'Silberlicht'

Robinia pseudoacacia 'Frisia'

This yellow-leaved tree can be seen in gardens throughout the country. It is a fast-growing tree, reaching 15m (50ft) in time, with soft yellow foliage that is divided into leaflets, rather like an ash tree. White flowers are produced in early summer but these are not the main reason to grow this tree. It grows well on light soils but has rather brittle branches that can break off large trees. It can sucker if planted in dry, poor soils, responds well to pruning and, in small gardens, can be pruned back to a main stem every spring to maintain a small head of large, bright foliage.

Summer companion
Hypericum x *inodorum* 'Elstead'

Spring companion
Aconitum carmichaelii 'Arendsii'

Rosa glauca

Roses are essential components of the summer garden and modern roses flower longer than almost any other summer shrub. They have many uses in the garden and *Rosa glauca*, a wild rose, is one of the most beautiful. It grows to about 2m (6ft) high and has grey-purple leaves that are the perfect background for the single, almost scentless flowers that are deep pink with a white centre. These are produced for about a month in early summer and are followed by deep red or orange hips in autumn. It is easy to grow in most soils and develops its best foliage colour in full sun, usually immune to most diseases. It makes a good garden shrub and is also excellent for hedges.

Summer companion
Fuchsia magellanica var. *gracilis* 'Tricolor'

Autumn companion
Miscanthus sinensis 'Flamingo'

Rosa – yellow

Yellow roses are popular and are available in the large-flowered or hybrid teas, the cluster-flowered or floribunda types and in other groups. 'Freedom' (pictured) is a good, scented rose with large flowers in bright yellow and resistant to disease. Korresia is compact, has healthy foliage and clusters of fragrant flowers with wavy petals. 'Graham Thomas' is one of the most popular of the English Roses, combining old-fashioned scent with repeated flowering throughout summer. The large, yellow flowers are carried on vigorous plants that can be used as pillar roses or up a trellis, growing to about 1.5m (5ft).

Summer companion
Nepeta 'Six Hills Giant'

Autumn companion
Phygelius aequalis 'Yellow Trumpet'

Rosa – red

Red roses may be romantic, but they do not always have as much fragrance as we would like them to have. There are lots of shades of red, and 'Brown Velvet' is a particularly unusual shade of rusty red. Its' deep green foliage shows off the flowers very well. 'Eye Paint' has single, red flowers with a bright white centre. 'Royal William' is everyone's idea of the perfect red rose, with dark green foliage and large, high-centred deep crimson flowers with a good perfume. However, 'The Times' is one of the best for a rose bed, because it is compact at 60cm (2ft) high with lustrous, purple new growth and clusters of dazzling red flowers all summer. Most roses grow best in heavy soils and, unless you know they are resistant to disease, they should be sprayed against blackspot and mildew every two weeks from late spring throughout the summer.

Summer companion
Lysimachia ciliata 'Firecracker'

Spring companion
Chionodoxa luciliae

Rosa – pink

There are many pink roses with flowers from palest shell pink to vibrant magenta. 'Flower Carpet' (pictured) is the latter and has clusters of small, almost scentless, double flowers from early summer through to late autumn. It has a spreading habit and is sold as a groundcover rose, though it will reach 1m (3ft) high, but its main merit is that it is almost always free from any disease. 'Flower Carpet Coral' has pretty, single flowers. 'Bonica' is a neat shrub rose that produces its double, mid-pink flowers all summer and reaches about 1m (3ft) high. 'Felicia' is a hybrid musk rose

with glorious scent that reaches 1.5m (5ft) high, often reaching its floral crescendo in late summer. 'Mary Rose' is an English Rose with cupped, double, heavily scented flowers. 'Brother Cadfael' has large, mid pink flowers with a glorious fragrance.

Summer companion
Paeonia 'Felix Crousse'

Autumn companion
Abelia x *grandiflora* 'Confetti'

Rosa – white

White roses are valuable when you need a long season of white flowers, including some of the most popular roses of all time. 'Iceberg' has masses of pure white flowers, sometimes tinged with pink in wet weather, on thin shoots with few thorns. It has a pleasant fragrance. 'Margaret Merril' has larger flowers with fewer petals and displays its' red stamens when the fragrant flowers are fully open. 'Blanc Double de Coubert' is a large shrub with double flowers made up of papery white petals. It is related to *Rosa rugosa* and is easy to grow, thriving on light soils.

Summer companion
Nepeta grandiflora 'Dawn to Dusk'

Winter companion
Euonymus fortunei 'Emerald Gaiety'

Rosa – patio

Patio roses are simply, short, cluster-flowered roses, most of which are 60cm (2ft) or less in height and can be grown in borders or in pots of John Innes compost in a sunny spot. Most are modern and fairly resistant to disease, but spraying will prevent blackspot and mildew. 'Surrey' is a ground cover rose with large, semi-double, frilly-petalled pink flowers and 'Sweet Dream' (pictured) has apricot flowers. 'Angela Rippon' has salmon pink flowers.

Summer companion
Potentilla x *hopwoodiana*

Spring companion
Brunnera macrophylla

Sambucus nigra 'Black Beauty'

Elderberry (*Sambucus nigra*) is a weedy shrub that often turns up uninvited in gardens, the gift of fruit-eating birds. But this very ease of cultivation is also a blessing because the many forms with interesting and coloured foliage are foolproof shrubs for almost any spot in the garden. They thrive in any soil and can be pruned at will and will bounce back with beautiful foliage. One of the best is 'Black Beauty', which has deep-purple foliage and clusters of pink flowers on lightly pruned or un-pruned plants. It can be kept to 2m (6ft) but can reach 4m (13ft) after a few years.

Summer companion
Lychnis coronaria

Spring companion
Ribes sanguineum 'Red Pimpernel'

Sambucus racemosa 'Sutherland Gold'

This elder has pyramidal clusters of white flowers and red berries, but only on plants that are lightly pruned. And, because the main feature of the plant is the feathery, bright yellow leaves, encouraged by hard, spring pruning, these are not always seen. It will grow in any soil, but the leaves develop brown edges if grown in dry soil and bright sun. It grows best in rich, moist soil and light shade. It will reach 2m (6ft) in a season and 3m (10ft) ultimately.

Summer companion
Berberis thunbergii 'Golden Ring'

Autumn companion
Cotinus coggygria 'Royal Purple'

Santolina chamaecyparissus

Santolinas are dwarf shrubs with feathery, aromatic foliage and are called cotton lavenders. They are not related to lavenders at all but appreciate the same conditions, flourishing in well-drained soil in full sun and being useful for dry, sunny borders. They quickly become floppy and should be pruned hard in spring to maintain a neat habit. They are also useful as a low hedge and as an edging plant beside paths. In summer they produce round clusters of tiny flowers in shades of yellow, but many gardeners trim these off before they open. *Santolina chamaecyparissus* grows to about 50cm (20in) and has grey leaves and bright

yellow flowers, and *S. pinnata* subsp. *neopolitana* 'Sulphurea' has grey leaves and pale yellow flowers.

Summer companion
Sisyrinchium striatum 'Aunt May'

Spring companion
Arabis alpina 'Flore Pleno'

Spartium junceum

The Spanish broom is a fast-growing, upright shrub that is ideal for dry soils where little else will grow. The green stems have narrow green leaves that cast hardly any shade. Throughout summer it produces large, pea-like flowers in bright yellow that are fragrant. It can be planted almost anywhere but needs a sunny spot, in time reaching 3m (10ft). It can be kept smaller by pruning in spring, but young plants are most attractive and it is easy to grow from seed, which is freely produced. Seedlings start to flower in their second year.

Summer companion
Buddleia 'Nanho Blue'

Autumn companion
Perovskia atriplicifolia 'Blue Spire'

Spiraea japonica 'Goldflame'

Spiraeas are useful, hardy, deciduous shrubs, and different kinds flower throughout spring and summer. *Spiraea japonica* 'Goldflame' is one of the most popular, being a shrub up to 75cm (30in) high with thin, interlocking branches. In spring the new growth is bright orange, but this fades to pale yellow as it matures. New growth, however, which emerges throughout summer, is orange, again. The plant also produces small clusters of dusky pink, small flowers throughout summer. If pruned hard in spring or early summer, it will produce a glorious display of vivid foliage. It will grow in most soils but is best in moist, rich soils in sun or partial shade.

Summer companion
Agastache 'Apricot Sprite'

Spring companion
Ajuga reptans 'Catlin's Giant'

Teucrium fruticans

Among the most brilliantly silver of all shrubs, this has long stems with small, narrow foliage, everything being covered in white hairs. It is aromatic, and throughout summer a mass of pretty, pale blue flowers is produced to create a luminous silvery blue haze up to 1m (3ft) high. It needs light, well-drained soil and a sunny spot, tolerating drought. It is useful to plant against a hot, sunny wall where it will grow taller than usual. It is not hardy in cold areas but is an ideal plant for coastal gardens.

Summer companion
Eryngium planum

Spring companion
Corokia virgata 'Red Wonder'

Teucrium scorodonia 'Crispum'

This teucrium has broad, pale green leaves on a dwarf shrub that prefers a semi-shaded spot. The leaves are beautifully wavy around the edges and the rather insignificant but pretty greenish flowers appear in summer. It tolerates drought but can look miserable by mid-summer, in which case you should cut it off close to the base, thus enabling it to produce fresh foliage.

Summer companion
Dicentra 'Pearl Drops'

Winter companion
Arum italicum 'Marmoratum'

Thymus pulegioides 'Aureus'

Thymes are dwarf, evergreen shrubs with aromatic foliage and small heads of pink, white or red flowers in mid-summer. They like an open, sunny position and tolerate drought. They do not grow well on clay soils or in borders that are wet in winter but do tolerate chalky soils. Their flowers attract bees and the smallest, creeping types can be used as an alternative to lawns in hot, dry positions. They are also useful in rock gardens. *Thymus pulegioides* 'Aureus' grows to 15cm (6in) high and has golden foliage. *Thymus citriodorus* 'Silver Queen' has tiny leaves with cream edges and pink flowers and

grows to about 30cm (12in) high, forming neat mounds. *Thymus serpyllum* 'Pink Chintz' has greyish foliage and pale pink flowers. *Thymus vulgaris* is the common, culinary thyme, which forms a small shrub up to 30cm (12in) high.

Summer companion
Dianthus deltoides

Spring companion
Pulsatilla vulgaris

Weigela 'Briant Rubidor'

Weigelas are useful shrubs because they flower in mid-summer, when few other shrubs show much colour. They are upright at first and then arch outwards with pairs of lance-shaped leaves and clusters of tubular flowers in shades of white, pink and red. They prefer moist, well-drained soil and a sunny spot, though they will also grow in most soils as well as in part shade. Most grow to about 1.5m (5ft) high and should be pruned immediately after flowering by cutting out a few of the oldest stems, near ground level. Any 'overall' pruning to restrict size will reduce flowering. 'Briant Rubidor' has golden leaves often splashed with green

and bright, wine red flowers. 'Jean's Gold' is similar but less bright. 'Florida Variegata' has green leaves edged with creamy yellow and pink flowers.

Summer companion
Iris 'Butter and Sugar'

Spring companion
Forsythia 'Courtalyn' (Weekend)

Begonia semperflorens 'Olympia Red'

This begonia is a perennial – though it is treated as an annual – and most grow to about 20cm (8in) high with glossy, fleshy leaves and stems that 'squeak' when moved. The small, four-petalled flowers open all summer in shades of white, pink and red, with some bicolours. 'Olympia Red' is typical, with neat habit and a never-ending display of red flowers. If you pot up a few plants at the end of summer they will continue to bloom on the windowsill all winter. They are ideal for edging and for small borders and pots because of their neat habit. They are best when grown in a spot with moist soil and a little shade because they tend to scorch in dry soil and hot sun. Tuberous Begonias can be bought as plants or tubers or grown from seed, though all Begonias can be difficult to grow from seed unless you have ideal conditions. Tuberous Begonias have fleshy stems with large leaves and flowers up to 15cm (6in) across though most are 8cm (3in) across. The tubers can be dried in autumn and kept for the following season. All are killed by the lightest frost.

Summer companion
Festuca glauca 'Blaufuchs'

Summer companion
Pelargonium 'Crystal Palace Gem'

Brachyscome iberidifolia

This Australian annual has feathery foliage and daisy-like flowers in shades of white, mauve, blue and purple. It is easily grown from seed though the seedlings are small at first and need careful handling – it is best to transplant a small cluster of seedlings rather than try to plant them singly. Growing to about 25cm (10in) high, they form a cushion of colourful flowers for several months. Many perennial types are now available. These flower all summer but are propagated by cuttings.

Summer companion
Diascia 'Twinkle'

Summer companion
Santolina chamaecyparis

Brugmansia x candida 'Variegata'

Brugmansias are perennial shrubs that can exceed 3m (10ft), with large leaves and spectacular, trumpet-shaped flowers 30cm (1ft) long. These have a pervasive scent that is heaviest and most noticeable in the evening. They are frost tender but require only frost protection in winter if they are kept quite dry, keeping the soil from drying out completely. They respond to heavy feeding and plants in pots on the patio should be fed at least once a week in summer and repotted regularly to maintain growth. The pure white, fragrant flowers of B. candida are difficult to improve but the white-splashed foliage of 'Variegata' enhances them and it is among the most beautiful of all. 'Grand Marnier' has soft orange flowers and B. arborea 'Knightii' has double, white blooms. Brugmansias are prone to many pests and are easy to increase from cuttings taken in spring or summer. They differ from daturas primarily in their pendent flowers. Most daturas grown from seed are annuals.

Summer companion
Ricinus communis 'Carmencita'

Summer companion
Canna 'Durban'

Calendula officinalis

Calendulas or English marigolds are one of the best plants for beginner gardeners to grow. Their seeds are large and easy to handle and they can be sown where they are to bloom. Most grow to 45cm (18in) high with aromatic leaves and long stems with daisy-like flowers in shades of yellow and orange. The flowers are good for cutting and the petals are edible and can be scattered in salads. Alternatively, sprinkle some in the bath for their skin-toning properties. Calendulas usually self-seed in the garden but successive generations will become closer to the wild types with single, orange flowers.

Summer companion
Cerinthe major 'Purpurascens'

Summer companion
Spiraea 'Gold Flame'

Canna 'Durban'

Cannas are dramatic, bold plants with large, paddle-shaped foliage and showy flowers. They send up leafy stems from a creeping rhizome and you can either buy growing plants or dried rhizomes. These rhizomes should be started into growth in small pots in a warm place in spring and then planted out in late spring when the danger of frost has passed. Cannas grow best in full sun and in rich, moist soil. In dry soils and if deprived of fertilizer or water they will be stunted. Cannas can also be grown successfully in large pots. They vary in height from 60cm (2ft) to 2m (6ft) when in flower, according to the variety and the foliage can be green or purple and the flowers yellow, orange, spotted, red or pink. 'Durban' is the most dramatic of all, with purple leaves, striped and speckled with orange and the flowers are tangerine.

Summer companion
Nicotiana sylvestris

Summer companion
Ricinus communis 'Carmencita'

Cerinthe major 'Purpurascens'

This annual is easily grown from its large, black seeds and has attractive, silvery leaves. It grows to about 60cm (2ft) high and the upright stems carry clusters of purple bracts and tubular purple flowers. These are attractive to bees. If the seeds are sown in spring, where the plants are to flower, they will bloom for many months in late summer but in well-drained soil seeds may germinate in late summer and survive the winter to flower in late spring. It requires a sunny spot and thrives in dry soils.

Summer companion
Cistus 'Silver Pink'

Summer companion
Nigella damascena

Cosmos bipinnatus 'Sonata Carmine'

The tall, annual Cosmos, with flowers in shades of pink and white, are wonderful plants to fill large areas of the border and they make excellent cut flowers. They are easy to grow from seed and the seeds are large enough to be spaced individually in cell-trays or small pots. The seedlings are easy to handle if you do need to transplant them and they grow rapidly. They cannot be planted out until the last frost has passed. Most grow to 1.2m (4ft), with masses of 10cm (4in) daisy-like flowers with yellow centres above the delicate, divided foliage, but the 'Sonata' series are a dwarf version with single flowers on neat plants that grow to 60cm (2ft) high.

Summer companion
Physocarpus opulifolius 'Diabolo'

Summer companion
Lavatera trimestris

Cosmos atrosanguineus

This perennial Cosmos is often sold as a bedding plant though it can also be grown as a herbaceous perennial. It is not completely hardy and the small, tuberous roots are often lifted in autumn. It has coarsely divided foliage and tall stems that carry solitary flowers 5cm (2in) across. The flowers are deep maroon and have a distinctive cocoa smell that is particularly noticeable in warm weather. It is not a showy plant and can be rather straggly, reaching 75cm (30in) when in flower, but its unique scent makes it a popular novelty. In well-drained soils in mild areas it may act as a perennial.

Summer companion
Cerinthe major 'Purpurascens'

Summer companion
Senecio cineraria 'Silver Dust'

Ensete ventricosum

This relative of bananas is commonly sold simply as a banana but it differs because bananas have rhizomes and send up offsets once the main stem has flowered. Ensete dies after flowering, but this is not likely in gardens. It can be grown from seed if the seeds are soaked in warm water for 24 hours and kept in warmth. Once they germinate they grow rapidly and will reach 1.5m (5ft) in the first year. Plants can be planted outside in summer but must be kept free from frost in winter. They form large shuttlecocks of huge leaves, 2m (6ft) or more long, and they must be given rich soil and a sheltered spot or the leaves will be torn by strong winds. The foliage is green with a central red midrib and in 'Maurelii' (pictured) they are a wonderful purple shade.

Summer companion
Ricinus communis 'Carmencita'

Summer companion
Nicotiana sylvestris

Gazania 'Daybreak Series'

Gazanias are short, almost stemless plants with clustered rosettes of bright green or grey, linear leaves and bright, daisy-like flowers. The colour of the blooms varies widely but orange and yellow are the most common and many have intricate markings around the centre. The flowers usually only open fully in bright sunlight but modern strains such as the 'Daybreak Series' stay open in warm, dull weather. The series has bright green foliage and plants grow to about 20cm (8in) high with flowers 8cm (3in) or more across in a wide range of bright colours, often with contrasting central zones. Plant gazanias in an open, sunny spot. Although they tolerate drought, they will give best results in average soil and benefit from watering and feeding in poor, dry soil. The dead flowers can look unsightly and deadheading keeps the plants tidy. Although most gazanias are grown from seed, some, such as 'Aztec', have creeping stems and are propagated by cuttings.

Summer companion
Senecio cineraria 'Silver Dust'

Summer companion
Pelargonium 'Crystal Palace Gem'

Helichrysum petiolare 'Variegatum'

This rambling, grey-leaved plant is a popular ingredient in hanging baskets but its long, arching stems, that can exceed 60cm (2ft), make it suitable only for the biggest containers. It is also useful to mix with larger bedding plants and to fill in bare areas in borders. Its round, grey leaves are soft to the touch and, in dry conditions, it produces dull, pale yellow flowers but these are not particularly attractive. 'Variegatum' adds a touch of interest because its leaves are irregularly edged with creamy yellow and it is a little less vigorous too. In moist soil a single plant will cover a large area and clamber through small shrubs.

Summer companion
Sidalcea 'Elsie Heugh'

Summer companion
Verbena 'Quartz Burgundy'

Lavatera trimestris 'Silver Cup'

This annual lavatera is easy to grow from seed. The large seeds can be planted direct into small pots, placing two in each and removing the second seedling if both seeds germinate. It will rapidly grow to 75cm (30in) high with many large, satin pink flowers. It can also be sown in late spring, directly where it is to grow. It is useful for filling large borders because of its bushy habit and is informal enough to fit into shrub and herbaceous borders. 'Noevella' is a recent introduction with similar flowers but it blooms as a younger plant.

Summer companion
Siberian iris 'Shirley Pope'

Summer companion
Physostegia virginiana 'Summer Snow'

Linaria maroccana 'Fairy Bouquet'

This dainty plant with narrow leaves, a bushy habit and delicate flowers like miniature snapdragons, is one of the easiest of all annuals. It is usually treated as a hardy annual and sown, in spring, where it is to flower. It will survive in dry soil but plants will be bigger and healthier in average soil, and it needs a sunny spot. It will then grow to 25cm (10in) with flowers in a Dolly mixture blend of yellow, pink, purple and orange. It flowers rapidly from seed but does not have a long flowering period and is best used as a filler, either to disguise late gaps or to provide colour before planting perennials in September.

Summer companion
Carex comans bronze

Summer companion
Geranium endressii

Lobelia erinus 'Crystal Palace'

Bedding lobelias are useful plants and there are two main groups: those that trail and those that form neat mounds about 10cm (4in) high which are used mainly for edging borders. They are grown from seed in spring and usually transplanted in small clusters of seedlings because they are so small and fiddly to handle. Lobelia grows best in moist soil in sun, though it also succeeds in part shade. 'Crystal Palace' is a popular variety with dark purple leaves and intense blue flowers. If plants set seeds and cease flowering they can be trimmed back and will produce a fresh crop of flowers if they are given extra water. *L. valida* is taller and produces stems up to 30cm (12in) high with pale blue flowers, marked with white.

Summer companion
Lysimachia nummularia 'Aurea'

Summer companion
Nemesia 'Blue Lagoon'

Lunaria annua 'Variegata'

Lunaria (honesty) is a biennial that is sown in summer and flowers the following year, in early summer, bridging the two seasons. But after the four-petalled flowers have faded it produces its distinctive seedpods that can be dried for use in the home. It thrives in most soils, particularly if the soil is alkaline, and will self-seed in many gardens. It can be grown in sun or part shade and, if grown in rich soil, can reach 1m (3ft) high. *L. annua* 'Variegata' has leaves that are

splashed with white, especially around the purple flowers, and var. *albiflora* 'Alba Variegata' is the most beautiful of all, with white-splashed foliage and white flowers.

Summer companion
Allium 'Globemaster'

Summer companion
Physocarpus opulifolius 'Diabolo'

Nemesia 'Blue Lagoon'

Nemesias have long been popular annuals but those grown from seed, although they are usually in a jewel-like mix of vibrant colours, tend to look tatty after the main flush of flowers. In recent years, new varieties that are strictly perennial, have become popular and these flower throughout summer and many are fragrant. 'Blue Lagoon' is one of many fine varieties which all grow to about 30cm (12in) high and are useful for borders and containers.

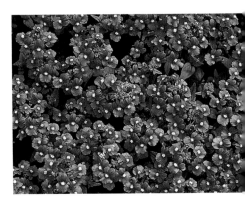

Summer companion
Hosta 'Halcyon'

Summer companion
Eryngium bourgattii

Nerium oleander

The Oleander is a tough shrub that will be familiar with anyone who has holidayed in warmer climes. Eventually reaching 2m (6ft) or more, it is an evergreen with long, deep green leaves and clusters of five-petalled flowers 3cm (1in) or more across throughout summer. Pink is the most usual colour, but white, apricot and yellow are also available as well as doubles and most have a sweet scent. It is an ideal patio plant for a pot and may survive winter outside in mild areas where hard frosts are rare. It requires a sunny spot and

although it will tolerate drought and poor soil, it will reward better conditions. All parts of the plant are poisonous.

Summer companion
Senecio viravira

Summer companion
Ricinus communis 'Carmencita'

Nicotiana sylvestris

Flowering tobaccos (Nicotiana) have tubular flowers that open out into five lobes and bloom for most of summer. The hybrids often have colourful flowers although most have lost their fragrance, but *N. sylvestris* not only smells wonderful, it is a bold, tall plant that does not look out of place in a border of shrubs. From a tiny seed it grows into a rosette of large, pale green leaves 30cm (12in) or more long and then sends up a tall, branching stem with many clusters of pure white flowers with tubes 15cm (6in) long. Their scent is strongest in the evening. It grows best in moist, rich soil in sun or partial shade and plants should be planted out before they become potbound. If they are starved or restricted, they will start to flower at a young age and will not achieve their full height.

Summer companion
Fuchsia magellanica var. *gracilis* 'Tricolor'

Summer companion
Canna 'Durban'

Nicotiana x sanderiana 'Domino'

'Domino' is one of many modern strains that have been bred for their compact habit, wide range of colours and day-blooming habit – many of the older kinds had flowers that wilted and looked miserable at midday. Growing to about 40cm (16in) high, with flowers in pinks, mauves and white, it is suitable for mass bedding and is also short enough for containers. Nicotiana grow best in average soil that is not too dry in summer and in

full sun, though they will grow in partially shaded spots.

Summer companion
Senecio cineraria 'Silver Dust'

Summer companion
Lavatera trimestris

Nigella damascena

Nigella (love-in-a-mist) is a hardy annual that can be sown in late spring where it is to flower and it often self-seeds. The plants grow to about 45cm (18in) high and have finely divided leaves that are attractive from the start. As the plants reach maturity, the round, inflated buds open to reveal intricate blue, pink, purple or white flowers in the mixture 'Persian Jewels' and these are followed by attractive seed pods which can be dried and used for flower arranging. It is one of the easiest and prettiest annuals and always welcome wherever it is planted.

Summer companion
Sidalcea 'Elsie Heugh'

Summer companion
Astrantia major 'Ruby Wedding'

Osteospermum

Osteospermums are frost-tender perennials from southern Africa with evergreen foliage and large, daisy-like flowers that open in the sun throughout summer. They thrive in well-drained, light soils but are frequently used in containers. *O. jucundum* is hardiest, and often survives winter cold in sheltered areas, forming a mat of green foliage 15cm (6in) high, but the purple flowers are mostly produced in early summer. The more tender cultivars have a longer flowering period. offer a greater range of colours and are more bushy, reaching 45cm (18in). 'Nairobi Purple' has a spreading, low habit and purple flowers, 'Buttermilk' has soft yellow flowers with a white and bronze eye, 'Silver Sparkler' has white flowers and variegated leaves and 'Whirligig' has white flowers with unusual, spoon-shaped petals.

Autumn companion
Nerine bowdenii

Summer companion
Cosmos bipinnatus 'Sonata Carmine'

Papaver rhoeas

Annual poppies are hardy annuals that can be sown in spring, directly where they are to bloom, or sown in small clumps in cell-trays and planted out without disturbing the roots. Like all hardy annuals, the best plants are produced if the seedlings are thinned at an early stage to allow the plants room to grow. *P. rhoeas* can also be sown in September, to flower the following summer, and these plants will flower earlier than spring sowings. 'Angel's Choir' is a superb mixture of pastel colours with double flowers. Height 60cm (2ft). Most poppies will self-seed.

Summer companion
Lupinus Gallery Series

Summer companion
Calendula officinalis

Papaver somniferum var. paeoniflorum

The garden forms of *P. somniferum*, the opium poppy, are beautiful hardy annuals that are best sown where they are to flower. Most grow to about 1m (3ft) and although there are single-flowered varieties, it is the doubles that are most popular, with large, peony-like flowers above the broad, greyish leaves. 'Black Peony' is particularly striking with deep blackcurrant-coloured flowers packed with petals. Although the flowering season is short, the blooms are followed by large, attractive seed pods that can be picked and dried or left for sparrows to peck and extract the seeds.

Summer companion
Phalaris arundinacea var. *picta* 'Picta'

Summer companion
Nicotiana sylvestris

Papaver commutatum

This, the ladybird poppy, is one of the most brilliant of all annuals, with large scarlet-petalled flowers marked at the base with a large, black blotch. Although it looks like the classic, cornfield poppy, it is native to south-east Europe, usually self-seeds in the garden and is a hardy annual. The best plants are produced from an autumn sowing in September. Then plants will reach 60cm (2ft) high and as much across, flowering for several months and combining well with yellow and orange flowers.

Summer companion
Oenothera fruticosa 'Fyrverkeri'

Summer companion
Calendula officinalis

Pelargonium 'Crystal Palace Gem'

Most bedding pelargoniums (geraniums) are grown from seed, but the finest varieties are still grown from cuttings and these include those with variegated leaves. 'Crystal Palace Gem' combines vigour, bright flowers and wonderful foliage that is bright yellow with a central green splash and is ideal for bedding in the garden and in containers. The bright red flowers are not as big as some others but contrast well with the foliage. Bred in 1869, it is still going strong. Other excellent variegated pelargoniums for bedding are 'Frank Headley', with salmon flowers and white-edged leaves, 'Caroline Schmidt' with white-edged leaves and double red flowers and its pink-flowered sport, 'Mrs Parker'.

Summer companion
Cosmos sulphureus 'Polidor'

Summer companion
Gazania 'Daybreak Series'

Pelargonium 'Sensation'

Seed-raised pelargoniums allow gardeners to raise plants without having to keep plants through the winter and the 'Sensation' series is one of the best, offering compact plants in a wide range of colours. Although the individual flower clusters are not large, there are masses of them on each plant and they provide a bright show all summer in beds and containers. Sow the seed in early spring and plant out when the chance of frost has passed.

Summer companion
Begonia semperflorens

Summer companion
Tagates patula

Pelargonium crispum 'Variegatum'

Scented-leaf pelargoniums usually have small flowers, but there is a great variation in leaf shape and fragrance and *P. crispum* 'Variegatum' is the most popular of all. The small leaves are edged with cream and the plants have an upright, neat habit, ideal for the windowsill, and the foliage has a biting, citrus scent. It is easy to grow in the greenhouse or outside but is rather slow growing, so is better for containers than general bedding. It is sensitive to overwatering in winter.

Summer companion
Lobelia erinus 'Crystal Palace'

Summer companion
Nicotiana x sanderae 'Domino'

Perilla frutescens var. *crispa*

The purple, frilly foliage of *P. frutescens* var. *crispa* contrasts well with pink and white flowers and silver foliage in the summer garden and has a pleasant, spicy scent when bruised. It is a tall, upright plant, grown from seed sown in spring in the greenhouse and can reach 60cm (2ft) by the end of summer. Young plants should be pinched out in spring to induce branching and they prefer warmth and sun to grow well. If they thrive, you can pick a few leaves to add a pungent taste to salads.

Summer companion
Sidalcea 'Brilliant'

Summer companion
Nerium oleander

Petunia 'Million Bells Terracotta'

Petunias are essential in the summer garden for their long display of bright flowers. Though they have a reputation for being poor in wet summers, the smaller-flowered Multiflora types perform well in wet summers. Always look out for F1 hybrids when sowing your own seed as these offer improved flowers, habit and vigour over older types. Perennial types that are raised from cuttings include the 'Million Bells' type. These are spreading, bushy plants with masses of small flowers that are rarely damaged by wet weather, though the brittle stems can break in strong winds unless they are given some shelter.

Summer companion
Dicentra spectabilis

Summer companion
Pelargonium 'Sensation'

Petunia 'Surfinia Series'

Surfinias are perennial petunias, raised from cuttings, though most gardeners discard their plants at the end of the season and buy new plantlets each spring. Although usually planted in hanging baskets, they are ideal for containers and also for borders, where their stems, that can reach 1m (3ft) will cover large areas of soil and even clamber through taller plants. There is now a wide range of colours, including vibrant purple, greenish white and bright red. Surfinias grow best

in full sun and should be well watered and fed to achieve their full potential, flowering from early summer through to the first frost.

Summer companion
Cordyline australis 'Albertii'

Summer companion
Lobelia erinus 'Crystal Palace'

Plumbago auriculata

The pale blue flowers of *P. auriculata* (formerly *P. capensis*) are carried in small clusters all summer. The plant is a large shrub and has thin, straggly branches and is often grown as a climber in greenhouses, but it also thrives in the summer outside in a sheltered spot in full sun. Because it appreciates plenty of water and fertilizer, it usually thrives best in a container on a patio. Plants should be overwintered in a cool greenhouse. Large plants can reach 2m (6ft) high and will reach 1m (3ft) in their first summer.

Summer companion
Cerinthe major 'Purpurascens'

Summer companion
Lavatera trimestris

Ricinus communis 'Carmencita'

Ricinus communis, the castor oil plant, is a tender shrub that is usually grown as an annual in the garden. It has large, lobed leaves and rapidly grows to 1m (3ft) or more in a single summer, to give a bold, tropical look to borders in a sheltered, sunny spot. Sow the seeds in individual pots in spring and keep them in a warm, light place. The most vigorous plants have green leaves but 'Carmencita' has attractive, purple-bronze foliage. The flowers are not large but are followed by 'conker-like' bright red fruits. All parts of the plant are harmful and the seeds are fatal if eaten.

Summer companion
Dahlia 'Tally Ho'

Summer companion
Canna 'Durban'

Tagetes 'Lemon Gem'

African and French marigolds are closely related and form the basis of many summer bedding schemes – they are colourful, reliable and easy to grow from seed. They are not frost hardy but are among the toughest of all half-hardy bedding. French marigolds (*Tagetes patula*) are generally shorter, less than 30cm (1ft), and have smaller flowers than African marigolds (*T. erecta*) with flowers in shades of yellow, orange and red that may be double, single or crested. 'Juliette' has double flowers that are yellow splashed with orange. Most African marigolds grow more than 30cm (1ft) high and the old variety, 'Crackerjack' has gold, lemon and orange flowers on plants 60cm (2ft) high. Modern hybrids such as 'Sahara' can be as short as 20cm (8in) with large, double flowers. *T. signata* is usually called Tagetes and these are bushy plants with masses of tiny flowers. 'Lemon Gem' (pictured) has fresh, acid yellow flowers.

Summer companion
Pelargonium 'Sensation'

Summer companion
Gazania 'Daybreak Series'

Tropaeolum majus 'Alaska Mixed'

Nasturtiums (*Tropaeolum majus*) are often described as easy to grow, but they are prone to being devoured by cabbage white butterfly caterpillars and are also attacked by blackfly. They can be sown where they are to flower, in late spring, and the large seeds are easy to handle, but the plants are not frost hardy and cannot be overwintered outside. In rich soil the plants produce masses of leaves and are shy to flower. What flowers they do produce may be hidden by the foliage, so it is usually recommended that plants are grown in dry, poor soil. 'Alaska Mixed' has foliage that is splashed with white and flowers in a wide range of colours on compact plots. The 'Gleam' series are semi-trailing and suitable for banks and hanging baskets. The leaves and flowers of nasturtiums are edible and can be added to salads.

Summer companion
Calendula officinalis 'Pink Surprise'

Summer companion
Euphorbia dulcis 'Chameleon'

Tropaeolum peregrinum

The canary creeper (*T. peregrinum*) is a fast-growing climber easily raised from seed that can be allowed to ramble through shrubs or up trellis. The dainty foliage is interspersed with curious, frilly, yellow flowers all summer that contrast especially well with purple foliage and can brighten an otherwise dull corner of the garden. A hardy annual, you can sow a few of the large seeds at the base of the support in late spring and let the plants grow as they wish. It thrives in most soils, in sun or part shade and is useful for containers and anywhere an easy, quick climber is needed.

Summer companion
Berberis thunbergii 'Dart's Red Lady'

Summer companion
Euphorbia dulcis 'Chameleon'

Verbena bonariense

This tall, willowy plant is quite unlike most bedding verbenas, with tall, almost leafless stems that can reach 2m (6ft) tall, with tight clusters of small, tubular, mauve flowers from July until the first frosts. It is easily raised from seed and may be perennial in well-drained soils but is best grown as a bedding plant, though it often self-seeds too. It is useful to give height to bedding schemes and among herbaceous plants such as grasses.

Summer companion
Nicotiana sylvestris

Summer companion
Veronica spicata

Verbena 'Quartz Burgundy'

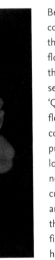

Bedding verbenas are useful plants for containers and the front of borders where their flat or domed heads of small, bright flowers provide colour all summer. Among the seed-raised varieties, the 'Quartz' series have large, bright flowers and 'Quartz Burgundy' has rich, deep purple flowers on low, spreading plants, combining well with yellow marigolds and purple heliotrope. 'Quartz Waterfall' is a lovely blend of white and blues. The newest types are propagated from cuttings, have a long flowering season and are generally better for containers than the seed-raised types because of their finer foliage and more spreading, dense habit. They are not frost hardy though some may survive the winter in sheltered positions. In cold areas the old plants can be overwintered in a cool greenhouse and propagated by cuttings in spring. The 'Temari' series are compact and ideal for containers, the 'Tapien' series have finer leaves and a trailing habit and the 'Aztec' series are resistant to mildew, a common problem with verbenas.

Summer companion
Osteospermum 'Silver Sparkler'

Summer companion
Perilla frutescens var. *crispa*

Zinnia haageana 'Persian Carpet'

Zinnias are unashamed sun-lovers and thrive in warm summers. They are easy to grow and have long-lasting, bright flowers that are good for cutting, but they have a reputation for being difficult to grow. They dislike root disturbance and cold weather, so sow them in late spring, putting one or two seeds in each small pot or compartment in cell-trays so they can be planted out without transplanting the small seedlings. Alternatively, sow them direct in late spring, where they are to flower. They vary from small, spreading plants to tall varieties 1m (3ft) high, but among the best is 'Persian Carpet', with dazzling scarlet and gold flowers on compact plants 25cm (10in) high.

Summer companion
Hakonechloa macra 'Alboaurea'

Summer companion
Tagetes

Clematis 'Alionushka'

Among the most useful of clematis for summer colour, especially where they have to be grown in containers or where there is not much space, are the herbaceous hybrids which usually reach no more than 2m (6ft) by the end of summer. They flower for many months and sprawl across or through other plants. They are pruned in spring by cutting back all the stems to about 30cm (1ft). 'Alionushka' has nodding, bright pink, four-petalled flowers that resemble elongated bells. *C. x durandii* has a rather stiffer habit and large, deep blue-violet, cross-shaped flowers all summer.

Summer companion
Phlomis fruticosa

Autumn companion
Aster amellus 'Sonia'

Clematis 'Comtesse de Bouchard'

There is a bewildering variety of summer-flowering clematis with new additions every year. Among the best of the reliable old kinds is 'Perle d'Azur' with a long succession of clear, soft blue flowers 8cm (3in) across on stems up to 3m (10ft) high. Prune hard in spring. 'Comtesse de Bouchard' is also recommended and combines the easy pruning of the late-flowering kinds with large flowers 10cm (4in) across. They are bright pink and produced from mid-summer onwards on stems up to 2.5m (8ft) high. Prune hard in spring. Both are easy to combine with shrubs because you simply prune out all the growth in spring and they are unlikely to swamp their host plants. 'Vyvyan Pennell' is one of the most beautiful of all double clematis, with 13cm (5in) wide, fully double, lilac flowers in early summer with a later crop of single flowers. It grows to 2.5m (8ft) and should be lightly pruned in spring.

Summer companion
Rosa glauca

Autumn companion
Miscanthus sinensis 'Flamingo'

Eccremocarpus scaber

The Chilean glory vine is an unusual climber with ferny foliage and tendrils that hoist it into shrubs or up trellis. For many months throughout summer it produces bright, tubular flowers that are usually orange but may also be yellow, red, pink or cream. It prefers a sunny spot and may not survive the winter on clay soils or in cold gardens but it is easy to grow from seed and will flower the first summer after sowing. It is suitable for the border and containers and will reach 3m (10ft). Prune hard in spring.

Summer companion
Sambucus nigra 'Black Beauty'

Spring companion
Kerria japonica 'Picta'

Humulus lupulus 'Aureus'

This vigorous climber has bristly stems and leaves and twines around any supporting plant or trellis. The leaves are bright golden yellow all summer, but they can become scorched in hot sun in dry soils. It will reach 3m (10ft) once established and is a herbaceous climber, dying down to the ground in autumn, so it will not get too tall. However, it is vigorous and the rootstock increases in size every year and may send up suckers,

so it is unsuitable for confined spaces or among delicate shrubs. In late summer it produces attractive hops that can be dried.

Summer companion
Physocarpus opulifolius 'Diabolo'

Spring companion
Pulmonaria 'Occupol'

Itea ilicifolia

This evergreen shrub can be grown as a free-standing plant but is usually grown as a wall plant, in sun or part shade. The glossy foliage looks like holly but is only softly spined. It has an upright habit and in summer it produces long catkins of pale green flowers that have a sweet scent and the young foliage is usually an attractive bronze colour. It tolerates most soils.

Summer companion
Lilium 'Black Beauty'

Winter companion
Helleborus argutifolius

Jasminum officinale 'Fiona Sunrise'

The common jasmine has flowers with a beautiful fragrance but is vigorous and hard to control in a small space. 'Fiona Sunrise' is a better plant for small gardens, with the same, deliciously scented flowers in summer but the yellow foliage is attractive from spring to autumn. It is also less vigorous and will slowly reach 3m (10ft) but is easily maintained on an arch or pergola. The foliage develops its best colour in sun but it can scorch in very dry soil. In shade the leaves are lime green and it will not flower freely. The blooms of jasmine are not showy or prolific, but just a few will perfume the air on a warm, summer's day.

Summer companion
Eccremocarpus scaber

Spring companion
Chaenomeles x superba 'Knap Hill Scarlet'

Lathyrus latifolius

The common everlasting sweet pea is an easy plant to grow and is an herbaceous climber, scrambling to 2m (6ft) in summer but dying to the ground in winter. The flowers are usually bright pink but 'White Pearl' has pure white flowers that are especially lovely, except that none have any fragrance. Each year the rootstock gets bigger and plenty of space is needed. However, it is a superb plant for screening in summer, especially up chain-link fencing. It thrives in sun and is best on light, well-drained soils; it does not do well in wet, clay soils. *L. latifolius* is easy to grow from seed but may not breed true to type.

Summer companion
Forsythia 'Courtalyn' (Weekend)

Spring companion
Aruncus dioicus

Lathyrus odoratus

Sweet peas are essential summer flowers and everyone loves their scent. They thrive best in full sun and in moist, rich soil. The most popular types are the 'Spencer' and 'Multiflora' types that have large, frilly flowers and are ideal for cutting, but the 'Grandiflora' sweet peas are best to climb through other plants and in containers because they branch more freely and have smaller, more intensely fragrant flowers on shorter stems. Sweet peas can be sown in pots in spring or directly where they are to flower in late spring. However, the best plants are grown from seed sown in autumn, the plants overwintered in a coldframe. Sweet peas stop flowering if they are allowed to produce seedpods so spent flowers should be removed.

Summer companion
Buddleia davidii 'Nanho Blue'

Autumn companion
Persicaria affinis 'Superba'

Lonicera japonica

Honeysuckles are vigorous climbers which twine up their supports and thrive in moist soils in partial shade. In dry soils, when grown against walls they are prone to aphid attack that can cause their buds to drop. The evergreen *L. japonica* 'Halliana' is a rampant climber with small flowers throughout summer and, though not showy, provides perfume all summer and shade when grown over a pergola. *Lonicera periclymenum* is the most popular honeysuckle, with tubular, fragrant flowers, but the flowering period is all too brief. 'Graham Thomas' has golden flowers which, although never as spectacular as the traditional kinds, bloom and produce fragrance all summer. The newer 'Scentsation' is similar and both will reach 3m (10ft).

Summer companion
Monarda punctata

Autumn companion
Cotoneaster frigidus 'Cornubia'

Passiflora caerulea

The common, hardy blue passion flower is a strong climber that will remain evergreen in a sheltered spot but will lose its leaves in a cold winter. It will grow to 3m (10ft) but can be lightly pruned in spring to control its size. Hard pruning will delay flowering till late summer. The intricate white and blue flowers never create a spectacular display but are worth close inspection. In warm summers they are followed by egg-shaped, pale orange fruits that are edible, though not very tasty. It will grow in a pot or the open ground but benefits from the reflected heat of a sunny wall and often flowers most freely in dry, light soils.

Summer companion
Canna 'Durban'

Autumn companion
Hedychium gardnerianum

Rosa – climbing 'Mme Gregoire Stachelin'

Climbing roses usually flower all summer and require similar pruning to shrubby roses, shortening the shoots on a permanent framework of branches in spring. There is a wide choice of varieties and most are suitable for walls and fences in sun or part shade. The main stems should be trained as near to horizontal as possible or most will produce flowers only at the top of the plants where they cannot be well seen. 'Mme Gregoire Stachelin' is a beautiful rose with huge, double pink flowers and a glorious fragrance. Unfortunately there is only one flush of flowers but they are followed by large orange hips. The flowers have weak stems so hang their heads but this is ideal in a climber so you can look into the blooms from ground level! 'Bridge of Sighs' is a recent variety with frilly, semi-double flowers in soft apricot. It is scented, has healthy foliage and is not too vigorous. 'Zephyrine Drouhin' is a popular choice because the pink flowers are highly scented and the stems are usually thornless but it is prone to diseases.

Summer companion
Gladiolus callianthus

Autumn companion
Phygelius 'New Sensation'

Rosa – rambler 'Albertine'

Rambling roses differ from climbers because they produce long stems that are covered in flowers the following year. The floral display is brief but spectacular. After flowering these shoots are cut out and the new stems are trained in their place. 'Albertine' is the gardener's favourite because of the relatively large, pink, highly fragrant flowers that open from copper-coloured buds. But it is prone to disease and is viciously thorny. 'American Pillar' is also popular and has masses of deep pink, white-eyed, single flowers in early summer. Both will grow to 5m (16ft) high. *Rosa filipes* 'Kiftsgate' is also popular and is spectacular when covered in its small, single, white flowers or small orange hips in autumn. It is commonly planted to grow up trees but it is rampant and will easily reach 10m (33ft), smothering everything in its path.

Summer companion
Thalictrum delavayi 'Hewitt's Double'

Autumn companion
Anemone x hybrida 'Honorine Jobert'

Solanum crispum

This exotic scrambler, which has no means of supporting itself, is often called the potato vine because its lilac, yellow-centred flowers are just like the blooms of potato plants. It is rather tender and requires a sheltered spot on a sunny wall but will then grow vigorously and produce masses of blooms in tight clusters at the end of the shoots in summer. Although sprawling and needing some support, perhaps tying the main shoots to horizontal wires or trellis, it is easily controlled by pruning in spring or whenever it gets out of control. It can reach 5m (16ft) high but is usually smaller.

Summer companion
Romneya coulteri

Autumn companion
Salvia guaranitica

Arisaema consanguineum

Arisaemas are exotic and curious, tuberous plants with striking foliage and bizarre flowers. Most are woodland plants and prefer light shade and moist, humus-rich soil that is acid or neutral. *A. consanguineum* is one of the most spectacular to grow outdoors and the tuber should be planted, 15–20cm (6–8in) deep in part shade. The plants do not appear until late spring, often as late as early summer, but then the purple-spotted shoots grow at a rapid rate to 1m (3ft) and the single, divided leaf unfurls. Below this, mature plants produce a sombre, hooded, striped, brown and white bloom which may be followed by a head of red berries. This is not a colourful plant, but one that adds drama to the woodland garden.

Summer companion
Matteuccia struthiopteris

Spring companion
Primula denticulata

Crinum x powellii

Sometimes sold as elephant lilies because of the huge bulbs, which can be 30cm (1ft) long, this is a dramatic plant for rich soil and full sun. Bulbs should be planted so the top is at the soil surface and mulched with rich compost or other organic matter to retain moisture in summer and feed the plants. Broad, long leaves create large clumps of foliage 1m (3ft) high and established clumps can be 1m (3ft) or more across. In late summer the flower stems are produced which carry clusters of pink, funnel-shaped, fragrant flowers 15cm (6in) long. Frosts cause the foliage to 'dissolve' and the crowns should be given a dry mulch in cold areas.

Summer companion
Zantedeschia aethiopica

Spring companion
Narcissus 'Geranium'

Crocosmia 'Lucifer'

Crocosmias bring vibrant colour to the garden in mid- to late summer and their clumps of upright foliage also relieve the flatness of herbaceous borders. Although they are corms and can be bought dried in packets, they are best bought as growing plants. They grow best in full sun but, despite being South African natives, need plenty of moisture in summer and will not thrive in dry, poor soil. 'Lucifer' is the best known and also one of the largest, reaching 1m (3ft) when in flower with branched spikes of deep red flowers above bright green leaves. 'Solfatare' is a choice but old variety with yellow flowers above unusual bronze foliage and 'Dusky Maiden' is a newer variety with rusty red flowers and bronze leaves. Both these grow to about 60cm (2ft) high and are more subtle in colour than most.

Summer companion
Hypericum 'Hidcote'

Spring companion
Lamium 'Golden Anniversary'

Dahlia 'Bishop of Llandaff'

Dahlias grow from tubers and can be planted as dried tubers in spring or bought in flower during summer. The dwarf bedding dahlias are useful small plants but the taller types offer more variety. For ease of growth and general garden effect, some of the dark-leaved, taller dahlias are hard to beat. Their purple foliage is attractive even before the flowers appear and their moderately sized, single flowers are less prone to damage by the wind and rain than large doubles. 'Bishop of Llandaff' has vibrant, scarlet flowers over many months and are ideal for garden display and for cutting, 'and 'Fascination' has shocking pink, semi-double blooms.

Summer companion
Philadelphus coronarius 'Aureus'

Autumn companion
Helenium 'Butterpat'

Eremurus 'Cleopatra'

Eremurus attract as much attention when they are sod as when they are in flower because the roots look like huge spiders. They should be planted in full sun in rich but well-drained soil, spreading the roots horizontally with the bud about 5cm (2in) below the surface. In spring the shoots produce a tuft of long leaves and then, from the centre, a tall spike of starry flowers appears. 'Cleopatra' is one of the best, being easy to grow and relatively inexpensive. The 1.2m (4ft) spikes carry hundreds of soft orange flowers in midsummer. *E. robustus* is even more spectacular with flower spikes up to 2.5m (8ft) high with hundreds of pale pink flowers.

Summer companion
Lysimachia ciliata 'Firecracker'

Autumn companion
Aster novi-belgii 'Apple Blossom'

Gladiolus callianthus

Sometimes called Acidanthera, this tender corm produces upright, pleated foliage and, in late summer, spikes of long-necked, white flowers. These are marked with maroon and have an exquisite fragrance. Because it can flower late if planted outside after frosts have finished, it is best started in pots in a greenhouse in early spring. It needs full sun and plenty of moisture when in growth and the corms are usually discarded after flowering because they rarely flower the second year. If you want to keep them the plants should be lifted in autumn and the corms stored in a cool, frost-free place in winter.

Summer companion
Perilla frustescens var. *crispa*

Autumn companion
Aster 'Little Carlow'

Gladiolus communis subsp. *byzantinus*

This hardy gladiolus from the Mediterranean spreads rapidly to form large clumps of narrow foliage in well-drained soils. It prefers light soils that are dry in summer and needs full sun. The bright magenta flowers open on 1m (3ft) stems in early summer and are good for cutting. In some gardens it can be invasive.

Summer companion
Iris – bearded 'English Cottage'

Spring companion
Euphorbia characias subsp. *wulfenii*

Lilium – Asiatic 'Grand Cru'

The Asiatic lilies are bright, colourful plants with upward-facing, star-shaped flowers and most bloom in early to mid-summer. They are among the easiest to grow and shorter varieties are especially suitable for pots. All lilies prefer a sunny spot with shade at the roots and soil that is not wet in winter but that contains plenty of organic material. They are not ideal for clay soils, where they are best grown in pots. Slugs and snails can attack the new shoots and the bright red lily beetle is becoming an increasingly common pest. Though few lilies like alkaline soils, these will tolerate them. 'Grand Cru' has striking yellow flowers with red centres and grows to 75cm (30in) and 'Lollipop' has unusual white flowers, tipped with bright pink on stems just 40cm (16in) high. 'Aphrodite' has double flowers in soft pink and grows to 75cm (30in).

Summer companion
Campanula 'Kent Belle'

Spring companion
Euphorbia polychroma

Lilium – trumpet 'African Queen'

The trumpet lilies flower in mid- to late summer and are among the giants of the lily world. They can be grown in pots but are best in the border where, if conditions suit, they will increase in size and may grow to 2m (6ft) or more. They tolerate mildly alkaline soils. They have large, trumpet-shaped flowers and most have a strong, sweet perfume. The most popular are 'Pink Perfection' and 'African Queen'. 'Pink Perfection' has tall stems with deep pink flowers and 'African Queen' has large flowers that are rich, apricot orange. *Lilium regale* has been a favourite ever since it was introduced from China in 1912. The 1m (3ft) stems carry many white, fragrant flowers, flushed with maroon on the back of the petals. It is easy to grow and adaptable.

Summer companion
Delphinium 'Magic Fountains'

Autumn companion
Miscanthus sinensis 'Sioux'

Lilium – oriental 'Casa Blanca'

Oriental lilies usually flower in mid- to late summer and have large, flat or re-curved flowers that face outwards from the stems or downwards, usually in shades of pink and white or red and white. They are spectacular, but most do not tolerate lime in the soil and they are ideal for containers. Old varieties are generally tall but increasingly they are short with upward-facing flowers. 'Casa Blanca' is a real summer treat with huge, pure white flowers with a heady scent, and grows to 120cm (4ft). The most popular of all is 'Stargazer', which has fragrant, upward-facing flowers in crimson and pink on stems 1m (3ft) high.

Summer companion
Dryopteris filix-mas

Autumn companion
Anemone 'September Charm'

autumn

Aconitum napellus

Aconitums (monkshood) are tough perennials that superficially look like delphiniums, but their flowers are hooded and usually deep blue, though there are also pale yellow species. They will grow in any soil and tolerate summer drought when established and thrive in sun or part shade, producing tall spikes of blooms in late summer. *A. napellus* grows to about 1.2m (4ft) high with spikes of deep blue flowers. *A. carmichaelii* 'Arendsii' also has deep blue flowers and 'Stainless Steel' has unusual, pale grey flowers. All parts of the plant are poisonous.

Summer companion
Euphorbia griffithii 'Dixter'

Autumn companion
Salvia guaranitica

Anemone x *hybrida* 'Honorine Jobert'

Japanese anemones are long-lived plants with coarsely divided foliage that forms dense ground cover about 45cm (18in) high. Though sometimes slow to establish, plants then spread to form large clumps and grow well in sun or part shade in most soils including clay. They produce tall stems with many white or pink flowers with neat 'button' centres and are among the most valuable and beautiful of all late flowers. 'Honorine Jobert' has pure white, single flowers and 'Konigin Charlotte' has semi-double pink flowers on 1.5m (5ft) stems. 'September Charm' is shorter and has single, pink flowers. Height 1m (3ft).

Summer companion
Geranium endressii

Autumn companion
Persicaria amplexicaulis

Aster amellus 'Sonia'

Autumn asters bring masses of colour to the autumn border but they are associated with mildew, a common problem on many. However, *A. amellus* is usually free from all pests and diseases and is a neat plant, forming dense clumps about 45cm (18in) high, that are covered in large daisy flowers for several months. 'Sonia' has beautiful, pale pink, yellow-eyed flowers, 'King George' has large, violet-blue flowers and 'Rudolph Goethe' (pictured) has lavender-blue flowers.

Spring companion
Omphalodes cappadocica
'Starry Eyes'

Autumn companion
Pennisetum alopecuroides 'Hameln'

Aster x frikartii 'Mönch'

Of all the autumn asters, this old variety, bred in 1918, is still possibly the finest. It begins to bloom in late summer and remains beautiful for many months, with 8cm (3in) wide flowers covering the mounded plants that grow to 60cm (2ft) or more. It flowers best in full sun but will tolerate all but wet soils.

Summer companion
Catananche caerulea

Autumn companion
Echinacea purpurea 'Kim's Knee High'

Aster 'Little Carlow'

This beautiful variety is a hybrid of *A. cordifolius* and *A. novi-belgii* and unfortunately suffers from mildew when grown in dry soil, but that should not prevent you from planting it. Plants grow to 1m (3ft) or more high and form dense clumps that become covered in masses of lavender blue flowers with a yellow eye that ages to pink. It is perfect for cutting, each stem forming a bunch in itself.

Spring companion
Malva moschata

Autumn companion
Miscanthus sinensis 'Sioux'

Aster novae-angliae 'Andenken an Alma Potschke'

The New England asters (A. novae-angliae) are native to the east of the USA and form clumps with woody stems with bristly foliage and rather compact heads of daisy flowers. They are not affected by mildew and are better for dry soils than the New York asters, but they are generally all tall and there is not such a wide range of colours. 'Andenken An Alma Potschke' is the best known and has vibrant flowers in a harsh shade of cherry red, difficult to combine with other colours, though very cheerful in autumn. 'Barr's Pink' has deep pink flowers and 'Harrington's Pink' has

pale pink flowers. All grow to 1.2m (4ft) high, more in rich soil.

Summer companion
Phalaris arundinacea var. *picta* 'Picta'

Autumn companion
Hydrangea 'Geoffrey Chadbund'

Aster novi-belgii 'Sandford White Swan'

A. *novi-belgii* is better known as the Michaelmas daisy or New York aster, and a mass of these looks superb in autumn with single or double flowers in white and every shade of pink, blue and purple. They vary in height from 30cm (1ft) to 1.5m (5ft) and are excellent for cutting but most are prone to mildew. This can be partially prevented by dividing the clumps every spring and planting them in moist soil but spraying is advised if you want green, rather than grey foliage at flowering time. 'Apple Blossom' has pale pink flowers 90cm (3ft), 'Climax' is one of the tallest, growing to 1.5m (5ft), with pale lavender flowers, 'Sandford White Swan' has large white flowers 90cm (3ft) and 'Jenny' has double, deep red flowers and is dwarf, reaching just 30cm (1ft).

Summer companion
Nepeta grandiflora

Autumn companion
Hibiscus syriacus 'Oiseau Bleu'

Cortaderia selloana 'Pumila'

Pampas grass (Cortaderia) is a popular evergreen grass, often grown as a lawn specimen, and thrives in full sun and in dry soils but is adaptable and easy to grow, even in exposed, windy gardens. In time it can attain monstrous proportions and cheap plants may be seedlings which do not always flower at an early age so it is advisable to buy a named plant such as 'Pumila'. This is useful because, although it flowers freely, it is dwarf and only reaches 1.2m (4ft) when in bloom. 'Aureolineata' is of the usual proportions but has leaves that are striped with yellow,

creating a golden mound, still with the normal, silvery plumes in autumn. 'Sunningdale Silver' is the best 'standard' pampas grass producing fluffy flower heads on stems 3m (10ft) high.

Autumn companion
Abelia x *grandiflora*

Winter companion
Phormium 'Pink Panther'

Deschampsia caespitosa 'Goldschleier'

For most of the year, this evergreen grass has little to commend it but in autumn the flowers stems create a cloud of golden mist that floats over the green foliage and you almost wish for autumn nights to cool so the stems are covered with dew or frost. It thrives in light soils in full sun and 'Goldschleier' grows to 1m (3ft) high. 'Northern Lights' is grown more for its pink-tinged, variegated foliage.

Spring companion
Scilla sibirica 'Spring Beauty'

Autumn companion
Sedum 'Purple Emperor'

Echinacea purpurea

Echinaceas are more famous as pills than as garden plants, but they are rapidly becoming popular because of their large, daisy-like flowers with pink petals and golden brown, domed centres. These flowers last for many weeks and a clump is beautiful for many months. It is easy to grow in well-drained soil in full sun and it is suitable for gardens that suffer from drought in summer. 'Kim's Knee High' has masses of pink flowers on 60cm (2ft) high plants, shorter than usual, but any are worth growing and will delight you and attract butterflies. 'White Lustre' has greenish white petals and reaches 1m (3ft) when in bloom.

Summer companion
Lilium 'Lollipop'

Autumn companion
Stipa tenuissima

Eupatorium rugosum 'Chocolate'

This unusual plant is grown for its foliage and its flowers. The nettle-like foliage is deep, brownish purple and the plants grow to about 1.5m (5ft) high, making a substantial clump and in late summer the ends of the stems carry small, fluffy white flowers. The best foliage colour is produced when the plant is grown in sun and it thrives best in soils that do not get too dry in summer.

Spring companion
Narcissus 'Ice Follies'

Autumn companion
Anemone x *hybrida* 'Honorine Jobert'

Eupatorium purpureum subsp. *maculatum* 'Atropurpureum'

Where a bold foliage plant is required, this eupatorium should fit the bill, reaching 2.5m (8ft) in height. Its upright, red stems bear whorls of rather coarse, deep green leaves and, in autumn, each stem carries a large head of tiny, fluffy, pink flowers that are besieged by bees and butterflies. It needs plenty of room and moist soil to do well, but does prefer alkaline soil. It often self-seeds where conditions suit and is useful for naturalizing in moist gardens.

Summer companion
Crocosmia 'Lucifer'

Autumn companion
Aconitum carmichaelii 'Arendsii'

Gaura lindheimeri

Few plants bloom for as long as Gaura, which is a rather shrubby plant with narrow leaves and long, wiry stems that seem to bear an infinite number of white, four-petalled flowers that sway in the breeze. It requires a sunny, warm spot and can die over the winter if the soil is wet and heavy. Although there are now dwarf varieties, most plants grow to about 60cm (2ft) tall and across. 'Corrie's Gold' has white flowers and yellow-variegated leaves and 'Siskiyou Pink' has pink blooms and red stems.

Spring companion
Allium albopilosum

Autumn companion
Nerine bowdenii

Gentiana sino-ornata

The autumn-flowering gentians are jewel-like plants that are without equal if you need a splash of intense blue. *G. sino-ornata* is a creeping evergreen plant with narrow foliage that forms a carpet of foliage studded with 7cm (2½in) long trumpets in autumn. They are usually intense, deep blue, striped with white inside, but there are varieties with other shades of blue. It thrives in sun or part shade, but must have an acid, humus-rich soil that never dries out in summer.

Summer companion
Carex siderosticta 'Variegata'

Autumn companion
Crocus speciosus

Hedychium gardnerianum

This is one of the hardiest of the ginger lilies and among the most exotic plants that can be grown outside. It needs a sheltered spot in sun and plenty of moisture and fertilizer in summer and then forms large clumps of stems up to 1.5m (5ft) high with long leaves from the base to the top. In late summer these stems produce a 30cm (1ft) spike of spidery cream flowers that have a rich, sweet scent. In most areas this can be grown at the base of a south-facing wall if given a protective mulch in winter, but in cold areas it can also be grown in large pots.

Summer companion
Alstroemeria 'Ligtu hybrids'

Autumn companion
Nandina domestica

Helenium 'Moerheim Beauty'

Heleniums are useful plants for late summer, forming great mounds of bright green leaves that become almost swamped with daisy-like flowers in orange, yellow and russet shades. They are easy to grow, though usually need staking and flourish in sun in most soils. They are hardy and free from pests and diseases and flower for many weeks. Divide plants in spring every three or four years to maintain vigour. 'Moerheim Beauty' has copper-orange flowers and 'Indianersommer' has dark, brownish copper flowers. 'Butterpat' is neat and grows to 90cm (3ft) high and has masses of golden flowers.

Summer companion
Thalictrum flavum subsp. *glaucum*

Autumn companion
Eupatorium rugosum 'Chocolate'

Helianthus multiflorus 'Capenoch Star'

Helianthus are perennial sunflowers and, though rarely grown, are valuable because they flower in autumn, bringing much-needed colour, and are easy to grow. In fact, a few can be rather invasive but they are easy to control by digging up unwanted growth in spring. They are mostly tall, but usually do not need staking, and they have bright, golden flowers. Plant them in a sunny spot in any soil. 'Capenoch Star' has deep green leaves and 1.5m (5ft) stems with 12cm (5in) lemon yellow blooms. 'Loddon Gold' is the same height but has beautiful, double flowers and 'Monarch' (pictured) has large, single flowers with dark eyes over a long period. All are good for cutting.

Spring companion
Kerria japonica 'Pleniflora'

Autumn companion
Solidago 'Goldenmosa'

Helianthus salicifolius

This is the willow-leaved sunflower and is a vigorous plant that needs plenty of space. Not only does it creep, especially in light soils, to form large clumps, its stems can reach 3m (10ft) high. But it is attractive all summer because the stems are clothed with long, narrow leaves that move in the wind. The flowers, which are only of moderate size, are carried at the top of the stems in small, tight clusters. It is best at the back of a large border, or you can plant it among shrubs in large gardens.

Summer companion
Physocarpus opulifolius 'Diabolo'

Autumn companion
Cotinus coggygria 'Royal Purple'

Indigofera heterantha

Although this is strictly a deciduous shrub, it is usually pruned hard in spring and may be cut to the ground by frost in cold areas so it usually grows more like a herbaceous plant than a shrub. It is an elegant plant with vetch-like foliage and slender spikes of small pink flowers in early autumn. When pruned hard in spring it usually reaches about 1.5m (5ft), making an arching clump of graceful habit. It grows best in light soils that are not too wet in winter and in a sunny spot.

Summer companion
Phlomis fruticosa

Autumn companion
Caryopteris x *clandonensis* 'First Choice'

Liriope muscari 'John Birch'

Neat, flowering evergreen plants are not common, so this tough, clump-forming plant solves lots of problems. It forms dense, slow-growing clumps of leathery, deep green, grass-like leaves that are attractive all year. It thrives in shade or sun, but bright sun and dry soil may cause the foliage to scorch and it thrives best in light shade in moist, acid soil, though it will grow perfectly well in neutral soil and where the soil is dry in summer. In autumn it produces 30cm (1ft) spikes of small, bobbly, violet flowers that last for several months. There are variegated forms such as 'John Burch', but these are not quite as tough as the plain green plant, although you do get lovely leaves all year round. Divide plants in spring so you have more clumps to use as ground cover.

Summer companion
Santolina chamaecyparissus

Autumn companion
Colchicum speciosum

Melianthus major

Among the most beautiful of all foliage plants, Melianthus is actually a shrub with huge, coarsely divided foliage that is silvery grey, however, in all but the mildest areas, frosts kill the stems and it produces new shoots from the base, acting as a herbaceous plant. If the stems do survive the winter, perhaps if the plant is grown against a warm wall, they produce curious, blood red flowers that drip with nectar. But it excels as a foliage plant and is best when given water and fertilizer to maintain strong growth and can form the basis of a subtropical foliage scheme. If cut back each spring, to remove frosted growth, it will reach 2m (6ft) in a season, but it can reach 3m (10ft) in sheltered areas.

Summer companion
Verbena bonariensis

Autumn companion
Hydrangea paniculata 'Grandiflora'

Miscanthus sinensis var. *condensatus* 'Cosmopolitan'

Miscanthus are large, clump-forming grasses that may be used as a substitute for bamboos. However, they are not evergreen and die back to soil level in winter. Most form great sheaves of long foliage on upright stems and are useful for screens as well as noble foliage and flowering plants and do not need staking. The dead stems, clothed with foliage can be left all winter but should be trimmed back hard in spring before the new foliage appears. They prefer a sunny site and well-drained soil. *M. sinensis* var. *condensatus* 'Cosmopolitan' is among the most beautiful, with white-edged foliage, but it needs a warm soil and is rather slow to start into growth in spring. It rarely flowers and reaches 2m (6ft) tall. 'Sioux' is small and has attractive autumn colour and 'Flamingo' has great plumes of deep pink flowers in autumn 2.5m (8ft). 'Zebrinus' has green foliage, banded with yellow and grows to 1.2m (4ft).

Spring companion
Cytisus x *praecox* 'Albus'

Autumn companion
Perovskia atriplicifolia 'Blue Spire'

Origanum laevigatum 'Herrenhausen'

This aromatic, woody-based plant has purple-tinted winter and spring foliage which grows into mounds of deep green foliage that is later covered in clusters of deep pink flowers which attract masses of bees. The old flower stems should be cut back in spring to make room for the new growth and it needs a warm, sunny spot and prefers a dry soil. It reaches 45cm (18in) when in bloom. It flowers for a long period and is ideal for poor soils where it associates with lavender and other fragrant herbs.

Summer companion
Thymus vulgaris 'Silver Posie'

Autumn companion
Crocus speciosus

Origanum vulgare 'Aureum'

This is the common, yellow-leaved oregano, but is too good a plant to confine to the herb garden. The foliage is bright yellow and always cheerful, though it can become scorched if the soil is too dry, especially in summer. The pink flowers are produced in late summer and though not showy, they do attract bees. If the plant gets straggly it can be pruned hard to provide a new flush of bright foliage for autumn. The foliage is edible.

Spring companion
Crocus 'Yellow Mammoth'

Autumn companion
Ceratostigma plumbaginoides 'Palmgold' (Desert Skies)

Pennisetum alopecuroides

Pennisetums are often called fountain grasses and they are among the most beautiful of all flowering grasses. Their foliage is usually narrow, evergreen and rather unremarkable but the flowers, which are carried on thin, arching stems above the leaves, form fluffy clusters that are often tinged with pink at first and catch the dew in autumn. They dislike cold, wet soils where they often flower very late or may die in winter and are best in light soils in a sunny spot. *P. alopecuroides* 'Hameln' is a compact, popular plant that flowers earlier than most and is about 60cm (2ft) high when in flower.

Summer companion
Crocosmia 'Solfaterre'

Autumn companion
Caryopteris x *clandonensis* 'First Choice'

Pennisetum setaceum 'Rubrum'

This is one of the most beautiful of all the fountain grasses but, coming from warm parts of Africa, is not totally hardy and must be planted in a sheltered place or in a container so it can be kept free from frost in winter. All this effort is rewarded by a plant reaching 1m (3ft) high with lustrous, burgundy foliage and large, fluffy, pink flower spikes. It is worth trying in a bed at the base of a warm wall, in a raised bed or on a bank with well-drained soil or in a large pot with purple-leaved Cannas and lilies.

Spring companion
Tulip praestans

Autumn companion
Yucca filamentosa 'Bright Edge'

Persicaria affinis 'Superba'

The knotweeds (persicarias) are often dismissed as weedy plants but several deserve a place in the garden and *P. affinis* is both useful and beautiful. The creeping, rather woody stems have green leaves and form a mat that cover the ground, covering slopes, banks and soil. Planted in well-drained soil in full sun, the plants are covered in upright spikes, 25cm (10in) high, of tiny pink flowers that, in 'Superba', turn deep red as they mature. The mix of pink and cherry red flower spikes in autumn is very striking and after the first frosts the leaves turn rusty brown and remain on the plants all winter. It is ideal for large rock gardens.

Summer companion
Potentilla 'Abbotswood'

Autumn companion
Schizostylis coccinea 'Jennifer'

Persicaria campanulata

Plants that are attractive and that will grow in dryish shade are not common, which is why this persicaria is so valuable. The creeping stems form wide-spreading clumps that send up stems reaching 75cm (30in) by autumn, with deep green leaves that are white underneath, and tight clusters of small, pink, bell-like flowers. These are produced for many months and provide a quiet but pretty display. It will be at its best in light shade in moist soil but will survive the shade under deciduous trees if watered well in the first year to get it established.

Spring companion
Muscari armeniacum 'Blue Spike'

Autumn companion
Cotoneaster horizontalis

Phygelius x *rectus* 'Moonraker'

Cape fuchsias (Phygelius) are semi-shrubby plants that can reach 1.5m (5ft) high if pruned lightly, but to prevent them becoming straggly they are best treated as herbaceous plants and pruned hard in spring to remove the old stems and any frosted shoots. They then produce upright stems with deep green leaves and large, pyramidal clusters of drooping, tubular flowers from summer till late autumn. *Phygelius* x *rectus* has masses of orange flowers and *P. aequalis* 'Yellow Trumpet' has pale, creamy yellow flowers, 'New Sensation' has rich, cherry-pink flowers and 'African Queen' has bright orange blooms. Also look for the 'Funfare' series which are more compact. All thrive in a sheltered spot in full sun but also tolerate a little shade. They respond well to watering and feeding in hot, dry weather.

Summer companion
Fuchsia 'Mrs Popple'

Autumn companion
Physalis alkekengi

Physalis alkekengi

The Chinese lantern (Physalis) is such a desirable plant in autumn that it seems remarkable that more gardens do not contain this hardy, easily grown plant. The papery husks around the fruits become bright orange as they mature and when the leaves turn yellow and start to fall, there are few more beautiful plants in the garden. However, this is a rampant spreader that can become a nuisance in some gardens, and the white flowers in summer are not very showy. This means you have to put up with large clumps of foliage, about 60cm (2ft) high, for many months when you could be enjoying something prettier in summer. Is it worth it? If you have plenty of room, and if you like flower arranging, the answer is yes.

Spring companion
Potentilla 'Elizabeth'

Autumn companion
Solidago 'Crown of Rays'

Rehmannia elata

This beautiful perennial is easy to grow in well-drained soil in sun or partial shade and spreads slowly to form rosettes of hairy, lobed leaves. In summer the plants produce branched stems up to 1m (3ft) high that carry trumpet-shaped, deep-pink flowers, spotted with red in the throats, from summer to autumn. In heavy soils it is best to lift the plants and overwinter them in a greenhouse. Plants can also be grown from seed and will flower in their first year.

Spring companion
Corokia cotoneaster

Autumn companion
Pennisetum setaceum 'Rubrum'

Rudbeckia fulgida var. sullivantii 'Goldsturm'

This comes close to being the perfect herbaceous perennial and is deservedly popular. It is tough, will tolerate most soils and though it flowers best in full sun, will tolerate light shade. It forms a dense clump of rough, deep-green foliage and for many months in summer and autumn it produces stems, about 60cm (2ft) high with golden daisy flowers. These can be 12cm (5in) across, especially those at the tips of the stems, and later flowers on side branches are usually smaller. The blooms are deep golden orange with dark, central eyes and are excellent cut flowers.

Spring companion
Erysimum cheiri

Autumn companion
Aster x frikartii 'Moench'

Rudbeckia 'Herbstsonne'

The most common rudbeckias, including the popular, bedding varieties of R. hirta, are compact plants for the front or middle of the border, but 'Herbstsonne', which translates as 'autumn sun', is a tall plant for the back of the border. It is a majestic plant with upright stems that may need support, reaching 2m (6ft) by the end of the season, with bright green, attractive foliage. The flowers are up to 12cm (5in) across and bright yellow with green

centres. They form a bright mass at the top of the plants for many weeks in early autumn.

Summer companion
Campanula 'Kent Belle'

Autumn companion
Aconitum carmichaelii 'Arendsii'

Salvia patens

Blue flowers are always welcome in the garden and salvias provide some of the most beautiful. Forget scarlet bedding salvias: these are taller and more varied, and many of the Mexican and South American salvias are hardy if planted in light soils, in sheltered positions in sun, or given a mulch in winter to protect the roots form freezing. Among the most beautiful is *S. patens*, which grows from a tuberous root and has branching stems bearing a long succession of clear blue, 5cm (2in), claw-like blooms through summer and autumn. The roots can be lifted and kept in a frost-free greenhouse in winter, but it usually survives if mulched.

Summer companion
Convolvulus cneorum

Autumn companion
Pennisetum alopecuroides 'Hameln'

Salvia guaranitica

This beautiful, upright plant from Brazil and Argentina brings a tropical touch to the border, with many spikes of intense, deep blue flowers from summer until the first frost of winter. The plants reach 2m (6ft) high and have deeply veined foliage that is aromatic. Though tall, the plants rarely need staking and are trouble-free. Mulch the roots with straw or compost in autumn and cut down the stems.

Spring companion
Tulipa 'Blue Parrot'

Autumn companion
Helianthus multiflorus 'Capenoch Star'

Salvia uliginosa

Among the very best of all garden plants, this salvia, that prefers more moisture in the soil than most others, has thin, wiry stems that reach 2m (6ft) high with small oval leaves and dense, small clusters of pale blue and white flowers from early autumn till the first frost. The flowers are small, but create a pale blue mist when seen en masse. Its colour is unusual and especially welcome in autumn, contrasting with the mass of orange and yellow autumn shades.

Summer companion
Ligularia dentata
'Britt-Marie Crawford'

Autumn companion
Anemone x hybrida 'Honorine Jobert'

Schizostylis coccinea 'Jennifer'

Schizostylis form clumps of grassy foliage and once they start to produce their 60cm (2ft) stems of starry flowers in late summer they do not seem to want to stop, often flowering well into winter. They prefer a sunny spot and moist soil and do not grow well or flower freely if the soil is too dry in summer. The blooms have a silky freshness that is welcome in autumn and they are good for cutting. 'Jennifer' has large, pink flowers, 'Major' is bright red, 'Sunrise' has large, salmon pink flowers and 'Viscountess Byng' has small pink flowers.

Spring companion
Leucojum vernum

Autumn companion
Aster amellus 'Sonia'

Sedum 'Herbstfreude'

The large, herbaceous sedums are essential to the autumn garden, their large, flat heads of small, starry flowers remaining attractive for many months and attracting bees and butterflies when in full bloom. They thrive in sun and survive poor, dry soils; in rich soils, they can become too soft and flop over just before flowering. 'Herbstfreude' has bright pink flowers, 'Purple Emperor' has deep purple foliage and *S. telephium* 'Matrona' has purple-tinged leaves and pink flowers.

Summer companion
Liatris spicata

Autumn companion
Gaura lindheimeri 'Siskiyou Pink'

Solidago 'Goldenmosa'

Solidagos (golden rod) are often regarded as rather weedy plants and it is true that they sometimes seed onto waste ground, bringing welcome colour in autumn, but the superior, named varieties have their place in the garden. They are easy to grow, though rather dull in summer, as they build into large clumps of green foliage. They prefer a sunny site and tolerate most soils, though they may get mildew if the soil is very dry in summer. 'Goldenmosa' has conical heads of fluffy, yellow flowers on 75cm (30in) stems, 'Crown of Rays' is just 60cm (2ft) high and *S. rugosa* 'Fireworks' is resistant to mildew, with loose clusters of flowers on 90cm (3ft) stems.

Summer companion
Hemerocallis 'Corky'

Autumn companion
Helenium 'Butterpat'

Stipa gigantea

This is one of the most beautiful of all ornamental grasses and deserves pride of place in the garden, so that its beautiful, oat-like flower spikes can be seen where the sun catches them. It is evergreen and forms a tussock of narrow foliage 45cm (18in) high and in summer the flower stems reach 2m (6ft) or more. As these age they mature to a beautiful straw yellow and continue to look good through autumn, until finally destroyed by winter gales when they should be cut down.

Spring companion
Knautia macedonica

Autumn companion
Echinacea purpurea 'White Lustre'

Stipa arundinacea

This is another spectacular stipa which forms low clumps that can be 1m (3ft) high when in flower but are usually wider and create a waterfall of green and bronze. The evergreen foliage is pale green streaked with orange in summer and the flower spikes, which are lax and fluffy, mature to reddish-orange in autumn. In autumn the foliage turns orange-brown and remains this colour all winter.

Spring companion
Armeria 'Joystick Series'

Autumn companion
Nerine bowdenii

Stipa tenuissima

Sometimes called ponytail grass, this is one of the most delicate-looking grasses. It is deciduous, forms neat clumps of narrow green foliage and in summer produces a mass of extraordinarily delicate flowers clusters that are creamy green at first but age to pale, straw-brown in autumn and move in the slightest breeze. Like all deciduous grasses, it should be cut back in late winter or spring and if plants need to be divided, this should be done in spring.

Spring companion
Allium albopilosum

Autumn companion
Colchicum speciosum

Strobilanthes attenuata (S. atropurpureus)

Although not commonly seen, this is a valuable, large herbaceous plant that brings colour to the autumn border. Native to Northern India, it forms dense clumps of large, rather coarse, deep green leaves and, in autumn, the plants are crowned by clusters of upright, curved, tubular flowers in indigo and purple. It is not as showy as more common plants such as Michaelmas daisies but this makes it a welcome and interesting addition.

Summer companion
Fuchsia magellanica var. *gracilis* 'Tricolor'

Autumn companion
Pyracantha Saphyr Orange

Tricyrtis formosana

Rejoicing under the rather unpleasant common name of toad lilies, because of their spotted blooms, Tricyrtis are beautiful plants for the autumn garden. Most of the common varieties are upright in habit with oval leaves alternating up the stems and clusters of upward-facing, six-petalled flowers about 2.5cm (1in) across. Some have spotted foliage and most have flowers that are spotted in shades of purple and white. *T. formosana* reaches 80cm (32in) in height and 'Samurai' has gold-edged foliage and grows to just 45cm (18in). 'White Towers' has white flowers on 60cm (2ft) stems and

'Empress' has heavily-spotted blooms that are larger than usual on 70cm (28in) stems. They thrive in sun or part shade but prefer moist, humus-rich soil.

Summer companion
Thalictrum delavayi 'Hewitt's Double'

Autumn companion
Rehmannia elata

Uncinia egmontiana

This pretty, red-leaved sedge is suitable for the front of the border in sun or partial shade, prefers moist, well-drained soil and is ideal for containers on the patio. The leaves are deep, beetroot red and glossy but the flowers have no beauty.

Spring companion
Anemone blanda 'Radar'

Autumn companion
Sedum 'Purple Emperor'

Vernonia crinata

Despite the fact that there are more than 1,000 species of Vernonia, only two have become anything like common garden plants. They are tall, robust plants with coarse leaves and heads of fluffy purple flowers resembling giant Ageratum. They grow best in moist soils in full sun and grow to 2m (6ft).

Summer companion
Phlox 'Red Feelings'

Autumn companion
Eupatorium purpureum 'Atropurpureum'

Veronicastrum virginicum

This unusual perennial adds interesting foliage and flowers to the garden and is easy to grow in any soil in full sun. It has tall, upright stems to 1.5m (5ft) with rings of leaves along their length and spikes of small flowers in shades of white, pale pink or pale lavender. It associates well with grasses and contrasts with the dumpy shapes of Michaelmas daisies and sedums.

Summer companion
Physostegia virginiana 'Summer Snow'

Autumn companion
Aster 'Little Carlow'

Abelia x grandiflora

Autumn-flowering shrubs are not common and this attractive, evergreen or semi-evergreen shrub is one of the best. In late summer the small, pink, fragrant flowers start to open and continue into autumn. It grows best in a sunny, sheltered spot and tolerates most soils. It can grow to 3m (10ft), but plants can be hard-pruned in spring if they grow too large. 'Frances Mason' has small, glossy foliage that is golden with a green splash and forms an arching shrub 1.5m (5ft) high and wide and 'Confetti' has pretty leaves splashed with pink and white.

Summer companion
Hypericum 'Hidcote'

Autumn companion
Cortaderia selloana 'Pumila'

Acer palmatum 'Dissectum Atropurpureum'

Japanese maples are beautiful hardy small trees or large shrubs, with a wide variety of foliage shapes and colours. Although often grown in pots on patios, this is not the best way to treat them. They require moist, acid or neutral soils that are rich in organic matter and must be sited out of strong winds and burning sun. A semi-shaded position is best and sunny patios, where heat is reflected from paving and walls, are totally unsuitable. Most grow rather slowly but can eventually reach 3m (10ft) and generally have superb autumn colour. They are hardy but the new growth is prone to damage by late spring frosts. 'Dissectum Atropurpureum' has a low, rather lax habit and finely divided, purple foliage. 'Garnet' is similar but has better colouring and 'Butterfly' has leaves variegated in pink and white. 'Trompenburg' is vigorous and has purple foliage.

Autumn companion
Liriope muscari

Winter companion
Luzula sylvatica 'Aurea'

Arbutus unedo

The strawberry tree is one of the most beautiful small, evergreen trees and has many seasons of beauty. It has attractive, dark brown bark, glossy, evergreen, oval leaves and a neat, rounded crown. The small, urn-shaped, white flowers open in autumn and eventually mature into round, yellow, red-flushed fruits that ripen twelve months later, so trees display fruits and flowers together. These fruits are edible but not very palatable. It thrives best in moist, humus-rich soil in sun or part shade but, unusually for a plant that is related to rhododendrons, it tolerates lime in the soil. It is slow growing but eventually makes a beautiful specimen. *A. unedo* f. *rubra* has flowers that are dark pink.

Autumn companion
Cotoneaster conspicuus 'Decorus'

Winter companion
Euonymus fortunei 'Emerald Gaiety'

Callicarpa bodinieri var. giraldii 'Profusion'

It is difficult to create interest in autumn without berrying shrubs, but if you cannot bear another red or orange berry in your garden, consider the beauty berry (Callicarpa). This deciduous shrub grows to about 1.5m (5ft) with rather dull leaves in summer and small clusters of tiny pink flowers, but these develop into shiny, small, round berries that ripen to bright purple. They are hidden by the foliage at first but this turns pink, yellow and purple and then drops to reveal the gorgeous berries on the bare stems. It is easy to grow in a sunny site and is untroubled by pests and diseases.

Spring companion
Chionodoxa 'Pink Giant'

Autumn companion
Perovskia atriplicifolia 'Blue Spire'

Caryopteris x clandonensis

The greyish foliage and small, blue flowers of Caryopteris bring a welcome, soft mound of colour when most plants are past their best. Thriving in dry soils and in full sun, they associate naturally with Cistus, Cytisus and lavenders, but flower much later. They should be pruned hard in spring to maintain a compact shape and can then be kept at about 75cm (30in) high, but they will grow a little larger, and be rather less compact, if left to grow unchecked. They are deciduous and when cut back, this allows underplanted bulbs to show off to advantage. Most have soft

blue flowers, but 'First Choice' is brighter than most and 'Worcester Gold' has yellow foliage. 'Summer Sorbet' is a recent introduction with yellow-edged foliage.

Spring companion
Muscari 'Valerie Finnis'

Autumn companion
Hydrangea quercifolia 'Snowflake'

Ceratostigma plumbaginoides 'Palmgold'

The hardy plumbago (Ceratostigma) is a low shrub that often acts as a herbaceous plant and should be hard-trimmed in spring. It often produces suckers to form a broad clump 45cm (18in) and considerably wider in time. It prefers a sunny site and well-drained soil and will survive drought when established. All summer it increases in size, forming a mound of wiry stems and neat, green foliage and just when you wonder if it is ever going to bloom, it starts to open small, intense blue flowers. A little later, when it is in full bloom, the leaves start to change to bright red and

the flowers and foliage make a wonderful combination. 'Palmgold' (Desert Skies) is rather slow growing but has leaves that are bright yellow all summer.

Summer companion
Lavendula angustifolia 'Imperial Gem'

Autumn companion
Nandina domestica 'Fire Power'

Clerodendrum bungeii

Although this shrub has a nasty habit of throwing up suckers 1m (3ft) or more from the main plant, but it deserves consideration for your autumn border. It produces upright, mostly unbranched stems with large, heart-shaped, deep green leaves that have an unpleasant smell if bruised, making a dense thicket. At the top of the stems, which grow to about 1.5m (5ft), dense domes of deep pink buds form which open to starry, pink flowers that have a lovely scent. These stems can be cut down in winter and, if you live in a cold area, the crowns should be covered with

a mulch to protect them from severe frost. It is not fussy about soil but flowers best in full sun. 'Pink Diamond' has greyish, white-edged leaves and is much less vigorous but is usually grafted onto the plain green plant so suckers should be removed.

Spring companion
Leucojum aestivum

Autumn companion
Vernonia crinata

Clerodendron trichotomum

This clerodendron is a large shrub or small tree and though it also produces suckers, these should be removed if you want a well-balanced tree. It rapidly grows to about 3m (10ft) and eventually forms a broad crown. It is hardy but needs a warm summer to 'harden' the stems and it is best in light soils and in full sun. The leaves are heart-shaped and have an unpleasant smell when crushed but, in early autumn, the plant is covered with masses of white, starry, intensely, fragrant flowers, rather like those of jasmine. If the weather is warm and sunny these are followed by bright turquoise berries surrounded by a star-shaped, crimson calyx and these last well into autumn – an extraordinary display. 'Carnival' has yellow-variegated leaves.

Autumn companion
Cyclamen hederifoilum

Winter companion
Euonymus fortunei 'Emerald Gaiety'

Colletia paradoxa

In autumn it is impossible to resist the perfume of Colletia; the tiny, tubular, white flowers crowd the stems and pump out an intoxicating scent. But do not be tempted to put your nose too close to the plants because this is one of the most spitefully prickly plants imaginable. It is basically a column of triangular, blue-green spines in pairs, at right angles to each other, and is the plant equivalent of barbed wire. It is hardy but is best planted against a sunny wall in light soil so the reflected heat ensures that it flowers freely. It is rather slow-growing but can eventually reach 3m (10ft). It is a good plant to put below windows to prevent burglars, but do not plant it where you have to walk past it every day or have to prune it regularly or you may have cause to curse it!

Summer companion
Crinum x powellii

Autumn companion
Vitis vinifera 'Purpurea'

Coprosma 'Rainbow Surprise'

Coprosmas are slightly tender shrubs that can only be grown outside in mild areas or with the protection of a sunny wall, to keep severe frosts at bay. They are most commonly available in autumn when they are sold to include in autumn containers. They are admirably suited to these, due to their small, colourful foliage that is thick and shiny with a mirror-like finish. Their flowers are small and may be followed by attractive berries but only on female plants and if a male is nearby. 'Rainbow Surprise' has bright leaves in shades of red, green, apricot and yellow and 'Coppershine' has deep, bronze foliage. They vary in height and habit but most slowly reach 1m (3ft) and can be kept at that size by pruning in spring.

Summer companion
Verbena 'Temari Violet'

Autumn companion
Nerine bowdenii

Cotinus coggygria 'Royal Purple'

The smoke bush is a popular shrub that is grown mainly for the feathery flower clusters that cover the plant with pink 'candy floss' in mid-summer. As autumn approaches, this turns red and then disintegrates but the foliage then turns gold, orange and scarlet before it falls. In time, it can grow to 3m (10ft) and form a small tree but it can be pruned every spring to keep it small. It then will not flower as freely but will have larger, more attractive foliage. The most popular have purple foliage all summer, such as 'Royal Purple', but 'Golden Spirit' has yellow leaves and the larger 'Grace' has glowing, claret leaves. All are easy to grow in a sunny spot, in any soil, including clay and chalk.

Summer companion
Dahlia 'Tally Ho'

Autumn companion
Clematis viticella 'Purpurea Plena Elegans'

Cotoneaster horizontalis

All cotoneasters are tough, useful plants with small white or pink flowers in summer and most have attractive red berries in autumn. *C. horizontalis* is deciduous and is often grown against walls where its 'herring bone' branches fan out against the bricks, showing their shape especially well in winter, but it can be grown as a shrub in the border, too. The stems are covered in small, pink flowers in spring that attract bees. Tiny leaves, which turn red and orange in autumn, are followed by red berries which last well after the stems are otherwise bare, unless they are eaten by birds. It will grow in any soil, in sun or part shade and reach about 1m (3ft).

Summer companion
Spiraea japonica 'Goldflame'

Autumn companion
Euonymus alatus

Cotoneaster conspicuus 'Decorus'

Evergreen cotoneasters are useful background shrubs and the larger varieties can be used as screens or to give structure to the winter garden. C. conspicuus 'Decorus' makes a mound of small, deep green leaves on plants about 1.5m (5ft) high and across with little white flowers in summer. These develop into small red berries that are usually borne in vast numbers, glowing in the autumn and winter sun.

Autumn companion
Clematis 'Gravetye Beauty'

Winter companion
Euonymus fortunei 'Emerald 'n' Gold'

Cotoneaster frigidus 'Cornubia'

This is one of the larger Cotoneasters and can be trained as a single stem when young to create a small, standard tree. It is evergreen or semi-evergreen and a few of the leaves turn red and fall in autumn. The leaves are dark green, 12cm (5in) long, and the clusters of white flowers are followed by bright red berries.

Autumn companion
Malus 'Evereste'

Winter companion
Aucuba japonica 'Crotonifolia'

Eucalyptus gunnii

Eucalyptus are fast-growing, evergreen trees and have many attractions, though none of the species that are frost-hardy have showy flowers. Young plants produce round, usually grey-blue foliage, but as they get taller this changes to oval foliage that is often greener in colour. If young plants are hard pruned every year or so to prevent them developing into trees, they retain their juvenile foliage; E. gunnii is often treated in this way. Eucalyptus prefer light soil and full sun and young plants should be planted in preference to large specimens to ensure that they develop strong roots to support their tall stems. If not pruned, E. gunnii will become a tree 25m (80ft) high, with pale bark and masses of small, fluffy flowers in autumn. E. pauciflora subsp. niphophila, the snow gum, is one of the hardiest and grows to 6m (20ft), with beautiful, smooth, white, peeling bark and fluffy cream flowers in spring.

Autumn companion
Euonymus europaeus 'Red Cascade'

Winter companion
Viburnum tinus 'Eve Price'

Eucryphia x nymansensis 'Nymansay'

Evergreen shrubs with showy flowers are few and far between and any that flower in autumn are even harder to find. Eucryphias fill this gap and can be planted in any garden that is moderately sunny and has acid or neutral soil. Some are not fully hardy, but *E. x nymansensis* 'Nymansay' is the toughest and forms an upright shrub that slowly grows to 15m (50ft) high with deep green, glossy foliage and masses of white flowers, rather like single roses, in early autumn. It is usually available as small plants, so give them plenty of room to grow and

keep well watered in their first years until they are established.

Summer companion
Sambucus nigra 'Black Beauty'

Autumn companion
Sorbus 'Joseph Rock'

Euonymus alatus

The evergreen Euonymus are so common that many gardeners are unaware of the deciduous species. They have tiny flowers and the foliage is rather dull in summer, but many have wonderful autumn colour. *E. alatus* is not only the best Euonymus for foliage colour, it is probably the best of all shrubs. If you hanker after a Liquidambar but do not have room, or a Japanese maple but your garden is too cold and windy, plant this instead. It forms a rounded shrub 2m (6ft) high with winged, corky stems and the leaves turn deep crimson pink in autumn lasting for many

weeks, sometimes with the added bonus of red, round fruits. It will colour best in full sun but will tolerate any soil including chalk and dry soils.

Summer companion
Physocarpus opulifolius 'Dart's Gold'

Autumn companion
Ligustrum lucidum
'Excelsum Superbum'

Euonymus europaeus 'Red Cascade'

E. europaeus is the native spindle berry, a deciduous shrub with an arching habit that can grow to 3m (10ft) in time, with dull green leaves and tiny flowers. These blooms develop into beautiful crimson fruits that split open in autumn to reveal orange seeds, and at the same time the foliage turns red, too. 'Red Cascade' is the best variety and is spectacular in autumn and into winter because the fruits remain on the plants for many months. Easy to grow in any soil, its only problem is that it

is the place where blackfly like to spend the winter before leaping onto your broad beans in spring.

Autumn companion
Sorbus vilmorinii

Winter companion
Rubus cockburnianus 'Goldenvale'

Heptacodium miconioides

This unusual shrub was only introduced to our gardens in 1981, so it is not found in many books. However, it is an unusual and beautiful shrub that will reach about 3m (10ft) high. It has large, deeply veined leaves and attractive, peeling bark – even on young plants – and in early autumn it is covered in clusters of small, fragrant, white flowers. These last many weeks, but when they have finished, their calyces grow and turn bright red, lasting for weeks, until the foliage drops at the onset of winter.

Spring companion
Ribes sanguineum 'Red Pimpernel'

Autumn companion
Rose 'Geranium'

Hibiscus syriacus

Most gardeners are surprised to find that there are hardy Hibiscus, associating the plants with tropical holidays. However, *H. syriacus* has been decorating our gardens for centuries and is one of the most beautiful of hardy, deciduous shrubs. It tolerates drought but must be grown in a sunny place and in cold areas it is best grown against a sunny wall or the flowers may start to open so late in autumn that they do not have a chance to fully open. Most grow to about 2m (6ft) high, but they can be pruned in spring to restrict their size and they are often grown as standards. They do not start to produce leaves until very late in spring and you may think they are dead at first, but they then grow rapidly and produce masses of flowers that open over several months. There are single and double-flowered varieties but the doubles often do not open well, especially in wet weather, so should be avoided. 'Oiseau Bleu' has lilac flowers with a maroon centre and is the most beautiful, with flowers 8cm (3in) across. 'Red Heart' has white flowers with red centres and 'Diana' has large, pure white blooms. The foliage usually turns bright yellow in autumn before falling.

Spring companion
Kerria japonica 'Picta'

Autumn companion
Hydrangea 'Altona'

Hydrangea 'Altona'

In mild areas, the Hortensia or mophead Hydrangeas create masses of colour in late summer and autumn. They are best suited to areas that do not suffer from cold winters and that have acid or neutral soil. They dislike dry soils and need plenty of water in summer. On chalky soils they do not thrive and develop sickly, yellow foliage, though they are suitable for growing in large pots and tubs if they are watered well. Most varieties have flowers that change colour according to the soil acidity: blue in acid soil, mauve in neutral soils and pink in slightly alkaline soil. They should be lightly pruned in spring, just removing the old flowerheads. If pruned too hard they may not bloom. 'Altona' has large heads of rich pink,

'Geoffrey Chadbund' is the best lacecap, with lacy flowerheads of deep pink, 'Pia' has bright red flowers on compact plants just 60cm (2ft) high and 'Hamburg' is a large plant with showy, dense heads of pink or mauve. Most grow to 1.5m (5ft) when mature and should be given plenty of space because of the problems with pruning.

Summer companion
Aruncus dioicus

Autumn companion
Anemone x hybrida 'Konigin Charlotte'

Hydrangea paniculata 'Grandiflora'

In cold gardens where the mophead Hydrangeas are difficult to grow, *H. paniculata* should be considered. It is tough, hardy, tolerates most soils and has large flowerheads of small white blooms that start pale green, change to white and then turn pink as they age. This hydrangea can be pruned and if it is cut back hard in spring, produces strong stems 2m (6ft) high with flower clusters that may be 45cm (18in) long – pyramids packed with hundreds of flowers. 'Grandiflora' is the most popular because of the large

flowerheads, but 'Pink Diamond' has blooms that change to pink at an early stage. These do not change flower colour according to soil acidity and if not pruned, can grow to 3m (10ft).

Spring companion
Narcissus 'Ice Follies'

Autumn companion
Liriope muscari

Hydrangea quercifolia 'Snowflake'

This unusual hydrangea has large, lobed foliage that is striking in summer but spectacular in autumn when it changes from green to purple and red before it falls. The clusters of white flowers open in late summer and in 'Snowflake', which has double flowers, are especially showy, turning to pink as they age. It prefers a sunny spot, sheltered from strong winds and will eventually reach 2m (6ft) high.

Summer companion
Euphorbia dulcis 'Chameleon'

Autumn companion
Melianthus major

Ligustrum lucidum 'Excelsum Superbum'

Most gardeners only think of privet (Ligustrum) as a hedging plant, but *L. lucidum*, a Chinese species, is a large shrub or small tree, 5m (15ft) high, that has large, glossy foliage attractive at all times of the year. It is easy to grow in any soil and in autumn is covered with large clusters of small, white flowers. The plain green plant is beautiful but 'Excelsum Superbum' is the finest, with beautiful foliage that is broadly edged with butter yellow. It can be pruned to form a large shrub or allowed to become a tree.

Autumn companion
Clerodendrum bungeii 'Pink Diamond'

Winter companion
Lonicera purpusii 'Winter Beauty'

Liquidambar styraciflua

Liquidambar, the sweet gum, gets its common name because the foliage, when crushed, has a sweet scent. It looks like a maple but the leaves are arranged singly on the stems and not in pairs as found on all maples (Acer). Liquidambars are large trees, reaching 25m (80ft) high and grow best in full sun in moist, rich soil. They are planted primarily for their autumn colour, which is among the finest of all deciduous trees. Individual leaves on the tree change to a variety of colours, from yellow to red and purple. 'Worplesdon' is a popular variety, with foliage that is predominantly orange and purple in autumn.

Autumn companion
Parrotia persica

Winter companion
Prunus lusitanica 'Variegata'

Malus 'Evereste'

Crab apples are ideal small trees with several seasons of interest. In spring they have colourful white or pink, fragrant flowers and in autumn they are laden with attractive fruits that feed the birds through winter. Most do not grow too tall and they are not fussy about soil, though they grow, flower and fruit best in a sunny spot. They are also good pollinators for edible apples. Some old varieties are rather prone to diseases such as mildew and scab, but modern varieties are generally fairly resistant. Most grow to about 5m (16ft) eventually. 'Evereste' has masses of white flowers that open from red buds in spring and red and orange fruits in autumn. *M. x*

zumi 'Golden Hornet' has an upright habit and branches laden with bright yellow fruits and 'John Downie' has large, red-flushed apples that are ideal for crab apple jelly.

Spring companion
Narcissus 'Bell Song'

Autumn companion
Crocus speciosus

Malus tschonoskii

This Japanese crab apple is unusual because of its upright, almost pyramidal habit, making it useful for small gardens. It can reach 12m (40ft) eventually but is slow-growing. The flowers in spring are not as showy as most and the apples themselves are rather dull but the leaves turn brilliant shades of orange, red and purple in autumn and last on the trees for many weeks before they fall.

Spring companion
Anemone blanda

Autumn companion
Eucalyptus gunnii

Nandina domestica

Sometimes called the sacred bamboo, this is not a bamboo at all, but is related to Berberis. However, it is spine-free and has beautiful, finely divided foliage that is purple at first and then deep, lustrous green. Some leaves drop in autumn, after turning scarlet, but it is essentially evergreen. Throughout summer it produces large clusters of small, white flowers and these are followed by red berries. Growing to about 1.5m (5ft), it is always elegant and beautiful and thrives in sun or part shade in most soils, but preferably in moist, acid soil. It is also

suitable for large pots and is a welcome addition on the patio. 'Fire Power' is a dwarf plant, 45cm (18in) high with broad foliage that is bright red but it does not flower or berry.

Summer companion
Hemerocallis 'Corky'

Autumn companion
Tricyrtis formosana 'Samurai'

Parrotia persica

In autumn there are few more beautiful sights than a large, spreading parrotia covered in its glorious foliage. The leaves that have been deep green all summer turn gold, red and purple and last for many weeks, longer than most other shrubs grown for autumn foliage. It is a large shrub, up to 8m (25ft) high and even more across, and the branches, that twist and turn in all directions, have beautiful, peeling bark. In spring, the bare branches produce tiny, spidery, red flowers. It will grow in most soils but autumn colour is best when it is grown on acid soil.

Autumn companion
Helianthus 'Capenoch Star'

Winter companion
Acer griseum

Perovskia atriplicifolia 'Blue Spire'

Perovskia is a fast-growing shrub that thrives in dry soil in a sunny spot and is an ideal companion for other silver-leaved plants and herbs. It will reach about 1m (3ft) high and is usually pruned hard each spring to keep it neat and encourage the growth of strong, upright shoots that are the most attractive because they are covered in a white powder. The deeply cut, small leaves are also silver and the ends of the shoots are covered in small, violet blue flowers in autumn. The whole plant is aromatic.

Summer companion
Iris 'Edith Wolford'

Autumn companion
Gaura lindheimeri

Pyracantha 'Teton'

Pyracanthas are adaptable, spiny evergreens that can be used in many ways in the garden. They are often planted against walls but can also be used as shrubs in the border or as hedges and screens. They grow and flower best in full sun but they can suffer when planted against a sunny wall where the soil is dry and they then become prone to scab, a disease that affects the foliage and causes the developing berries to go black at an early stage. The bright yellow, orange or red berries are usually freely produced and look attractive all autumn and winter unless blackbirds strip them. Saphyr Orange is a recent introduction with orange berries that is resistant to scab. 'Sparkler' has variegated leaves but fewer berries, 'Soleil d'Or' has yellow berries and 'Golden Charmer' and 'Teton' have pale orange berries. All grow to 2.5m (8ft) in time but can be regularly pruned to keep them smaller.

Summer companion
Eccremocarpus scaber

Autumn companion
Phygelius aequalis 'Yellow Trumpet'

Rhus typhina

Rhus typhina, the stag's horn sumach, has rather fallen from favour in recent years but was once a common shrub in gardens. It is easy to grow in most soils and forms a low, spreading tree 5m (16ft) high, but usually rather less, with thick, furry branches and strange, red flower clusters that remain on the plants for many months like velvety cones. The 60cm (2ft) leaves are divided into many leaflets which are bright green in summer but turn brilliant red and flame colours in autumn. Its only problem is that it is prone to produce suckers considerable distances from the trunk, especially in dry soil, which can make it a nuisance when grown as a lawn specimen.

Spring companion
Berberis darwinii

Autumn companion
Physalis alkekengi

Rosa 'Geranium'

Most roses are grown for their beautiful, fragrant flowers but many have attractive hips and a few are grown primarily for these. 'Geranium' is a large, sprawling shrub with thorny stems and neat, deep red flowers in summer in one flush but it is for the hips that most people grow it. These are bright red and hang on the shrubs for many months, usually long after the leaves have fallen. It will grow in any soil, in sun or part shade, and will reach 2.5m (8ft) high, though it can be kept a little smaller by pruning lightly in spring.

Spring companion
Viburnum x burkwoodii

Autumn companion
Cotinus coggygria 'Royal Purple'

Rosa rugosa

Roses have a reputation for being prone to diseases such as blackspot and mildew, but *R. rugosa* is usually free from any troubles and is a good choice for organic gardeners. Unlike most roses, it also thrives in light, sandy soils and produces suckering stems, forming a thicket of branches up to 1.5m (5ft) high. The branches are covered in bristly thorns and make a good hedge, covered in large, pink, fragrant, single flowers in summer. These are followed by heavy crops of large, fleshy hips that birds love to devour, and when the leaves turn bright yellow in autumn, the contrast is beautiful.

Summer companion
Leycesteria formosa

Autumn companion
Hydrangea paniculata 'Grandiflora'

Sorbus hupehensis

Sorbus are best known as mountain ash (*S. aucuparia*) with its ferny foliage and bunches of red fruits in late summer, but there are many more interesting species and *S. hupehensis* is not only beautiful, it will have your neighbours green with envy. It is a small tree, 5m (16ft) high with blue-green leaves in summer and clusters of white flowers. The leaves turn yellow and red in autumn and the berries, carried on red stalks, are white, sometimes flushed with pink. It grows best on moist, acid or neutral soil.

Spring companion
Corylopsis pauciflora

Autumn companion
Persicaria affinis 'Superba'

Sorbus aucuparia

Of the many sorbus suitable for small gardens, this is probably the best known. It is always elegant, with finely divided foliage, that does not cast too much shade on plants underneath and has small white flowers in summer. These are followed by berries that ripen to orange in late summer. They contrast well with the foliage that changes from green to yellow. It grows to 8m (25ft) high eventually and is tolerant of most soils. Unfortunately, most sorbus are prone to a disease called fireblight in some areas. This spreads through the flower clusters and causes short, flowering shoots to turn brown and die. Affected shoots should be cut out as soon as they are seen.

Spring companion
Chaenomeles superba 'Knap Hill Scarlet'

Autumn companion
Cotoneaster horizontalis

Sorbus cashmiriana

This small tree is a fine addition to the garden in autumn and winter when it is laden with large, white berries. It reaches 8m (25ft) high and has fine, dark green leaves. The flowers are unusual because they are larger than most and pink rather than white. The berries are pink at first but ripen to white. These last well into the winter, hanging from the chunky twigs and are not as eagerly devoured by birds as the berries of most other sorbus trees.

Spring companion
Rhododendron 'Blue Diamond'

Autumn companion
Colchicum 'Waterlily'

Yucca filamentosa 'Bright Edge'

Yuccas are drought-tolerant, evergreen plants with long, spine-tipped foliage that bring an exotic look to the garden. Though primarily grown as foliage plants, they also produce dramatic, bell-shaped flowers. These are waxy in texture, cream in colour and are produced on tall spikes, well above the foliage. Although most yuccas are frost tender, many are hardy enough to grow in our gardens but need a well-drained soil that is not wet in winter and a sunny spot, to remind them of their homes in the south of the USA and Central America. *Y. filamentosa* is a dwarf yucca that can be fitted into most gardens and forms rosettes of foliage about 45cm (18in) high and flower spikes 1m (3ft) high in summer and autumn. 'Bright Edge' has colourful leaves edged with yellow.

Summer companion
Iris 'Sarah Taylor'

Autumn companion
Sternbergia lutea

Yucca flaccida 'Ivory'

If the sharp tips of most yuccas worry you, or if you have children, *Yucca flaccida*, which has relatively soft, harmless leaves, is the right choice. It is a dwarf species that spreads by underground shoots to form clumps of rosettes of grey leaves. The plant is only 30cm (1ft) high until it produces its upright stems of flowers, 60cm (2ft) high. The variety 'Ivory' produces more flowers than usual and is the one to choose if you want flowers as well as leaves. It is a good plant for dry, sunny borders or gravel gardens.

Summer companion
Convolvulus cneorum

Autumn companion
Sedum telephium 'Matrona'

Yucca gloriosa 'Variegata'

Unlike the previous species which barely form stems, *Y. gloriosa* is a big, bold plant with thick trunks that can reach 2m (6ft) high. On these there are long, thick, spine-tipped leaves, brightly edged with creamy yellow creating a head of foliage 1.2m (4ft) across. Although dramatic in appearance, this plant must be sited carefully because of the sharpness of these leaf tips. It is surprisingly hardy and will flourish in any soil, including clay soils, but must have an open, sunny sight. When mature, the plant will produce sideshoots and dramatic flower stems, usually in late summer and autumn. These appear as thick, red spears in the centre of the rosette and grow to 1.5m (5ft) high with masses of cream, bell-shaped flowers. This is just as easy to grow as the plain green but a bit more expensive. This is a bold, dramatic plant that will bring a touch of the exotic to your garden. Usually plants are small when bought and will take several years to develop a trunk and reach flowering size, so this is not a plant for the impatient.

Summer companion
Romneya coulteri

Autumn companion
Eucalyptus gunnii

Zauschneria californica 'Garrettii'

Sometimes called the Californian fuchsia, this is a superb plant for hot, dry soils. This small shrub, about 30cm (1ft) high and 45cm (18in) wide, is attractive all summer, with small, silvery grey leaves, and in autumn it is covered with tubular, scarlet flowers for many weeks. It can be shortlived and will only survive the winter if it is planted in a sunny spot in well-drained, light soils. Winter wet kills it. Plants should be trimmed hard in spring, cutting away any growth that has been killed by winter cold.

Spring companion
Tulipa 'Red Riding Hood'

Autumn companion
Pennisetum alopecuroides 'Hameln'

Campsis radicans

This is a vigorous climber that clings to buildings and other supports with roots that grow from its stems, in the same way as ivy. It is deciduous and its leaves turn bright yellow in autumn, but it is grown for its clusters of large, trumpet-shaped, deep orange flowers that open for many months from late summer to autumn. Plants that are scaling their support rarely flower and it is only when they run out of support, so the stems splay out horizontally, that they bloom freely. For this reason it is not a good climber for a house wall, where it will only bloom when it has filled the gutters. It is better on pergolas and posts. 'Indian Summer' is more compact than most and C. x *tagliabuana* 'Madame Galen' is the most common variety.

Autumn companion
Colletia paradoxa

Winter companion
Trachycarpus fortunei

Clematis 'Gravetye Beauty'

Autumn-flowering clematis have many advantages over summer-flowering clematis. They are easy to prune because all you have to do is cut back all the growth to about 30cm (1ft) from the ground in spring, so it is easy to combine them with shrubs in the border and roses on walls. They are also unlikely to suffer from Clematis wilt, which seems to attack mostly early summer-flowering varieties. Most grow to 2m (6ft) or slightly more, so will not smother supporting plants, and they produce masses of mostly small flowers for several months. 'Gravetye Beauty' is a hybrid of C. *texensis* and has tulip-shaped, deep red flowers. C. *viticella* produces showers of small, four-petalled, often nodding flowers. 'Alba Luxuriens' has white flowers, marked with pale purple and green, and 'Purpurea Plena Elegans' has sumptuous, burgundy, double flowers. 'Venosa Violacea' has beautiful purple and white blooms.

Summer companion
Physocarpus opulifolius 'Diabolo'

Autumn companion
Euonymus europaeus 'Red Cascade'

Parthenocissus tricuspidata

Virginia creeper is a plant you cannot miss in autumn when its growth, which covers the walls of many houses, turns bright red. But there are several species that each have their own merits. *P. henryana* is a Chinese species that is the most interesting in summer because the leaves, which are divided into five leaflets, are deep green, often flushed with bronze, with pale pink veins. The leaves turn bright red in autumn before falling. *P. quinquefolia* is the true Virginia creeper from Virginia in the USA and also has divided leaves, which are green all summer, but turns even brighter shades in autumn. *P. tricuspidata* is Boston Ivy and has three-lobed foliage with spectacular autumn colour. All produce 'sticky' tendrils that cling to walls and fences and are vigorous and may smother small buildings.

Summer companion
Sambucus racemosa 'Sutherland Gold'

Autumn companion
Parrotia persica

Trachelospermum jasminoides

This twiner is an ideal choice where you need fragrance in autumn and some evergreen foliage in winter. It prefers moist soil and a sunny, sheltered position and then is capable or reaching 5m (16ft) or more. The oval leaves are thick and glossy, though a few may go red and fall in autumn and the small, creamy white flowers open for several months in late summer and autumn, filling the air with their rich fragrance. It is vigorous but not rampant and is a good choice for planting in a pot on a sunny patio.

Summer companion
Leptospermum scoparium

Autumn companion
Clematis 'Venosa Violacea'

Vitis vinifera 'Purpurea'

Most gardeners only plant grapes in the hope of producing an edible crop but vines are ornamental, too, and *Vitis vinifera* 'Purpurea', the purple-leaved grape, is a lovely climber for a sunny wall, pergola or trellis. It has tendrils that will grip on to wires and trellis and will reach 3m (10ft) or more but is easily restrained by pruning in the depths of winter. The lobed, deep purple leaves are slightly grey when young but develop their full colour as they age, in sun. And when autumn arrives they develop some brighter, red tints before they fall. This plant is a good companion for pink or orange climbing roses or pale clematis and can even be used on banks as ground cover to clamber over cotoneasters.

Summer companion
Lavatera x *clementii* 'Bredon Springs'

Autumn companion
Strobilanthes attenuata

Colchicum speciosum

Colchicums are large bulbs that produce large, mauve or lilac flowers in autumn and large clusters of broad, glossy foliage in spring. They are unusual because they will produce their flowers without being planted and you can enjoy the flowers by simply placing the large bulb on the windowsill, but it must then be planted in the garden. The flowers are welcome in autumn, but you must remember that the leaves are large, 30cm (1ft) high and that they die down in early summer, flopping onto surrounding plants. *C. speciosum* has large, mauve, white-centred flowers and *C. autumnale* has many smaller flowers. 'Waterlily' has beautiful mauve, double flowers. Colchicums thrive in sun or part shade and can be planted in the border or naturalized in grass. All parts of the plant are poisonous.

Autumn companion
Liriope muscari

Winter companion
Euonymus fortunei 'Emerald Gaiety'

Crocus speciosus

Not all crocuses flower in spring and although colchicums may look like Crocus when in flower, their huge foliage betrays the fact that they are not Crocus at all. *C. speciosus* is a true crocus and flowers in late autumn but does not produce its grassy foliage until spring. The blooms grow to about 15cm (6in) high and look beautiful when planted in large clumps, their lavender flowers contrasting with fallen leaves on the border. The flowers are sweetly scented. It thrives in well-drained soil in sun or partial shade and will spread by self-seeding in most gardens, gradually increasing in beauty over the years.

Spring companion
Crocus vernus 'Remembrance'

Autumn companion
Hibiscus syriacus 'Oiseau Bleu'

Cyclamen hederifolium

Few plants are interesting and beautiful for ten months of the year– as well as easy to grow – but the hardy, tough, *C. hederifolium* earns its keep from early autumn till summer each year. There is nothing to see in summer but then the delicate pink or white flowers appear from the bare earth in early autumn. These are followed by grey and green marbled leaves that cover the ground throughout winter and into summer when they finally die down. It is completely hardy and will grow in sun or deep shade under trees and will seed itself to form large clumps. Dried corms are often offered for sale, but these do not always grow and it is best to buy plants that are in leaf or flower.

Autumn companion
Euonymus alatus

Winter companion
Arum italicum 'Marmoratum'

Nerine bowdenii

The bright pink flowers of South African *N. bowdenii* would be pretty at any time of the year, but they are especially welcome in autumn. This beautiful plant produces its 60cm (2ft) stems with clusters of spidery, bright pink flowers in late autumn and then has clusters of narrow, bright green foliage that eventually dies down in late summer. It requires a sunny, hot site to bake the bulbs in summer and often does not flower until it has produced offsets, so the clumps of bulbs are crowded. Certainly, old clumps that are pushing themselves out of the ground always seem to flower best. Plant the bulbs, so the tips are at ground level, at the base of a sunny wall.

Summer companion
Anthemis punctata subsp. *cupaniana*

Autumn companion
Origanum laevigatum 'Herrenhausen'

Sternbergia lutea

This bright bulb needs similar conditions to nerines; a hot, dry site that gets as much sun as possible, but the flowers, that look like those of crocuses, are bright, golden yellow. The flowers are followed by deep green, glossy foliage. Each bulb produces several flowers and the bulbs should not be disturbed once established so they form dense clumps that will flower freely. The flowers are carried on stems 15cm (6in) high and the foliage grows to 30cm (1ft).

Summer companion
Agastache 'Apricot Sprite'

Autumn companion
Ceratostigma plumbaginoides

winter

Asplenium scolopendrium

This hardy, evergreen fern contrasts with most others because of its glossy foliage that is undivided and forms lustrous 'shuttlecocks' of leaves 45cm (18in) tall. It is easy to grow in partial shade and prefers alkaline soils, though it will grow anywhere that is not too wet in winter. In shady places it may self-'seed' (through spores) into walls and in paving and seems to resist considerable drought in these conditions. There are many different varieties, with different leaf shapes such as 'Crispum' which has fronds with wavy margins and the 'Cristatum Group' which has broad, divided frond tips.

Winter companion
Euonymus fortunei 'Emerald Gaiety'

Spring companion
Lamium maculatum 'White Nancy'

Helleborus hybridus

Hellebores are useful plants that flower in late winter and have attractive, evergreen foliage. *H. hybridus* is easy to grow in most soils and thrives in light shade, but will also grow in full sun or complete shade if the soil is moist. The deep green, fingered foliage grows to about 40cm (16in) high and is attractive all summer with the nodding flowers starting to appear, on stems from soil level, in winter and continuing to bloom into spring. The flowers are usually in shades of pink but vary from white, green and pale yellow to deep purple and are often prettily spotted inside. In the right conditions, plants often self-seed freely and seedlings flower in their third year. To allow the flowers to be seen more clearly and prevent leaf spot disease, trim off the old foliage in early winter each year.

Winter companion
Gaultheria mucronata 'Bell's Seedling'

Spring companion
Primula vulgaris

Helleborus argutifolius

This evergreen hellebore prefers a warmer and sunnier spot than most and produces stems, up to 1m (3ft) high, with spine-edged leaves. In late winter the top of each stem produces a large cluster of round, pale green flowers. After flowering, the stems should be cut to the ground to allow new shoots to develop. It forms large clumps that are attractive all year with leaves that are deep green when grown in light shade and paler when in the sun.

Winter companion
Chimonanthus praecox

Summer companion
Teucrium fruticans

Helleborus foetidus

This is a useful plant for shade, producing 60cm (2ft) stems with deep green, finely divided foliage and eventually forming broad clumps. It may self-seed. The foliage is ornamental all year and in late winter the shoot tips produce flowerheads with pale green bracts and nodding, small, rounded green flowers, usually rimmed with purple. The flowers last many months and when they have finished, the flowered stems should be cut out at the base.

Plants vary in the amount of purple colouring on the blooms and 'Wester Flisk' also has red-flushed stems.

Winter companion
Euonymus fortunei 'Emerald 'n' Gold'

Autumn companion
Persicaria campanulata

Helleborus x nigercors

This is an unusual hybrid between *H. argutifolius* and the Christmas rose (*H. niger*). It is easier to grow than *H. niger*, which requires rich, moist soil, but is still compact in habit, with white flowers that have a green stripe through the petals. It produces deep green leaves and branched stems from the soil carrying several flowers that remain beautiful for many weeks. It thrives in semi-shade.

Winter companion
Ruscus aculeatus

Spring companion
Pulmonaria 'Occupol'

Iris unguicularis

This tough iris from Algeria is the ideal plant for dry, sunny borders where little else will survive. It forms clumps of narrow, long green foliage 40cm (16in) high which are not particularly attractive, but it excels in winter when it opens its lilac flowers. These open for several months, during mild spells, and nestle among the foliage. They are sweetly scented and deserve to be picked and brought into the house. It thrives on neglect and should not be divided once established because it can take a few years to settle down after planting. It prefers an alkaline soil and grows and flowers well at the base of sunny walls in association with nerines and sternbergias. The flowers should be protected from slugs and snails. *I. lazica* is similar but the foliage is brighter green and it prefers some shade.

Winter companion
Correa 'Mannii'

Spring companion
Crocus tommasinianus

Iris foetidissima

Few plants grow well in the dry shade under trees, but this evergreen iris will thrive here if the young plants are watered in their first season, until established. Forming clumps 60cm (2ft) high, the leaves are deep green and glossy. In late spring the small, pale lilac and brown or pale yellow and brown flowers open but are not showy. These develop into large, green seedpods that split open, in autumn, to reveal bright orange seeds that remain attached for many months throughout winter. If left intact they will eventually fall off and produce new plants, but can also be cut for indoor decoration. There is a variegated form but this does not flower.

Winter companion
Arum italicum 'Marmoratum'

Spring companion
Vinca minor 'Illumination'

Luzula sylvatica 'Aurea'

This woodsedge is perfect for ground cover in sun or shade and forms clumps of rosettes of narrow foliage. The plant is green in summer and not very exciting but, as temperatures drop, in autumn, the whole plant turns bright gold and remains that colour until the following spring when the small, insignificant flower clusters appear. It is not invasive and grows to 30cm (1ft) high.

Winter companion
Ilex crenata 'Golden Gem'

Spring companion
Omphalodes cappadocica 'Starry Eyes'

Ophiopogon planiscapus 'Nigrescens'

Plants with black foliage are rare, but this low evergreen is about as close as we can get. The leaves are narrow, grass-like and curve out from ground level to form a carpet 15cm (6in) high. In summer, pinkish flowers open on short stems and these develop into attractive, black berries. It grows best in part shade or sun in acid soil that is rich in organic matter but it will survive in other soils. As a contrast, you could plant *O. jaburan* 'Vittatus', which is more upright, reaching 45cm (18in) high, with brightly variegated green and white leaves. Both spread slowly by suckers and are useful for containers in winter.

Winter companion
Galanthus nivalis

Summer companion
Erica vagans 'Mrs D. F. Maxwell'

Phormium 'Yellow Wave'

Phormiums are bold evergreens with clumps made up of fans of long, narrow foliage. They are not always completely hardy, especially when grown in heavy, clay soil and when grown in containers where frost can penetrate the roots. They vary in height from 60cm (2ft) to 3m (10ft) and those with plain green or purple foliage are the toughest. Most produce tall stems of tubular flowers and seedpods when mature. The most popular have foliage that is brightly variegated with yellow, red and pink with green or bronze and most of these reach 1.5m (5ft) high and 2m (6ft) across. 'Yellow Wave' has arching foliage with a broad, pale yellow centre, 'Pink Panther' is marked with pink whilst 'Dazzler' has bright red and purple foliage. All prefer full sun, tolerate winds and thrive in coastal gardens.

Winter companion
Skimmia japonica 'Rubella'

Summer companion
Crocosmia 'Lucifer'

Polystichum aculeatum

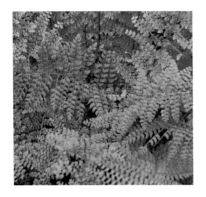

This is a tough, hardy fern that thrives in shade and forms shuttlecocks of finely divided, dark green foliage. It is evergreen and contrasts, in summer, with the softer-textured foliage of deciduous ferns and hostas. In winter it is useful ground cover for shrubs and spring-flowering bulbs. The fronds grow to 60cm (2ft) high and form dense clumps for ground cover, contrasting well with more common spreaders such as Vinca, Pachysandra and Lamium.

Winter companion
Lonicera purpusii 'Winter Beauty'

Autumn companion
Callicarpa bodinieri var. *giraldii* 'Profusion'

Ruscus aculeatus

Almost indestructible, butcher's broom is related to lilies, but you would hardly guess that from a quick glance. Also called Bath asparagus because the young shoots look like asparagus spears, you would have to be very hungry to eat such a tough, woody plant, even when it was young. The shoots grow to 60cm (2ft) and are covered in spine-tipped 'leaves' which are actually flattened stems. The tiny green and brown flowers are followed by red berries on female and hermaphrodite plants. It survives in dense shade in dry soil but is very slow to grow, gradually forming a dense, spiny clump. Each shoot lasts for several years and when they die they can be cut for indoor decoration. It is unusual and useful rather than beautiful, except when covered in the large, bright red berries. *R. hypoglossum* is even less common but just as tough and forms permanent, dense groundcover with broader, paler 'leaves'.

Winter companion
Corylus avellana 'Tortuosa'

Autumn companion
Cyclamen hederifoilium

Sempervivum arachnoideum

Sempervivums (houseleeks) are succulent but hardy plants that form mats or mounds of evergreen rosettes. The leaves are usually green but may also be tinged with purple and there are dozens of varieties with rosettes that vary from 1cm (½in) to 12cm (5in) across. They tolerate drought and can be grown where there is little soil such as in gravel, on paths and even on roofs. When mature, each rosette produces a stem, about 15cm (6in) tall, with pink, starry flowers in summer. *S. arachnoideum* has clumps of small rosettes covered in a fine webbing whilst *S. tectorum* is the most common and easiest to grow and find. All are attractive and need full sun, especially to help purple colouring to develop, and are easy to grow though often falling prey to vine weevil grubs, which eat the roots.

Winter companion
Cyclamen coum

Spring companion
Chionodoxa lucillae

Acer griseum

Most maples are renowned for their elegant, beautiful foliage and spectacular autumn colouring, but some have beautiful bark. *A. griseum* is one of the finest and has striking, peeling, papery bark that is cinnamon coloured and especially beautiful in winter when the tree is leafless. It is ideal for small gardens, reaching 8m (25ft) high. The foliage is bronze when young and turns orange and scarlet in autumn. Few small trees are so beautiful for so many months of the year. Though it is usually available only as small plants, it is not difficult to grow and tolerates clay and chalky soils.

Winter companion
Sarcococca hookeriana

Spring companion
Erythronium 'Pagoda'

Acer davidii

The 'snake-bark' maples are among the most beautiful trees and have striped bark. *A. davidii* is a medium-sized tree, 15m (50ft) high when mature, with green, white-striped bark and good autumn colour. The variety 'George Forrest' has bold leaves up to 20cm (8in) long with red stalks. *A. pensylvanicum* is slightly smaller, up to 12m (40ft) high, with green, white-striped bark and good autumn colour. The most beautiful of all is its variety 'Erythrocladum' which has coral pink young shoots. It is slow-growing and grows best in a sheltered spot in full sun, out of strong winds. Most snake-bark maples do not tolerate chalky soils.

Winter companion
Mahonia x *media* 'Charity'

Spring companion
Photinia x *fraseri* 'Red Robin'

Aucuba japonica 'Crotonifolia'

Aucubas are robust evergreens with pairs of glossy, large foliage on green stems. They are useful shrubs that tolerate deep shade, under larger shrubs, but are seen at their best when planted in semi-shade in rich soil. They then form beautiful, rounded shrubs up to 2m (6ft) high, that can be kept smaller by pruning, at any time of the year. The flowers are small and brown but female plants, such as the yellow-speckled 'Crotonifolia', have large, attractive, red berries. 'Picturata' is also female and has foliage with a large yellow splash in the centre and 'Rozannie' is more compact, only growing to 1m (3ft). It has plain green leaves but is hermaphrodite so will produce berries without a nearby male and will also pollinate other females.

Winter companion
Cornus sanguinea 'Midwinter Fire'

Summer companion
Hypericum 'Hidcote'

Betula nigra

Betula (birch) are favourite garden trees because they are hardy, generally easy to grow, have pretty foliage and are usually upright and elegant in habit. They often have bright yellow autumn colour and bright bark that makes them especially attractive in winter. The best known is the common silver birch (*B. pendula*) with its white bark, but there are 60 species and many other bark colours. One of the most beautiful is *B. nigra*, the black birch, which grows wild in swampy conditions and is especially suitable for moist, clay soils, though it will grow in average conditions, too. It is a large tree, growing to 15m (50ft) with a more angular shape, when mature, than most birches, with deep brown bark that peels off in flakes to reveal younger, copper bark beneath. The foliage is glossy and dark green turning yellow in autumn.

Winter companion
Lonicera nitida 'Red Tips'

Autumn companion
Deschampsia caespitosa 'Goldschleier'

Betula utilis var. jacquemontii

The common silver birch has attractive, white bark but it looks decidedly dowdy when compared with the brilliant white of the best forms of *B. utilis*, a Himalayan tree that grows to 15m (50ft). It has large, deep green leaves that turn yellow in autumn but it is grown primarily for its peeling, bright white bark. When buying this tree, look out for one of the superior, named varieties such as 'Jermyns' or 'Silver Shadow', which have exceptional bark. All make imposing specimen trees of beautiful shape.

Winter companion
Rubus cockburnianus 'Goldenvale'

Summer companion
Buddleia x *weyeriana* 'Sungold'

Betula albosinensis

This Chinese birch is planted for its beautiful bark that peels in horizontal strips to reveal the pink and copper colouring underneath. It is a large tree, up to 25m (8ft) when mature, with small, deep green foliage and is conical in shape at first and later more spreading in outline. For bark colour choose *B. albosinensis* var. *septentrionalis*, which has exceptional copper-brown, orange and pink bark.

Winter companion
Prunus laurocerasus 'Otto Luyken'

Spring companion
Clematis alpina 'Frances Rivis'

Buxus sempervirens

The common box is best known as clipped, topiary specimens. The small foliage, twiggy habit and ability to withstand regular clipping makes it ideal for low hedges and topiary and the plant used is *B. sempervirens* 'Suffruticosa', a dwarf form that only reaches 1m (3ft) in height. But there are many other varieties of *B. sempervirens*, many of which are evergreen, that have other attractions, such as variegated foliage, and these grow to 2m (6ft) or more, though are easily kept smaller by pruning. 'Marginata' has leaves edged with yellow, 'Elegantissima' has foliage edged in white and 'Handsworthensis' has large leaves and a very upright habit, making it a good choice for hedges 60cm–150cm (2–5ft) high. All grow in sun or part shade and tolerate most soils, including chalk.

Winter companion
Lonicera purpusii 'Winter Beauty'

Spring companion
Anemone nemorosa 'Allenii'

Chamaecyparis lawsoniana 'Pembury Blue'

The huge group of conifers listed under Chamaecyparis all have small leaves on flat sprays of branches and are best known as evergreen hedging and screening plants. *C. lawsoniana*, the Lawson cypress from the north-west USA, is a large tree, 15m (50ft) or more high, but there are dozens of different varieties that are suitable for every purpose in the garden, from tiny dwarf plants for window boxes to tall windbreaks. 'Ellwoodii' is popular and has feathery, blue-grey foliage. It is useful for containers when young but can reach 3m (10ft). 'Pembury Blue' also has blue-grey foliage but reaches 15m (50ft). All can be trimmed to keep them more

compact but, like most conifers, they must not be trimmed hard because bare branches will not produce new shoots. *C. obtusa* 'Fernspray Gold' is slow-growing with fern-like, golden foliage and 'Nana Aurea' forms mounds of yellow foliage. All grow best in full sun.

Winter companion
Erica carnea 'Springwood Pink'

Spring companion
Allium karavatiense

Chamaerops humilis

This dwarf palm is unusual because it is the only one found wild in Europe. It has fan-shaped foliage with spiny stems and slowly grows to 2m (6ft) high, often producing sideshoots around the base. It is hardy if grown in well-drained soil in full sun but, in cold areas, it should be grown in a pot and kept in a greenhouse in winter.

Winter companion
Iris unguicularis

Summer companion
Myrtus communis

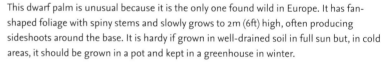

Chimonanthus praecox

This deciduous shrub is known as wintersweet because the small, straw-coloured flowers with red centres open in winter and early spring and have a pervasive, spicy, sweet fragrance. It is usually grown against a sunny wall to encourage flowering but it can also be grown as a free-standing shrub, when it should be planted in the sunniest possible site. It is rather dull in summer and its appearance can be improved by growing a summer-flowering climber through it. Late-flowering clematis are ideal, because they can be cut away in winter and should

not smother the plants in summer. It will grow in any soil and can reach 3m (10ft) in height. No pruning is necessary but you will want to cut stems to bring into the house when it is in bloom.

Winter companion
Iris unguicularis foetidissima

Autumn companion
Clematis viticella
'Purpurea Plena Elegans'

Choisya ternata

Choisya (Mexican orange blossom) is a beautiful rounded, evergreen shrub with three-fingered, glossy, dark green foliage and clusters of white, fragrant flowers in spring and autumn. It grows in most soils and flowers best in full sun but severe frost will damage the shoot tips which should then be trimmed off in spring; this reduces the first flush of flowers. It eventually can reach 2m (6ft) high but withstands severe pruning if necessary to maintain a smaller size. Plant in well-drained soil in sun or partial shade. 'Sundance' is a beautiful variety with bright yellow foliage. In bright sun and when planted in dry soil, the foliage may scorch and need trimming and if planted in shade the foliage will become lime-green. 'Goldfingers' is similar but has finely divided foliage.

Winter companion
Elaeagnus x ebbingei 'Gilt Edge'

Spring companion
Pulmonaria angustifolia 'Azurea'

Cornus sanguinea 'Midwinter Fire'

Many cornus are grown for the bright bracts that surround their small flowers in summer but another, important group are grown for their colourful winter stems. These are all easy to grow, most tolerate a wide range of conditions, including moist soils, and bring colour at the dullest time of the year. It is the young stems that have the best, brightest colour and they are usually pruned yearly or every other year, cutting them back to near ground level in early spring. *C. sanguinea* has small, white flowers in summer and good, bright, autumn colour and, in 'Midwinter Fire' and 'Winter Beauty' the stems are bright gold and orange in winter. Although it can reach 2m (6ft), it is usually half this height when regularly pruned.

Winter companion
Ilex x altaclerensis 'Lawsoniana'

Spring companion
Narcissus 'Jetfire'

Cornus sericea 'Flaviramea'

Formerly known as *C. stolonifera* 'Flaviramea', this tough, deciduous shrub is easy to grow in moist or wet soil and often produces suckering stems. Although it is rather dull in summer, when the leaves drop the bright, yellow-green stems are revealed which look attractive all winter. Like all cornus grown for their stems, it is strongest and most beautiful when grown in full sun.

Winter companion
Choisya ternata

Summer companion
Clematis x durandii

191

Cornus alba 'Sibirica'

C. alba is named for its attractive, white berries, but these are not often seen if the plant is pruned hard each year to promote the young, vigorous stems. These are red and at their most beautiful in the variety 'Sibirica'. The leaves are plain green but they do turn bright red in autumn, before they fall. A better, all-round plant is 'Elegantissima' which has colourful summer foliage that is variegated with white and also turns pink and red in autumn. 'Kesselringii' is an interesting alternative which has deep purple-black winter shoots and bright

purple and red autumn colour. Plants are compact and upright when annually pruned but the bushes become broader and carry small white flowers and white berries if allowed to grow naturally.

Winter companion
Helleborus hybridus

Spring companion
Doronicum x excelsum 'Harpur Crewe'

Correa 'Mannii'

Correas are sometimes called Australian fuchsias and are small, evergreen shrubs with nodding, bell-shaped flowers in winter. They are not completely hardy and should be grown in well-drained soil in a sunny spot, preferably against a sunny wall in all but the mildest gardens. C. 'Mannii' is one of the hardiest and will reach 1.5m (5ft) high and produce its bright red flowers throughout autumn, winter and early spring. In cold areas it can be grown

in a large pot and taken into a greenhouse in the coldest months.

Winter companion
Pittosporum tenuifolium 'Abbotsbury Gold'

Spring companion
Tulip 'Apricot Beauty'

Corylus avellana 'Tortuosa'

The corkscrew hazel is a popular and common garden shrub and at its best in winter. The branches twist and turn in all directions and gradually build up into a mound 2m (6ft) or more high. When leafless, in winter, and laden with golden catkins, it is a beautiful and intriguing sight. It will grow in any soil, in sun or part shade. Most plants are grafted and may produce upright stems from the base which must be removed. In summer, the plants have deep green, twisted leaves which look as if they are infested with aphids, but this is normal.

Winter companion
Euonymus fortunei 'Emerald Gaiety'

Spring companion
Ajuga reptans 'Catlin's Giant'

Elaeagnus x ebbingei 'Gilt Edge'

Elaeagnus include deciduous and evergreen shrubs but the evergreens are the most popular and usually have stems and foliage covered in tiny scales most obvious on the young shoots which often have a silvery appearance. E. x ebbingei is popular for its upright growth and deep green foliage that is silver underneath. It is useful for screening and for hedging and grows to 2m (6ft), but can be kept smaller by pruning. The flowers are small, silvery bells and are hidden by the foliage and open in autumn and they have a sweet, pervasive scent. 'Gilt Edge' has foliage that has broad, yellow margins and 'Limelight' has leaves with yellow centres. E. pungens 'Maculata' has yellow-variegated leaves and a rounder habit. All grow best in full sun, in well-drained soil and are prone to die-back. Any shoots that show signs of wilting should be cut out to prevent the problem spreading.

Winter companion
Mahonia x media 'Charity'

Summer companion
Rose 'Graham Thomas'

Euonymus fortunei 'Emerald 'n' Gold'

Evergreen euonymus are tough shrubs that are usually grown as small, trimmed shrubs or as ground cover, but the stems can produce roots that allow it to be used as a self-clinging climber, useful for shady walls. The small leaves are usually dark green but the most popular varieties are variegated and 'Emerald Gaiety' has deep green leaves with white edges. All thrive in moist soils in sun or shade but they also survive in dry shade. 'Emerald 'n' Gold' (pictured) has yellow-variegated leaves and is especially bright in spring when the new foliage is produced. The tiny flowers and fruits are rarely produced. They withstand pruning and can be planted as dwarf hedges. E. japonicus 'Ovatus Aureus' has a more upright habit and foliage that is boldly variegated with yellow, but is prone to mildew when grown in dry soils.

Winter companion
Cornus alba 'Sibirica'

Summer companion
Spiraea japonica 'Goldflame'

Erica carnea 'Springwood Pink'

Winter-flowering heathers bring colour to the winter garden and are more adaptable than most summer heathers because they tolerate lime in the soil. They prefer an open position, in full sun and should be pruned in spring, after flowering, to keep plants neat and compact. Many have foliage that turns bronze in the cold weather and their flower buds are attractive before the flowers open fully in early spring. *E. carnea* 'Springwood Pink' is a low-growing plant 16cm (6in) high but 45cm (18in) across, with pale pink flowers that mature to deep pink. 'Myretoun Ruby' is similar but has darker flowers and 'Anne Sparkes' has pink flowers and yellow foliage.

Winter companion
Cornus alba 'Sibirica'

Autumn companion
Liriope muscari

Erica x darleyensis

This winter-flowering hybrid heather is larger than *E. carnea* and grows to 30cm (1ft) high. It grows in any well-drained soil in full sun and has masses of small pink flowers in late winter. 'Darley Dale' has shoots that are creamy coloured at first and pink flowers whilst 'Silberschmelze' has white flowers and deep green leaves that are tinged with red in winter. *E. erigena* is larger still, sometimes reaching 2m (6ft) and has fragrant flowers but the many varieties are usually smaller. 'Golden Lady' has yellow foliage but only reaches 30cm (1ft) and 'Brightness' has leaves that turn purple in winter with pink flowers and reaches 60cm (2ft).

Winter companion
Helleborus hybridus

Autumn companion
Collettia paradoxa

Fatsia japonica

With large, lobed, evergreen foliage, Fatsia is a popular choice for patio pots and even as a houseplant but it is generally hardy and thrives in most soils, in partial shade or shade. Then its deep green, glossy-textured leaves can reach 45cm (18in) across and the plants, with stout, thick stems, can reach 2m (6ft) or more. In full sun the leaves often turn yellow and look rather sickly. Mature plants produce large clusters of small, white flowers in ball-shaped heads in autumn. Late spring frosts often damage new growth but plants usually recover quickly. However, this is a plant that grows best in milder areas. Variegated plants, with cream-edged leaves are often available but are expensive and grow more slowly.

Winter companion
Mahonia aquifolium 'Apollo'

Summer companion
Leycesteria formosa

Gaultheria mucronata

Until recently this was known as Pernettya and is a low-growing, evergreen shrub with small, spiky leaves that is valued for its bright, long-lasting berries. It is a lime-hater and must be grown in acid soil, in sun or partial shade. Only female plants produce berries and for every three or four females you should plant one male. This should be planted at the back of the groups because the small, white flowers of male and female plants are not very showy. Not all garden centres sell male plants but they are necessary unless you buy 'Bell's Seedling' which is one of the few that is hermaphrodite, so will pollinate itself and others. It has dark red berries.

'Crimsonia' has large, crimson fruits, 'Mulberry Wine' has deep purple berries and 'Lilian' has lilac berries. *G. shallon* is a tough, suckering evergreen for acid soils with clusters of pink flowers. It is useful for ground cover in sun and part shade and reaches 1m (3ft) high, spreading into large clumps.

Winter companion
Helleborus foetidus

Spring companion
Corylopsis pauciflora

Hamamelis x intermedia

Witch hazels (Hamamelis) are beautiful, large, deciduous shrubs that bloom in mid-winter with clusters of spidery, spicily fragrant flowers in shades of yellow, orange and red. The plants are fully hardy and the flowers, even if frosted, recover when they thaw and give colour for many weeks. Most are spreading in habit when young and have foliage like hazels that turns gold, red and purple in autumn. They prefer an acid or neutral, moist, humus-rich soil and a semi-shaded site but will tolerate full sun if the soil is moist. They dislike dry, windy

sites. *H. x intermedia* covers a group of hybrids which have some of the best flowers. 'Jelena' has large, coppery red flowers and 'Pallida' has masses of yellow blooms. Most grow to about 4m (12ft) when mature, but very slowly over many years.

Winter companion
Iris lazica

Summer companion
Hosta 'Halcyon'

Hamamelis vernalis

This is a smaller and rather upright plant, especially when young, that will reach 4m (12ft) when mature but is usually much smaller. It has smaller flowers than *H. x intermedia*, but they are carried in great numbers so still make a show in winter. The best is 'Sandra', which has purple new growth that is green in summer and the leaves turn red, purple and gold in autumn. The flowers are gold. It thrives in moist soil.

Winter companion
Cornus sanguinea 'Midwinter Fire'

Summer companion
Rodgersia pinnata 'Superba'

Hippophae rhamnoides

Sea buckthorn is an excellent choice for
seaside gardens but will grow well in any
well-drained soil, in full sun where its
rather airy crown of branches, with narrow,
silvery leaves contrast with most other
large shrubs. It is deciduous and spiny and
though the flowers are insignificant,
female plants usually carry heavy crops of
small orange or gold fruits that brighten
the winter garden. It is useful as a
windbreak and on poor, dry soils and
grows to 5m (16ft) high.

Winter companion
Ilex x *altaclerensis* 'Lawsoniana'

Summer companion
Spartium junceum

Ilex x *altaclerensis* 'Lawsoniana'

Hollies are adaptable evergreens that
withstand regular clipping, are attractive
all year round and thrive in sun or partial
shade in most soils, including chalk
though they dislike soil that is wet for long
periods. *I.* x *altaclerensis* 'Lawsoniana' is a
large shrub or small tree that can grow to
6m (20ft) high with large leaves, with few
spines, that are boldly marked with rich
yellow in the centre. It is female and bears
large red berries in autumn and winter.

Winter companion
Phyllostachys aureosulcata f.
spectabilis

Spring companion
Berberis darwinii

Ilex aquifolium

The common holly is a useful evergreen
that can be trimmed as a hedge, pruned to
keep as a shrub or allowed to grow into a
small tree. Like most evergreens, it drops
some of its oldest leaves in late spring as
the new growth is being produced and
these can make weeding surrounding
areas unpleasant. Most trees are either
male or female and only females carry
berries and then only if there is a male, or
hermaphrodite, plant nearby. One of the
most useful, for small gardens where
there is room for only one, is 'J. C. van Tol',
which is hermaphrodite and carries heavy
crops of berries and has few spines on its

leaves. There is a variegated form of this
called 'Golden van Tol'. 'Ferox Argentea' is
the variegated hedgehog holly, with small
leaves that are covered with spines on the
leaf surface as well as around the edge. It
is neat, compact and male.

Winter companion
Prunus laurocerasus 'Latifolia'

Spring companion
Berberis darwinii

Ilex crenata 'Golden Gem'

I. crenata is a small, compact holly from Japan that has small, spineless leaves and black berries and is a good substitute for box as a hedge or for topiary. 'Golden Gem' is a small shrub, reaching 1m (3ft) with bright yellow foliage and is female so bears small black berries. Although it will grow in sun or shade, the best foliage colour is produced when it is grown in sun.

Winter companion
Helleborus foetidus

Autumn companion
Physalis alkekengi

Juniperus x pfitzeriana 'Aurea'

Junipers are useful evergreen conifers that usually thrive in most soils, including dry soils and chalk. Like many fine-leaved conifers, they have different types of leaf according to the maturity of the plants: juvenile foliage is often rather spiny while when mature it is smaller and less painful. They have a wide variety of plant shapes and foliage colour and some are large and spreading while others are tiny, so it is advisable to check your plants carefully before you buy. *J. x pfitzeriana* 'Aurea' is a large, spreading shrub 1m (3ft) high and 2m (6ft) across with foliage that is yellow in summer and gold in winter. *J. communis* 'Compressa' is completely different and is a small, upright plant that is eventually 75cm (30in) high but is among the smallest and slowest-growing conifers with a dense, neat habit.

Winter companion
Cornus sericea 'Flaviramea'

Autumn companion
Stipa arundinacea

Juniperus squamata 'Blue Carpet'

J. squamata usually has blue-grey foliage and an arching habit. Small plants look perfect for the rock garden but the habit of the varieties varies hugely. The most common is 'Meyeri' but, despite the arching branches, this can grow to 5m (16ft) high and across. 'Blue Star' is much smaller and only 40cm (16in) high and 'Blue Carpet' is of similar height, with spreading stems that make excellent ground cover for dry banks.

Winter companion
Prunus laurocerasus 'Castlewellan'

Summer companion
Potentilla 'Abbotswood'

Ligustrum undulatum 'Lemon Lime and Clippers'

The common privet is usually planted solely as a hedging plant, but *L. undulatum* 'Lemon Lime and Clippers' is a recent introduction that has a neat, bushy habit and is useful for topiary and as a neat, evergreen, gold shrub. *L. ovalifolium* 'Aureum', is a fine evergreen that can bring a ray of sunshine to the winter garden. If pruned hard in spring every year it will produce strong, vigorous stems with larger than average foliage that remains beautiful all winter, providing a bright background to other winter shrubs. It has the added advantage of being cheap to buy and easy to grow, in any soil, and the leafy stems are useful for flower arrangers. Foliage colour of both varieties is best in full sun and will be lime green in shade.

Winter companion
Cornus alba 'Sibirica'

Summer companion
Spiraea japonica 'Goldflame'

Lonicera purpusii 'Winter Beauty'

Although climbing honeysuckles are frequently grown in gardens, the shrubby species are largely ignored but they include some easy to grow shrubs that will bring fragrance to your garden. They are rounded shrubs, about 1.5m (5ft) high with small clusters of white or creamy flowers that open in the depths of winter on the leafless branches. Although they are rather dull in summer, with plain green leaves, they will grow in most soils and in sun or part shade, though they flower most freely when grown in full sun. *L. purpusii* 'Winter Beauty' has lemon-scented flowers from mid-winter till spring. *L. standishii* and *L. fragrantissima* are similar and may carry red berries in summer that blackbirds quickly devour. They may be semi-evergreen in mild winters.

Winter companion
Ligustrum ovalifolium 'Aureum'

Autumn companion
Clematis 'Gravetye Beauty'

Lonicera nitida 'Baggesen's Gold'

This shrubby honeysuckle is a common hedging plant with narrow branches and tiny, glossy, deep green leaves. It can reach 2m (6ft) in height and spread but because the stems become weighed down with age, it is best as a hedge no more than 1m (3ft) in height. As a garden shrub, the varieties with coloured foliage are more attractive and 'Baggesen's Gold' is a good choice with bright yellow leaves. In summer, if the soil is dry and the plant is in full sun, the leaves may become bleached. 'Red Tips' has foliage that is burgundy red when young. All withstand slipping and will grow in all soils, in sun or partial shade. In some seasons, if the plants are not grown as a hedge and clipped frequently, small cream flowers will be followed by translucent, purple berries.

Winter companion
Phormium 'Yellow Wave'

Autumn companion
Cotinus coggygria 'Royal Purple'

Lonicera pileata 'Silver Lining'

Lonicera pileata is similar to *L. nitida* but has larger leaves, up to 2.5cm (1in) long, of the same glossy, deep green and the plants are lower and more spreading, making effective ground cover, about 60cm (2ft) high. It is a useful plant for filling space in sun or shade and can be pruned at any time to keep it neat. Small, white flowers are followed by purple berries. 'Silver Lining' is more attractive because each leaf is edged with white to create a lighter, greyish overall effect, useful for lightening dark areas of the garden.

Winter companion
Viburnum tinus 'Eve Price'

Summer companion
Fuchsia magellanica var molinae

Mahonia x *media* 'Charity'

Mahonias are spiny shrubs, related to Berberis, but their clusters of (usually) yellow flowers, often sweetly scented, open from autumn to spring and contrast well with the evergreen, glossy foliage. Most tolerate a wide variety of soils, including chalk, and they grow in sun or partial shade.
M. x *media* is a tall shrub with bold foliage that is divided into many spiny leaflets and young plants, with just a few stems, that look a little like palms. To encourage basal branching and a bushier habit, plants should be pruned hard in spring. Without pruning it will reach 2m (6ft) or more in height and spread. The flowers of the variety 'Charity' open in late autumn and each stem carries many long spikes of small, yellow, fragrant flowers. 'Winter Sun' has bright yellow flowers.

Winter companion
Ruscus aculeatus

Summer companion
Cotoneaster horizontalis

Mahonia aquifolium

This is a low-growing, suckering shrub with deep green, glossy foliage with weak spines around the edge and compact clusters of bright yellow flowers at the tips of the shoots in late winter. These are followed by deep purple berries. It reaches about 1m (3ft) high but can be pruned hard in spring if it gets straggly. In dry soils, mildew can sometimes be troublesome. In autumn, some of the leaves turn red and drop but it is evergreen. The new growth in spring is often flushed with purple and in the variety 'Apollo' it is particularly bright.

Winter companion
Helleborus foetidus

Autumn companion
Pyracantha Saphyr Orange

Mahonia x wagneri 'Pinnacle'

This hybrid of *M. aquifolium* is similar but is more upright and has dense clusters of bright yellow flowers in early spring. It is easy to grow and has glossy mid-green foliage. Thriving in most soils and in sun or shade, it is a useful shrub for 'difficult' places.

Winter companion
Aucuba japonica 'Crotonifolia'

Spring companion
Kerria japonica 'Picta'

Osmanthus heterophyllus

At first glance, this evergreen shrub looks like holly but the leaves are arranged in pairs on the stems and the 'spines' are soft, not sharp. It is a large shrub that can reach 4m (12ft) and as the shrubs mature the leaves often have no spines. The foliage is dark green and in autumn there are masses of small, white, fragrant flowers. It withstands clipping and can be used as a hedge or it can be pruned to keep plants smaller than their full height. It grows well in sun or shade and in most soils. The most popular forms have coloured foliage. 'Aureomarginatus' has leaves beautifully edged with bright yellow, 'Goshiki' has leaves splashed with yellow and green and 'Purpureus' has dark green foliage that is purple when young.

Winter companion
Phyllostachys nigra

Autumn companion
Rosa 'Geranium'

Phyllostachys nigra

Bamboos have a reputation for being invasive but many are good-natured and form dense clumps of tall stems with evergreen, elegant foliage. Most Phyllostachys are easy to grow and form neat clumps, though in warm climates they are more inclined to spread. They are hardy but the leaves become scruffy if they are grown in areas with strong, cold, winter winds. They grow best in moist soil but will not withstand waterlogged soils and they dislike soils that are dry in summer. *P. nigra* grows to 4m (12ft), has fine, green foliage and canes that are black when mature, when grown in full sun. *P. aurea* is taller and has yellow canes.

Winter companion
Fatsia japonica

Autumn companion
Sorbus 'Joseph Rock'

Picea pungens

Picea (spruce) are hardy conifers that are usually large trees, too large for average-sized gardens, but there are smaller species and compact varieties that bring interesting forms and foliage to the garden. Most Piceas prefer moist soil that is acid or neutral and they generally dislike chalky soils. *P. pungens* is the Colorado spruce and is a tall tree, up to 15m (50ft) high, with blue-green foliage. There are many varieties, most of which are more compact and have blue-grey leaves. 'Hoopsii' has particularly bright leaves and 'Montgomery' is dwarf, just 2m (6ft) high. All are prone to aphid which infest branches and can cause leaf drop.

Winter companion
Prunus 'Otto Luyken'

Summer companion
Acer negundo 'Flamingo'

Picea glauca albertiana 'Conica'

This neat plant is a dwarf form of the white spruce and has green foliage that is particularly bright in spring. It is a compact plant that is rarely seen more than 1m (3ft) high. At first it is a dense, pyramidal bush but eventually it becomes a rounded mound of dense branches, almost like a green anthill. Because shade from other plants will cause the foliage and then the branches to die, it must never be allowed to become swamped by surrounding plants.

Winter companion
Luzula sylvatica 'Aurea'

Autumn companion
Nandina domestica 'Fire Power'

Picea breweriana

When well grown, this evergreen tree, which reaches 10m (33ft) high, can be one of the most beautiful sights in the garden, with wide branches festooned with pendulous shoots. It requires a moist, acid soil and plenty of space to allow it to achieve its natural shape, and a site out of cold, drying winds.

Winter companion
Gaultheria shallon

Spring companion
Magnolia stellata

Pinus mugo 'Mops'

Unlike spruces, which require acid or neutral soils, most Pinus tolerate some lime, though they grow best without it. They are evergreen conifers with needles arranged in clusters around the stems and, when mature, decorative cones. Most are large trees but among the 120 species there are small trees and bushes and many varieties that have been selected for their decorative foliage or compact habit. These are ideal to add colour and form to the winter garden in full sun. *P. mugo* is the dwarf mountain pine, although it will grow to 3m (10ft) high in its natural form. It has

dark green foliage. It is most popular as the many dwarf forms such as 'Mops', which grows very slowly and 'Gnom', which are good associated with heathers to bring height and a different foliage texture.

Winter companion
Erica carnea 'Springwood Pink'

Autumn companion
Cotoneaster horizontalis

Pinus sylvestris 'Aurea Group'

The native Scots Pine is a tree that can grow to 30m (100ft) with dark green foliage and beautiful reddish bark. It tolerates a wide range of soil conditions including poor, dry soils and withstands strong winds. Although it is too big for most gardens, there are smaller varieties such as the 'Aurea Group' which is slower growing, but still potentially large, with green foliage that turns bright yellow in winter. 'Gold Coin' is a compact shrub, just 2m (6ft) high, with golden needles.

Winter companion
Mahonia aquifolium

Spring companion
Rhododendron 'President Roosevelt'

Pinus wallichiana

This large pine, 30m (100ft) high, is a beautiful tree with bluish needles, 20cm (8in) long, and large cones that are slender and can be 30cm (1ft) long that are covered in fragrant resin. It tolerates some lime in the soil but, like most conifers, prefers an open, sunny site and well-drained soil. Young plants are vulnerable to drought. In small gardens plant the variety 'Umbraculifera' which is a small, dense globe of long foliage but still bears the large cones.

Winter companion
Osmanthus heterophyllus

Summer companion
Kolkwitzia amabilis 'Pink Cloud'

Pittosporum tenuifolium 'Tom Thumb'

This is an evergreen with small, glossy foliage that is usually wavy at the edges and spaced out along the dark twigs. In spring the stems are covered in deep purple, fragrant flowers but this shrub is grown primarily for its foliage. It is not hardy in cold areas and on wet soils but can then be grown against a sunny wall. In milder areas it can be used as a hedge or screen because it tolerates regular or hard pruning and naturally grows to about 3m (10ft). There are many interesting varieties with coloured foliage. 'Abbotsbury Gold' has pale yellow foliage, 'Irene Paterson' is dwarf with green foliage speckled with white and 'Tom Thumb' is also dwarf, with green young foliage that matures to deep purple.

Winter companion
Ilex crenata 'Golden Gem'

Autumn companion
Nandina domestica

Pittosporum tobira

Although not hardy enough to survive outside except in the mildest areas or in urban gardens where frosts are rare, this dome-shaped evergreen is popular because of its flowers. These are carried in small clusters, are white, resemble orange blossom and have a sweet perfume. They open in spring and contrast with the deep green leaves. It is a drought-tolerant evergreen that makes a good patio plant which can be taken into the greenhouse or conservatory in winter. 'Variegatum' has foliage that is greyish in colour, edged with white. It can grow to 2m (6ft) or more but is usually smaller and can be pruned to keep it compact.

Winter companion
Chamaerops humilis

Summer companion
Leptospermum scoparium

Prunus lusitanica

The Portugal laurel is a useful evergreen for hedges and screens and it is tougher than the more common cherry laurel (*P. laurocerasus*), tolerating chalky soils, bright sun and drought. It is a twiggy, rounded tree with deep green leaves with reddish stalks and has spikes of white flowers in late spring. It can be trained as a small tree and will withstand clipping, so can be pruned into a formal shape. The variegated form is especially beautiful and has leaves that are edged with white and splashed with grey.

Winter companion
Phormium 'Pink Panther'

Summer companion
Lavatera x *clementii* 'Bredon Springs'

Prunus laurocerasus

The common cherry laurel is frequently used as a hedge but often looks yellow because it is grown in chalky soils or is planted in dry soils in full sun. It then also often suffers from mildew, which coats the leaves with white 'powder' and cause them to twist and curl. But when planted in good soil, watered, fed and given a little shade, it can be a magnificent evergreen and can be trained into a broad, evergreen tree which has showy flowers in spring and masses of berries that feed wildlife. Rather than accepting unnamed plants, look out for more interesting plants such as 'Castlewellan', which has leaves splashed and mottled with white. 'Latifolia' is a magnificent plant with leaves up to 25cm (10in) long, and 'Otto Luyken' (pictured) is a dwarf, spreading plant with dark green, narrow leaves and masses of upright spikes of white flowers, which is useful for ground cover.

Winter companion
Fatsia japonica

Summer companion
Philadelphus 'Manteau d'Hermine'

Pseudopanax lessonii 'Gold Splash'

Pseudopanax are slightly tender, evergreen shrubs with divided foliage and insignificant flowers. Plant them in full sun or partial shade in moist, fertile soil. Because they are not completely hardy they should be planted against a sunny wall in all but the mildest gardens, or they can be grown in pots on the patio and put into a greenhouse, conservatory or porch in winter. *P. lessonii* 'Gold Splash' has bright foliage that is mid-green with a bright yellow centre to each leaflet. It is an upright, neat shrub that grows to 3m (10ft) in favourable areas but can be pruned to keep it smaller.

Winter companion
Pittosporum tenuifolium 'Tom Thumb'

Summer companion
Crocosmia 'Lucifer'

Rubus cockburnianus

This spiny, vigorous bramble has small flowers and tiny 'blackberries' and is at its best in winter when the leaves have fallen to reveal the shoots that are covered in white 'bloom' (powder). Because young stems are the brightest, clumps should be cut to the ground in spring every few years. It will grow in sun or part shade and is best suited to wild areas of the garden because of its vigour and long stems that can reach 2m (6ft) high. A better choice for most gardens is 'Goldenvale' (pictured), which also has white stems but has golden

foliage. *R. thibetanus* has more delicate, ferny foliage and white stems and is slightly less invasive. All grow in any, average soil.

Winter companion
Arum italicum 'Marmoratum'

Spring companion
Narcissus 'Jetfire'

Salix alba var. *vitellina* 'Britzensis'

Salix (willow) are best known by the common weeping willow, which is only suitable for the largest gardens, but there are willows that can be grown in smaller areas and have other attributes. One of the best, which is still a large, vigorous plant, is *S. alba* var. *vitellina* 'Britzensis'. Thriving in moist or even wet soils, this is a large tree that can reach 15m (50ft) if not pruned, but is most often grown as a large shrub. It has long, green foliage, but the young stems, in their first few years, are golden orange-red in colour in winter. To encourage these shoots the plants are usually hard pruned each spring and by

the end of the summer these will be 2m (6ft) or more in height and look striking in winter. Even overgrown plants can be cut down to near ground level and will produce a mass of new, colourful shoots. It will grow more slowly in dry soils and will not thrive in shade.

Winter companion
Galanthus nivalis

Spring companion
Anemone x *lipsiensis*

Salix 'Erythroflexuosa'

The dragon claw willow (*S. babylonica* var. *pekinensis* 'Tortuosa') is a popular, contorted tree and cut, dried stems are often sold for household decoration. It is easy to grow and will eventually reach 15m (50ft), especially in moist soils, but can be pruned hard every spring to maintain a smaller plant. However, for most gardens, *S.* 'Erythroflexuosa' is a better choice, because it is much smaller. Even without pruning it rarely exceeds 4m (12ft) in height and, though upright at first, it

becomes a rounded, small tree with twisting and contorted stems that are deep, reddish brown.

Winter companion
Sarcococca hookeriana

Spring companion
Narcissus 'Jetfire'

Sarcococca hookeriana var. digyna

Sarcococcas are neat, evergreen shrubs with upright, suckering stems that form dense clumps. The flowers are small and do not have petals but, although not showy, they have a sweet perfume that wafts across the garden in the depths of winter. As a bonus, most have attractive red or black berries. They will grow in any moist, well-drained soil and prefer a semi-shaded or shady spot. S. hookeriana var. digyna is taller than most and grows to 1.2m (4ft) high with slender, shiny foliage and reddish stems. S. ruscifolia forms a rounded mound 1m (3ft) high with creamy flowers and red fruits whilst S. confusa has black fruits.

Winter companion
Euonymus fortunei 'Emerald Gaiety'

Spring companion
Narcissus 'Geranium'

Skimmia japonica 'Rubella'

The most common Skimmia in garden centres is *S. japonica* 'Rubella', which has large clusters of red buds throughout winter that contrast with the deep green foliage. In spring these open to white, pink-tinged flowers that are highly fragrant. Like most skimmias, it grows best in light shade in acid soil. In bright sun, especially in dry soils, the foliage turns yellow and looks rather sick and they do not thrive in chalky soils. *S. japonica*

'Rubella' is a male plant and does not produce berries, but female plants, which usually have smaller clusters of flowers, have the benefit of large, round, red berries. Most grow to about 1m (3ft) high and a little more across. *S. x confusa* 'Kew Green' is also male and has greenish buds and flowers but is particularly fragrant. *S. japonica* 'Nymans' has masses of red berries and 'Fructu Albo' is unusual for its white berries.

Winter companion
Erica carnea 'Myretoun Ruby'

Autumn companion
Callicarpa bodinieri var. *giraldii* 'Profusion'

Taxus baccata Fastigiata 'Aurea Group'

The common yew (*T. baccata*) is a useful evergreen and an unusual conifer with red, fleshy berries instead of cones. Unlike most conifers it tolerates shade and, if it gets too large, can be hard pruned and will grow with renewed vigour. It can become a huge tree but the upright forms, though they can reach 8m (25ft) high, are easier to accommodate in gardens because they are narrow in habit and can be clipped to keep them smaller. *T. baccata* Fastigiata 'Aurea Group' has an upright habit and yellow foliage. In small gardens plant 'Standishii', which also has

yellow foliage but grows slowly and forms a column 1.5m (5ft) high and 30cm (1ft) wide. The seeds in the red yew berries are poisonous and dried foliage is dangerous to grazing animals.

Winter companion
Lonicera nitida 'Red Tips'

Autumn companion
Euonymus 'Red Cascade'

Trachycarpus fortunei

Despite the exotic appearance of this palm, it is completely hardy and can slowly reach 20m (70ft) in height, though such large plants are rarely seen. Young plants with short trunks are unlikely to reach more than 3m (10ft) in an average (human) lifetime. The leaves are 45cm (18in) across and form crowns 1m (3ft) across on the trunks that are covered in brown fibres and old leaf stems. As the leaves age they become brown and droop and should be cut away, taking care not to be caught by the spiny leaf stalks. It grows best in full

sun in a position away from strong, cold winds and tolerates most soils except those that are wet in winter. It also makes a good plant for a large pot on the patio.

Winter companion
Osmanthus heterophyllus 'Aureomarginatus'

Autumn companion
Campsis x tagliabuana 'Madame Galen'

Viburnum tinus 'Eve Price'

Sometimes called Laurustinus, this Mediterranean shrub has been grown in our gardens for centuries. It forms large mounds 2m (6ft) or more high and wide of dark green foliage but can be kept smaller by pruning or clipping and can be used as a large hedge. In autumn it is decorative with its flower buds and these open to white flowers throughout late winter and spring and are followed by blue-black berries. It is easy to grow in most soils, including chalk. 'Eve Price' has a compact habit and pink flowers buds and 'Gwenllian' (pictured) has red flower buds

and pink-flushed flowers. 'Variegatum' has attractive foliage that is edged with pale yellow but does not grow as strongly or flower as freely.

Winter companion
Ligustrum ovalifolium 'Aureum'

Summer companion
Eccremocarpus scaber

Viburnum rhytidophyllum

This bold, evergreen shrub grows to 5m (16ft) tall and has an upright habit, especially when young, with large leaves. These can be up to 25cm (10in) long and are heavily veined on the upper surface and covered in dense, buff hairs on the underside. The flowers are rather dull, carried in flat heads, and creamy white and the berries, which are not always profuse, ripen to red and then black. It is a useful shrub for screening and has a distinctive habit and form, especially in cold, winter weather when the leaves tend to hang vertically from the stems. It thrives in sun or part shade and is one of the best large-leaved evergreens for chalky soils.

Winter companion
Lonicera purpusii 'Winter Beauty'

Autumn companion
Cotoneaster conspicuus 'Decorus'

Viburnum x *bodnantense* 'Dawn'

This deciduous shrub is one of the essentials for any garden. It is upright in habit, especially when young, and reaches 2.5m (8ft) high, though it can be kept smaller by pruning out a few of the older stems, near ground level, in spring. It has neat, small, red-stemmed foliage which drops in autumn to reveal angular branches. Throughout winter, from autumn to spring, often for almost six months, clusters of small, tubular, sweetly scented, soft pink flowers open. Although open flowers are killed by hard frosts, new buds open later to refresh the display. In severe winters, when few flowers open, there is a huge flush of flowers in spring before the new foliage appears. It grows in any well-drained soil and is completely hardy. It flowers best when grown in full sun. It is commonly available but the varieties 'Deben' with white flowers and 'Charles Lamont' with slightly larger flowers, whilst less common, are still worth planting.

Winter companion
Sarcococca hookeriana

Summer companion
Leycesteria formosa

Clematis cirrhosa

This Mediterranean clematis is unusual for its evergreen flowers and delicate, nodding flowers. Although most clematis prefer light shade to prevent problems such as mildew, this species likes a sunny spot and is ideal for covering walls and trellis in full sun and prefers a sheltered spot so the growth and flowers, which open from early winter through to spring, are not damaged by frost. The leaves are prettily divided and glossy green, usually bronze when young, and the plant will rapidly cover an area 2.5m (8ft) high and across. The bell-shaped, lightly fragrant flowers are cream and spotted with dark red, heavily spotted in 'Freckles' and almost without any marks in 'Wisley Cream' (pictured). The flowers are rather hidden by the foliage and best seen from below, so plant it through tough, mature shrubs in well-drained soil, where it can grow unhindered, or on a tall wall or pergola.

Winter companion
Hippophae rhamnoides

Summer companion
Physocarpus opulifolius 'Diabolo'

Garrya elliptica 'James Roof'

This evergreen shrub can be grown as a free-standing plant but is usually planted as a wall-shrub. It has stiff branches and leathery, deep green leaves that are grey underneath. In autumn you will notice the clusters of small catkins and these expand in winter and spring to 'drip' from the shrubs. They are grey and, in 'James Roof', can be 20cm (8in) long. It is often planted on shady, north-facing walls but will flower more prolifically when planted in sun. It is a good plant for coastal gardens and thrives in light soils, though it will also grow in clay soils. It is not a colourful plant, but its attractive foliage and unusual catkins give interest all year and it can be used to support a more colourful climber if it is not too vigorous.

Winter companion
Iris foetidissima

Autumn companion
Clematis 'Alba Luxuriens'

Hedera colchica 'Sulphur Heart'

Ivies are among the most useful climbers because they are evergreen and produce sucker-like roots along their stems so they can support themselves on any vertical surface. In addition, they can be planted as ground cover and they thrive in sun or shade, even under trees. They do not harm masonry that is in good condition and their overlapping, evergreen foliage can help keep walls dry and warm as well as providing cover for insects. When they reach the top of any support they change habit, becoming self-supporting, and then produce flowers that open in autumn and provide late nectar for bees and butterflies and, later, berries for birds. *H. colchica* has large leaves, up to 12cm (5in) long. They are dark green but 'Sulphur Heart' has leaves with a large splash of soft yellow in the centre.

Winter companion
Jasminum nudiflorum

Summer companion
Lathyrus latifolius 'White Pearl'

Hedera canariensis 'Gloire de Marengo'

This is one of the quickest growing ivies and has large, glossy, deep green foliage but, coming from North Africa, it is not hardy in the coldest gardens and is best planted in a sheltered spot. It is a good choice for a warm, sunny or part-shaded wall or on a wall behind a deciduous climber or wall shrub. Its green leaves are augmented by the deep red stems and leaf stalks. It is most beautiful in the variety 'Gloire de Marengo', which has foliage that is green and grey and edged with cream. It is often sold as a houseplant but, if planted out in spring or summer so it is established by winter, will survive well outside and can reach 4m (12ft) in height if not pruned. Young growth may be damaged by late frosts.

Winter companion
Garrya elliptica

Autumn companion
Clematis 'Gravetye Beauty'

Hedera helix 'Buttercup'

The common ivy is underused in our gardens. There are hundreds of varieties with many leaf shapes and colours and they are as useful on walls and fences as they are for ground cover, where they can be underplanted with small bulbs. Because it can be vigorous and difficult to pull from walls once established, it should be pulled away from gutters and areas where it is not needed every year. However, in the right place ivy can be beautiful and the flowers and fruits of the adult, arborescent form are beneficial to wildlife. These adult forms are sometimes sold as 'Arborescens', are usually plain green and are useful shrubs for deep shade, but the adult shoots of any ivy, with any leaf colouring, can also be rooted. The small pots of ivy, sold as houseplants, are completely hardy and can be planted out in the garden to cover walls and fences. 'Buttercup' is a superb variety, with pale green leaves in shade but bright yellow in sun. 'Eva' has leaves prettily edged with white and 'Manda's Crested' has deep green leaves that are deeply lobed and curled. 'Goldheart' has deep green leaves with yellow centres with bright red, contrasting stems and is particularly bright in winter.

Winter companion
Galanthus nivalis

Autumn companion
Cyclamen hederifolium

Jasminum nudiflorum

Although the winter jasmine has no means of attaching itself to walls or trellis and can be left to grow as a sprawling shrub with long, arching branches, it is usually grown as a wall shrub. It needs to be trained on wires or trellis and it thrives in sun or shade. The young stems are bright green and these flower most freely. Old stems should be cut out in spring after flowering and new shoots trained in their place. The small leaves drop in autumn and throughout winter the bright yellow, starry flowers open. It is easy to grow in any but wet soils and is hardy. Open flowers are damaged by severe frost but new flowers quickly open to replace them. Trained against a wall, it can reach 2m (6ft) high and 2.5m (8ft) across.

Winter companion
Elaeagnus x *ebbingei* 'Gilt Edge'

Summer companion
Paeonia lutea var. *ludlowii*

Arum italicum 'Marmoratum'

For much of summer this tuberous plant hides underground, but the arrowhead-shaped foliage appears in autumn and is at its best in winter, forming clumps 30cm (1ft) high. The lustrous, deep green leaves are veined and marbled with white and, though they collapse under the strain of a heavy frost, they recover when they thaw. In spring, strange 'cuckoo pint' flowers open and these are followed by clusters of bright red, poisonous berries that ripen after the leaves disappear. It grows in any soil, in sun or light shade and usually self-seeds.

Winter companion
Cornus alba 'Kesselringii'

Spring companion
Vinca minor 'Azurea Flore Pleno'

Cyclamen coum

Hardy cyclamens look delicate, but they are tough plants that are unaffected by cold and thrive in well-drained soil in sun or light shade. *C. hederifolium* is the easiest of the autumn-flowering cyclamen and *C. coum* is the best for winter flowers. The rounded foliage appears in late autumn and is deep green, usually marbled with grey, and the pink, white or bright magenta flowers open in winter. These are unaffected by frost or snow and make a vibrant contrast to snowdrops. It only grows 10cm (4in) high.

Winter companion
Helleborus hybridus

Autumn companion
Liriope muscari

Galanthus nivalis

The common snowdrop (*G. nivalis*) is one of the first flowers of spring, a sign that spring is not far away. It thrives in sun or shade and is often seen at its best under deciduous shrubs and trees. It will grow in most soils, provided they are not too dry in summer, and should be planted 'in the green' while the foliage is still intact, after flowering. Dried bulbs give poorer results. In addition to the common snowdrop there are many interesting varieties and other species. *G. elwesii* has broad grey foliage, the two leaves curled around each other at the base, and large white and green flowers, whilst *G. plicatus* has grey leaves and often more than one large white and green flower per bulb.

Winter companion
Lonicera purpusii 'Winter Beauty'

Summer companion
Dryopteris erythrosora

planting
combinations

A flowering cherry can be the high-light of your spring garden but the soil underneath will be dry in summer. A path beneath the tree may be a practical solution.

Forsythias are at their best in spring, so combine them with bulbs such as crocus and then simply ignore them for the rest of the year.

Spring combinations

Spring is the most eagerly awaited season, bringing colour and frgrance after what many gardeners feel is a long, dull, dark winter. Spring often starts slowly and the first flowers of snowdrops and aconites can mean more cold weather as often as the promise of warmer days. But those first, small flowers offer us hope and are always the start of nature's most frenetic season.

Blossom and catkins

Many of the earliest flowers on shrubs are catkins. Though not the most showy of blooms, they are usually carried in such profusion that they brighten the garden with their pendant clusters. The most common are hazels (Corylus) but alders (Alnus) can also be showy while other shrubs, such as Corylopsis and Stachyurus, have catkin-like clusters of flowers.

Once the days start to warm up, a host of shrubs begin to bloom, and when the forsythias and ribes are in full spate hardly a day goes by without new flowers appearing. Bulbs rocket through the soil and herbaceous plants cover the bare soil, many opening their blooms as soon as their leaves expand.

In summer, Corylus avellana 'Contorta' is not a thing of beauty; its foliage is curled and distorted. But when leafless, in winter, the beauty of the twisted branches is revealed and in spring it is superbly augmented by golden catkins.

Magnolias often have their magnificent displays cut short by late frosts, but M. liliflora *usually produces late flowers that escape this damage.*

Roses and grasses

In spring this rose, 'The Fairy', is pruned to keep it neat; however, this can make the surrounding bare soil look dull. To solve this problem, plant it with a host of spring-flowering ground cover plants or, if you want a more seasonal effect, with polyanthus and hyacinths. As the rose grows, throughout spring, its foliage will cover the untidy polyanthus and dying hyacinth foliage. By the time the rose is in bloom, the complemetary foliage of *Miscanthus* 'Cosmopolitan' is at its best.

Narcissus 'Tête-à-Tête' *is one of the best daffodils for every garden. It is short but showy, vigorous yet dainty in appearance.*

Bulbs

From the smallest, dainty blooms of snowdrops (Galanthus) to the showy blooms of huge Parrot tulips, bulbs bring a kaleidoscope of colours and shapes to spring gardens. Most are easy to grow and, when you buy them, the flowers are ready formed in the bulbs so you can be sure of a brilliant show.

The biggest criticism of spring bulbs is that the foliage is untidy after the flowers have faded but it is essential it is left so that it feeds the bulbs for the next season. You can hide the foliage of daffodils and other bulbs by planting hardy geraniums, peonies and other herbaceous plants beside or behind them. When used for bedding, you can lift tulips as soon as the flower stems start to wither at the top – something that can be speeded up by removing the dead flowers, complete with seed pods, as soon as they wither.

Bulbs in the border

Tall tulips are usually planted in bedding and then discarded. But they can be left in place in most gardens. Plant them deeply in autumn, so their bulbs are 20–25cm (8–10in) deep. In this way they are less likely to be damaged when you divide and

replant other plants and they will not 'break up' into small bulbs. This makes them more likely to bloom the following year, unlike bulbs which are planted close to the surface. This spring border would be dull without those red Darwin hybrid tulips.

Muscari armeniacum *can be a troublesome weed but is so spectacular that it is difficult to avoid. Plant it under shrubs where it will not be a nuisance.*

Tulipa 'Queen of Night' *is easily obtained and gives a touch of class to any planting scheme. Use it to reinforce sumptuous purple wallflowers or as a contrast to the silvery foliage of artemisias, lavender and sage.*

Erythronium revolutum *prefers light shade and moist soil and combines perfectly with hostas.*

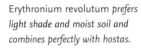

Crocus tommasinianus *(left) seeds freely and is perfect for naturalizing in sun or part shade.*

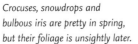

Crocuses, snowdrops and bulbous iris are pretty in spring, but their foliage is unsightly later.

Traditional combinations such as blue forget-me-not (Myosotis) and polyanthus are easy to create and always welcome.

On acid soils, spring flowering, deciduous azaleas bring colour and fragrance.

Spring Schemes

It often seems that spring flowers are only blue, yellow and white. It is not quite true, but they are certainly abundant. Fortunately these three colours combine harmoniously and with yellows varying from cream to rich gold and blues from pastel shades to vibrant midnight blues, your garden need never look dull. Look out for interesting varieties of common plants such as pale Muscari 'Valerie Finnis' and daffodils and tulips in very variation of yellow. Tulips give us the biggest range of colours with every shade except true blue.

Not all daffodils are yellow either! There are many daffodils with white petals and pink trumpets and these combine especially well with blue grape hyacinths (Muscari) and grey foliage.

Repetition of a simple colour palette always works well and blue myosotis and yellow tulips look fresh and bright.

Summer combinations

The abundance of summer flowers and foliage allows us to create luxurient displays to suit every taste. Though it is tempting to concentrate on flower colour, remember that many flowers are fleeting and that foliage provides a backdrop that can enhance bloms when they appear.

The longest displays of flowers are often provided by bedding plants, especially if they are deadheaded. But do not forget the colour and fragrance of roses. They may need spraying to keep them healthy but no shrub gives more colour over such a long period.

The finest sweet peas are grown up canes and given careful treatment but they can also be mixed with other plants such as here where they give complementary colour to a lilac buddleia.

Remarkable bedding

Bedding plants are perfect for a quick transformation. In a matter of weeks, the young plants get established and will bloom for months, until stopped by the first frost of autumn. Most are frost tender, so they cannot be planted until the last frost of spring has passed.

Because they grow so quickly and need to be replanted each summer, you can experiment with combinations of colours or stick with a single colour theme as here, with fiery reds and oranges.

Silver and purple

Silver and purple are a perfect match. The richness of purple foliage and flowers is accented by silver and grey foliage and both colours are at their best in sunlight. Purple-leaved plants may be dull and green when grown in shade and most plants with silvery leaves are naturally from sunny climes and will be straggly in shade. Most silver plants are also resistant to drought.

Both foliage colours are sympathetic partners to pink flowers and purple foliage gives richness to red flowers, as well. In shade and dull weather, silver leaves can look grey and purple foliage may look dull, so try not to have too much of a good thing!

This combination of purple ligularia and variegated grass offers good contrast in form and colour.

Pink flowers always look good when set against silvery or grey foliage, especially on a sunny day.

The architectural, silver foliage of cardoon at the back of this summer border forms the focus of this combination of alliums and aquilegias.

Richly hued heleniums and fiery crocosmia need sunlight to bring out their full beauty and are enhanced by splashes of yellow.

Hot Summer Schemes

It is satisfying to create a 'hot' border by combining red, orange and yellow flowers. They are abundant in summer and annuals such as Californian poppies, many petunias, dahlias, zinnias and marigolds give us planty of scope for a quick effect. Heleniums, crocosmias, monardas, rudbeckias, solidago and many more provide a perennial accent. Bright green foliage adds some 'zing' to the planting while purple leaves give depth to the display and extra richness. You can appply these principles to the smallest area and practice with plants in containers if you are uncertain of the effect

This summer border sizzles on a hot, sunny day, thanks to its bold colouring.

A simple pairing of self-sown Californian poppies and bronze Carex comans is especially effective.

Roses and clematis

Clematis are useful climbers to provide extra colour through shrubs in summer and, if planted with a rose that flowers at the same time, they create a sumptuous combination. Most clematis are climbers, but herbaceous clematis, such as *Clematis integrifolia*, *C. x durandii* and *C. 'Alionushka'* with pink blooms, reach about 1.5m (5ft) when in bloom and will scramble through shrubs including roses and those that flowered earlier in the season, such as Forsythia and Weigela. They are also useful for scrambling over winter-flowering heathers, because their foliage is not dense and will not harm the heathers.

The nodding blooms of Clematis integrifolia *brighten the foliage of* Rosa glauca *after its flowers have gone.*

Oriental maple

A Japanese maple can be the focus of a planting scheme that has an oriental theme. Here, a purple-leaved maple is planted in semi-shade in soil that is not too dry in summer, which is just the kind of spot that suits hostas and ferns. In spring, a white *Dicentra spectabilis*, another oriental plant, is shown off to perfection under the dark foliage and a herbaceous

clematis begins to climb the trunk, to open its pink flowers later in summer. By summer the dicentra will die down, but the expanding hosta foliage will soon cover any gaps and its flowers will provide extra colour and interest.

This bold and beautiful border depends on just three plants, carefully chosen; delicate pink astrantia, structural Allium cristophii *and spiky eryngium.*

Shape and texture

Colour is often the most obvious feature of a plant or flower, but successful combinations rely on much more. A good way to learn to consider plant shapes, forms and textures is to plan a single-colour border. Without care it can easily be dull, unless you are obsessed with your chosen shade. However: contrast plants with big leaves against small foliage; upright habits with weeping plants; round leaves of hostas with the delicate tracery of ferns; soft, felty foliage with shiny leaves; small flowers and big, bold blooms and rounded plants with spiky ones – and then suddenly everything becomes far more interesting.

Cultural requirements

Another way to achieve successful combinations is to combine plants that like similar growing conditions. Plants always grow best when planted in conditions that suit them and part of the skill of gardening is learning the needs of plants. If you have a favourite plant that suits your garden, learn what else likes similar conditions and plant these. The chances are that these will look perfectly at home. And if there is a gap in the season of interest, just add some bedding or bulbs for an extra shot of colour.

Yellow and purple

It is often easier to deal with plants in small groups and use one, major plant around which to build a combination. Here, *Sambucus nigra* 'Black Beauty' forms the basis of a scheme that is beautiful all summer. The dark foliage combines well with *Lysimachia* 'Alexander' from the moment its pink-flushed, variegated leaves appear to when the starry, yellow flowers open. A little

later the dark leaves show off the bright yellow flowers of lilies, though pink or orange lilies could be planted instead. The sambucus is easy to grow in any sunny spot and can be pruned at will whenever it gets too big. It produces elderberries, too.

Autumn combinations

The autumn sun traverses low in the sky and gives a warm light that enhances the beauty of golds, metallic browns and orange – the true colours of autumn. Though the plant palette is smaller than in summer, there is a greater variety of shapes, forms and textures, as seed pods, berries and both fresh and dying foliage are added to the mix. Use late flowers to give a shock of seemingly unseasonable colour, or rejoice in the mass of autumn foliage and fruit.

Grasses

Ornamental grasses are now firmly entrenched in our garden designs and their flowing shapes and constant movement enhance borders throughout summer. But many are at their most beautiful in autumn as their foliage and diaphanous seedheads turn gold and bronze and are jewelled with dew in the morning. Foggy days also enhance their lightness and frost outlines their beauty. Their brown tones complement red and russet chrysanthemums and the ageing flowers of herbaceous sedums.

The narrow foliage of senescent grasses and evergreen bamboos seems especially airy and delicate against evergreen shrubs.

The autumn border offers the last strong show of the garden year and the richness of asters, sedums and kniphofias is a splendid finale.

Seed heads

There are good reasons for removing dead flowers as they fade; it may encourage more flowers to be produced and keeps things neat and tidy. But some seed heads are attractive and add extra interest to the garden in late summer, autumn and winter. Some also provide seeds to feed birds and shelter for insects in winter. Among the best plants for structural winter seed heads are Siberian iris, alliums, thistles and globe artichokes, clematis, eryngium, sedums, teasels and sunflowers.

Most seedheads begin to decompose in the wet, frosty weather of winter, so pick and dry any that you want to preserve before they start to rot.

Few plants retain the structure of their flowers when the colour fades, but *Allium cristophii* (below) changes from metallic mauve to strawy brown while *A. aflatunense* (bottom) becomes a sphere of round seedpods.

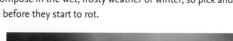

Cardoons and globe artichokes have huge 'thistle' heads of purple flowers which become golden seed heads in late summer and autumn – ideal for winter flower arrangements.

Teasels are bold, architectural plants and their tiny mauve flowers attract hordes of bees. Long after these are a memory, the seed heads feed our imagination, as well as finches!

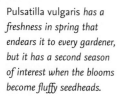

Pulsatilla vulgaris has a freshness in spring that endears it to every gardener, but it has a second season of interest when the blooms become fluffy seedheads.

Accents in borders

Pots and containers do not have to be planted to have a place in borders and you do not need a statue to create a centre-piece, as this unplanted urn (below) shows. It is the focus of the border in summer and its hard lines, brown colour and shiny texture stand out against the profusion of flowers and foliage. In autumn its colour blends with its surroundings, yet still stands out and gives a focus to the view.

The most important plants in the autumn garden are asters and chrysanthemums which, between them, provide every colour except true blue.

Berries and fruits

Autumn is always associated with heavy crops of apples, pears and other fruits and, in the ornamental garden, with a wide variety of berries. Though not edible raw, crab apples (Malus) are among the most popular small trees because of their dual season of interest; blossom in spring and colourful fruit in autumn. Other small trees with autumn berry interest include sorbus, which have delicate foliage and berries in shades of orange, yellow, white and pink. Many roses have attractive hips, though the best for this purpose, such as 'Geranium' have a short flowering period. Also, do not forget the common pyracanthas and cotoneasters which are easy to grow, have flowers that attract bees and berries that will feed the birds in cold, winter weather.

Fiery foliage

Autumn is the time when deciduous plants prepare to drop their leaves and many are transformed from green mounds into a blaze of glory. Maples of all kinds are the most famous but others that can be relied on to set the garden alight with colour are Rhus, Cotinus, Liquidambar, Parrotia, deciduous euonymus, particularly *E. alatus*, and deciduous berberis.

Sorbus cashmiriana *is a superb small tree with white berries that are rarely stripped by birds.*

Autumn-flowering bulbs such as pinkish colchicums have a freshness that contrasts with rudbeckias and grasses.

You cannot go wrong in autumn – as leaves turn to red, orange and gold, other plants such as grasses also change shades and old sedum flowers develop russet hues.

The red stems of Cornus alba *are hidden by green leaves in summer but revealed in all their glory in winter, augmented here by a background of golden conifer foliage.*

Winter wonders

It is easy to disregard winter as a dead time in the garden and to reduce your gardening activities to searching seed catalogues for bedding plants and reading books. These are worthwhile activities, but your garden can be just as fascinating in the darker days of winter as in summer; however, we need to look a little harder to spot the beauty of plants because their charms may be more subtle. As leaves drop from deciduous plants, interesting stems are revealed and evergreen foliage becomes more important. Cold weather may change the colour of foliage and there are still flowers opening on a select band of plants.

Sweet fragrance

What many winter flowers lack in size or colour they more than make up for with fragrance. Some of the most delightfully fragrant shrubs flower in winter and a waft of their intoxicating scent can lift the spirits on a dull day. *Viburnum* x *bodnantense* is one of the best, flowering from November to March, with bunches of small, pink, fragrant flowers. Other exceptional shrubs for scent are mahonias, *Daphne bholua*, *Lonicera purpusii*, Sarcococca, Hamamelis and the aptly named wintersweet (*Chimonanthus praecox*).

The bold, sword-like foliage of phormiums are especially welcome in winter, giving dramatic shapes among the fiery colours of bright cornus stems.

The winter garden need not be devoid of flowers. Bright witch hazel (Hamamelis) blooms rise above winter flowering heathers and between silver Rubus stems.

Solid evergreens

In summer, most evergreens provide a solid backdrop to the masses of other foliage and colourful flowers. They do not attract much attention, even though their height, texture and colour provide lots of interest – there are just so many more things to look at. But when winter cuts away all the extraneous foliage and bold, summer flowers, the importance of evergreens such as upright conifers and glossy laurels or hollies is suddenly obvious. Whether emerging from November fog or outlined with frost or a light covering of snow, they become the most important plants in the garden. You can make the effect more pronounced by clipping your evergreens into interesting shapes, such as cubes, balls and spirals – or more bizarre shapes if you are brave! But not all herbaceous plants dissolve at the first touch of frost. Tall, elegant Miscanthus might change colour, but their strawy stems and foliage are still elegant. Some seed heads remain beautiful and these include alliums, teasels, echinaceas, sedums and physalis (see page 227).

A winter garden

Some plants for winter interest can look rather dull in summer, so you may not want to plant the whole garden for winter display. But you can add a few plants to the garden, in strategic places, to enjoy in winter. It is best to plant them in easily accessible places so that you do not have to tramp across wet lawns to enjoy them. Plant fragrant sarcococcas and viburnums near paths or by a door so you can enjoy them every day. Group a few winter plants together in a border where you can see them from the house. An easy combination of plants that would look good all year as well as in winter could be created with *Fatsia japonica*, *Mahonia* 'Charity', *Cornus alba*, *Helleborus foetidus* and a coloured phormium.

Foliage

With a limited choice of plants to use in winter, evergreen foliage is especially important and there is a wide range of sizes, textures and colours. Bergenias provide lustrous, large, rounded leaves at ground level that often turn red or purple in winter. Shrubs with similar leaves include some viburnums and aucubas, often spotted with yellow. Bold, striking foliage is provided by phormiums, in many colours and sizes, and these contrast wonderfully with bergenias. Most evergreen berberis have tiny foliage that creates a dark green background for more interesting shapes such as Fatsia or Griselinia.

Conifers, with foliage in shades of green, grey, silver and gold, should not be ignored because only a few are giants and most are of moderate size and will withstand clipping if they get as big as you require.

Ivies are often considered too weedy to include in well-tended gardens, but they are adaptable and can be trained and clipped as here, with hart's tongue fern.

This low-maintenance border is simply planted with short, ornamental grasses and winter-flowering heathers. These heathers thrive in most soils, in full sun, and are easy to care for.

Pittosporum tenuifolium *is a neat, evergreen shrub with small, glossy foliage that is beautiful to look at all year round.*

If autumn gales do not destroy their airy stems, ornamental grasses add beauty in winter.

Covering the ground

Ground cover plants are sometimes considered the panacea for lazy gardeners, covering the soil and suppressing weeds. Few are as efficient at keeping weeds at bay as many gardeners hope, but plants such as Lamium, Vinca and Stachys will prevent some annual weeds from getting established and they help to unite clumps of other, more desirable plants in the

border. In winter, they not only give interest when other plants have disappeared under ground, they help prevent soil erosion and they provide cover for insects, toads and other wildlife, so are of benefit to the organic gardener. Their foliage also helps prevent soil splashing on the blooms of short, spring bulbs.

Planting Combinations

Frost brings a new glamour to evergreens. Though they may collapse as they freeze, as temperatures rise and the frost thaws, they pick up again and look as good as new.

Perfect partners

Helleborus foetidus is one of the easiest hellebores to grow and also one of the earliest to begin to flower. Its finely divided, deep green foliage is a wonderful contrast to the pale green flowers and it could be planted at the base of a wall-trained garrya for a subtle but pretty pairing. Winter-flowering jasmine (*Jasminum nudiflorum*) has a long season of interest and is often planted on a shady wall. Its effect can be enhanced by adding a golden ivy. Surround a clipped box ball with bergenias to reflect the rounded shape. Plant black-leaved *Ophiopogon planiscapus* 'Nigrescens' through a silver carpet of *Lamium* 'White Nancy', combine different coloured cornus and plant *Cyclamen hederifolium* through a carpet of green ivies in shade for a mosaic of fascinating foliage.

Leaving herbacous stems uncut in autumn allows you to enjoy the tracery of winter frost on the dead flowers and leaves. They also provide homes for ladybirds and other insects.

A simple, but brilliant, winter combination of red cornus stems, pale green Helleborus foetidus flowers and pink winter-flowering heathers.

profiled plants

Plant	Spring	Summer	Autumn	Winter	Height	Spread	Cultivation	Pests/Disease	Page
Abelia x grandiflora	★ ★ ★	★ ★ ★	★ ★ ★	★ ★ ★	2.5m	3m	well-drained soil in full sun	trouble-free	159
Abutilon x suntense	★ ★	★ ★	★ ★	★	4m	2m	well-drained soil in full sun	trouble-free	22
Acaeana microphylla 'Kupferteppich'	★ ★ ★	★ ★ ★	★ ★ ★	★ ★	6cm	60cm	well-drained soil in full sun	trouble-free	50
Acanthus mollis	★ ★	★ ★ ★	★ ★	★	1.2m	1m	well-drained soil in full sun	powdery mildew	50
Acer davidii	★ ★	★ ★	★ ★		8m	8m	fertile, well-drained soil	trouble-free	187
Acer griseum	★ ★	★ ★	★ ★		8m	8m	fertile, well-drained soil	trouble-free	187
Acer negundo 'Kelly's Gold'	★ ★	★ ★	★ ★		5m	5m	fertile, well-drained soil	powdery mildew	93
Acer palmatum 'Dissectum Atropurpureum'	★ ★	★ ★	★ ★		2m	3m	fertile, well-drained soil	trouble-free	93
Achillea 'Red Velvet'	★	★ ★ ★	★ ★		60cm	30cm	well-drained soil	powdery mildew	51
Aconitum napellus	★ ★	★ ★ ★	★		1.5m	40cm	well-drained soil	trouble-free	142
Agapanthus praecox	★ ★	★ ★ ★	★ ★	★	1m	60cm	well-drained soil in sun	trouble-free	51
Agastache foeniculum 'Golden Jubilee'	★ ★	★ ★ ★	★ ★		75cm	40cm	well-drained soil in sun	trouble-free	51
Ajuga reptans 'Catlin's Giant'	★ ★ ★	★ ★	★ ★	★ ★	20cm	40cm	moist soil in shade	powdery mildew	10
Alchemilla mollis	★	★ ★ ★	★ ★		40cm	60cm	sun or light shade	trouble-free	10
Allium cristophii	★ ★ ★				60cm	20cm	well-drained soil in sun	trouble-free	41
Allium 'Globemaster'	★ ★ ★				1m	20cm	well-drained soil in sun	trouble-free	41
Alstroemeria	★	★ ★ ★	★		30–90cm	40cm	well-drained soil in sun	trouble-free	52
Althaea rosea	★	★ ★ ★	★		1.5m	60cm	well-drained soil in sun	rust	52
Amelanchier lamarkii	★ ★	★ ★	★ ★		6m	66m	well-drained soil in sun	trouble-free	22
Anemone blanda	★ ★				10cm	10cm	sun or light shade	trouble-free	42
Anemone x hybrida 'Honorine Jobert'	★ ★	★ ★ ★	★ ★		1.2m	1m	sun or light shade	trouble-free	142
Anemone nemorosa 'Vestal'	★ ★				10cm	20cm	light shade, moist soil	trouble-free	42
Anthemis punctata subsp. *cupaniana*	★ ★ ★	★ ★	★ ★	★ ★	30cm	60cm	sun, well-drained soil	aphids	53
Anthemis tinctoria 'Wargrave'	★ ★ ★	★ ★	★ ★	★ ★	75cm	75cm	sun, well-drained soil	aphids	53
Aquilegia vulgaris 'William Guinness'	★ ★	★ ★	★ ★		90cm	45cm	sun or light shade	aphids and sawfly	53
Arabis caucasica 'Flore Pleno'	★ ★ ★	★ ★	★ ★	★ ★	25cm	35cm	sun, well-drained soil	aphids, mildew	10
Arbutus unedo	★ ★ ★	★ ★	★ ★	★ ★	8m	8m	sun, fertile soil	trouble-free	160
Arisaema griffithii	★ ★	★ ★	★		60cm	15cm	light shade, moist soil	slugs, vine weevil	136
Armeria maritima	★ ★	★ ★	★ ★	★	25cm	30cm	sun, well-drained soil	trouble-free	11

★ in flower   ★ in flower with leaf   ★ in leaf

Plant	Spring	Summer	Autumn	Winter	Height	Spread	Cultivation	Pests/Disease	Page
Artemisia absinthium 'Lambrook Silver'	★ ★	★ ★	★ ★	★ ★	80cm	80cm	well-drained soil, sun	aphids	54
Arum italicum	★ ★	★ ★		★ ★ ★ ★	30cm	30cm	sun or shade, moist soil	aphids	214
Aruncus dioicus	★ ★	★ ★ ★	★ ★		2m	1.5m	moist soil, sun or shade	trouble-free	54
Asplenium scolopendrium	★ ★ ★	★ ★ ★	★ ★ ★	★ ★	45cm	40cm	part shade or shade	trouble-free	182
Aster amellus 'Sonia'	★ ★	★ ★	★ ★ ★		45cm	45cm	sun, well-drained soil	trouble-free	143
Aster x frikartii	★ ★	★ ★	★ ★ ★		70cm	60cm	sun, well-drained soil	trouble-free	143
Aster 'Little Carlow'	★ ★	★ ★	★ ★ ★		1m	75cm	sun, well-drained soil	powdery mildew	143
Aster novae-angliae	★ ★	★ ★	★ ★ ★		1m	75cm	sun, well-drained soil	trouble-free	144
Aster novi-belgii	★ ★	★ ★	★ ★ ★		1m	75cm	sun, well-drained soil	powdery mildew	144
Aster thomsonii 'Nanus'	★ ★	★ ★ ★	★ ★		70cm	60cm	sun, well-drained soil	trouble-free	54
Astilbe 'Venus'	★ ★	★ ★ ★	★ ★		70cm	60cm	sun, moist soil	trouble-free	55
Astilbe chinensis var. pumila	★ ★	★ ★	★ ★		25cm	25cm	sun, moist soil	trouble-free	55
Astrantia major 'Ruby Wedding'	★ ★	★ ★ ★	★ ★		70cm	70cm	sun, well-drained soil	trouble-free	56
Athyrium filix-femina	★ ★	★ ★	★ ★		1m	70cm	sun or shade, moist soil	trouble-free	56
Athyrium nipponicum var. pictum	★ ★	★ ★	★ ★		40cm	45cm	sun or shade, moist soil	vine weevil	56
Aubrieta 'Whitwell Gem'	★ ★ ★	★ ★ ★	★ ★ ★	★ ★	15cm	40cm	sun, well-drained soil	aphids, white blister	11
Aucuba japonica	★ ★ ★	★ ★ ★	★ ★ ★	★ ★	2m	2m	sun or shade, any soil	trouble-free	188
Begonia semperflorens		★ ★ ★	★ ★ ★		25cm	20cm	sun or shade, moist soil	vine weevil	117
Berberis darwinii	★ ★ ★	★ ★ ★	★ ★ ★	★ ★	2m	2m	sun, fertile soil	trouble-free	23
Berberis linearifolia 'Orange King'	★ ★ ★	★ ★ ★	★ ★ ★	★ ★	2m	2m	sun, fertile soil	trouble-free	23
Bergenia 'Bressingham White'	★ ★ ★	★ ★ ★	★ ★ ★	★ ★	30m	60cm	sun or shade	trouble-free, snails	11
Berberis thunbergii 'Helmond Pillar'	★ ★	★ ★ ★	★ ★		1.5m	60cm	sun or shade, moist soil	powdery mildew	94
Betula albosinensis	★ ★	★ ★ ★	★ ★		25m	8m	sun, light, moist soil	powdery mildew	189
Betula nigra	★ ★	★ ★ ★	★ ★		15m	8m	sun, light, moist soil	powdery mildew	188
Betula utilis var. jacquemontii	★ ★	★ ★ ★	★ ★		25m	8m	sun, light, moist soil	powdery mildew	189
Brachyglottis 'Sunshine'	★ ★ ★	★ ★ ★	★ ★ ★	★ ★	1m	2m	sun, well-drained soil	trouble-free	94
Brachyscome iberidifolia		★ ★ ★	★		25cm	20cm	sun, well-drained soil	trouble-free	117
Brugmansia x candida		★ ★ ★	★ ★ ★		3m	2m	sun, moist, fertile soil	red spider mite	118
Brunnera macrophylla 'Jack Frost'	★ ★ ★	★ ★ ★	★		45cm	60cm	sun or part shade	trouble-free	12

★ in flower   ★ in flower with leaf   ★ in leaf

Plant	Spring	Summer	Autumn	Winter	Height	Spread	Cultivation	Pests/Disease	Page
Buddleja alternifolia					3m	3m	sun, well-drained soil	trouble-free	95
Buddleja davidii 'Nanho Blue'					2m	2m	sun, well-drained soil	trouble-free	95
Buddleja x weyeriana 'Sungold'					3m	3m	sun, well-drained soil	trouble-free	95
Buxus sempervirens					3m	3m	sun or shade, any soil	box sucker	189
Calendula officinalis					60cm	60cm	sun, well-drained soil	powdery mildew	118
Callicarpa bodinieri 'Profusion'					2m	1.5m	sun, well-drained soil	trouble-free	160
Callistemon citrinus					2.5m	2.5m	sun, well-drained soil	trouble-free	96
Calluna vulgaris					25cm	45m	sun, well-drained soil	trouble-free	96
Caltha palustris					45cm	60cm	sun, moist soil	powdery mildew	12
Camellia x williamsii 'Donation'					2m	1.5m	sun or shade, lime-free soil	scale, vine weevil	23
Campanula carpatica					30cm	45cm	sun, well-drained soil	trouble-free	57
Campanula glomerata					45cm	60cm	sun, well-drained soil	trouble-free	57
Campanula 'Kent Belle'					75cm	60cm	sun, well-drained soil	trouble-free	58
Campanula lactiflora 'Loddon Anna'					1.2m	1m	sun, well-drained soil	trouble-free	57
Campsis radicans					8m	8m	sun, well-drained soil	trouble-free	176
Canna 'Durban'					1.2m	60cm	sun, well-drained soil	virus	118
Canna elata 'Aurea'					45cm	45cm	sun, well-drained soil	trouble-free	58
Carex elata 'Aurea'					60cm	45cm	sun or shade, moist soil	trouble-free	58
Caryopteris x clandonensis					1m	1m	sun, well-drained soil	trouble-free	161
Catananche caerulea					60cm	40cm	sun, well-drained soil	trouble-free	58
Ceanothus 'Concha'					3m	3m	sun, well-drained soil	trouble-free	24
Ceanothus arboreus 'Trewithen Blue'					5m	5m	sun, well-drained soil	trouble-free	24
Cedronella canariensis					1.2m	60cm	sun, dry soil	trouble-free	59
Centaurea montana 'Gold Bullion'					45cm	60cm	light shade, rich soil	powdery mildew	59
Centranthus ruber					75cm	60cm	sun, well-drained soil	can be invasive	60
Ceratostigma plumbaginoides					75cm	1m	sun, well-drained soil	trouble-free	161
Cercis canadensis 'Forest Pansy'					8m	6m	sun, well-drained soil	trouble-free	24
Cerinthe major 'Purpurascens'					45cm	45cm	sun, well-drained soil	trouble-free	119
Chaenomeles speciosa 'Nivalis'					2m	3m	sun, well-drained soil	trouble-free	25

★ in flower   ★ in flower with leaf   ★ in leaf

Plant	Spring	Summer	Autumn	Winter	Height	Spread	Cultivation	Pests/Disease	Page
Chamaecyparis lawsoniana 'Elwoodii'	★ ★ ★	★ ★ ★	★ ★ ★	★ ★ ★	3m	1m	sun, any soil	aphids	190
Chamaerops humilis	★ ★ ★	★ ★ ★	★ ★ ★	★ ★ ★	1m	1m	sun, protect from cold	trouble-free	190
Chelone obliqua	★	★ ★ ★	★ ★		60cm	45cm	sun or part shade	trouble-free	60
Chimonanthus praecox	★ ★	★ ★ ★	★ ★	★	3m	2m	sunny, warm position	trouble-free	190
Chionodoxa lucilliae	★ ★ ★				10cm	5cm	sun or part shade	trouble-free	42
Choisya ternata 'Sundance'	★ ★ ★	★ ★ ★	★ ★ ★	★ ★	1.5m	1.5m	sun, protect from cold	trouble-free	191
Cistus 'Silver Pink'	★ ★ ★	★ ★ ★	★ ★ ★	★ ★	70cm	90cm	sun, well-drained soil	trouble-free	96
Clematis 'Alionushka'	★ ★	★ ★ ★	★		1.5m	1m	sun or part shade	trouble-free	131
Clematis cirrhosa	★ ★ ★	★ ★ ★	★ ★ ★	★ ★	2.5m	2m	sun, protect from cold	trouble-free	211
Clematis 'Comtesse de Bouchard'	★ ★	★ ★ ★	★		3m	2m	sun or part shade	trouble-free	131
Clematis x durandii	★ ★	★ ★ ★	★ ★		1.2m	1m	sun or part shade	trouble-free	131
Clematis macropetala 'Markham's Pink'	★ ★ ★	★ ★ ★	★		2.5m	1.5m	sun or part shade	trouble-free	40
Clematis montana 'Elizabeth'	★ ★ ★	★ ★ ★	★		4m	4m	sun or part shade	trouble-free	40
Clematis 'Gravetye Beauty'	★ ★ ★	★ ★ ★	★		3m	2m	sun or part shade	trouble-free	176
Clerodendron bungeii	★ ★ ★	★ ★ ★	★		2m	2m	sun - suckers freely	trouble-free	161
Clerodendron trichotomum	★ ★ ★	★ ★ ★	★		3m	3m	sun, well-drained soil	trouble-free	162
Colchicum speciosum	★ ★ ★		★ ★		20cm	20cm	sun or part shade	trouble-free	178
Collettia paradoxa	★ ★ ★	★ ★ ★	★ ★ ★	★ ★	2.5m	1.5m	sun, well-drained soil	trouble-free	162
Convallaria majalis	★ ★ ★	★ ★ ★	★		20cm	45cm	sun or part shade	trouble-free	12
Convolvulus althaeoides	★ ★ ★	★ ★ ★	★ ★		60cm	1m	sun, well-drained soil	invasive	97
Convolvulus cneorum	★ ★ ★	★ ★ ★	★ ★ ★	★ ★	70cm	70cm	sun, well-drained soil	trouble-free	97
Convolvulus sabatius	★ ★ ★	★ ★ ★	★		15cm	60cm	sun, well-drained soil	rather tender	97
Coprosma 'Rainbow Surprise'	★ ★ ★	★ ★ ★	★ ★ ★	★ ★	1.5m	1m	sun, well-drained soil	rather tender	162
Cordyline australis	★ ★ ★	★ ★ ★	★ ★ ★	★ ★	5m	1m	sun, well-drained soil	trouble-free	98
Coreopsis verticillata	★ ★ ★	★ ★ ★	★		60cm	45cm	sun, well-drained soil	trouble-free	60
Cornus alba 'Sibirica'	★ ★ ★	★ ★ ★	★		1.5m	1.5m	sun or shade, moist soil	trouble-free	192
Cornus mas	★ ★ ★	★ ★ ★	★		2.5m	2.5m	sun, well-drained soil	trouble-free	25
Cornus sanguinea 'Midwinter Fire'	★ ★ ★	★ ★ ★	★		1.5m	1.5m	sun or shade, moist soil	trouble-free	191
Cornus sericea 'Flaviramea'	★ ★ ★	★ ★ ★	★		1.5m	1.5m	sun or shade, moist soil	trouble-free	191

★ in flower ★ in flower with leaf ☆ in leaf

Plant	Spring	Summer	Autumn	Winter	Height	Spread	Cultivation	Pests/Disease	Page
Corokia cotoneaster	★ ★	★ ★	★ ★	★ ★	2m	1.5m	sun, well-drained soil	trouble-free	25
Correa 'Mannii'	★ ★	★ ★	★ ★	★ ★ ★	1.5m	1m	sun, well-drained soil	rather tender	192
Cortaderia selloana 'Pumila'	★ ★	★ ★	★ ★	★ ★	1.2m	1.2m	sun, well-drained soil	trouble-free	144
Corydalis solida	★ ★ ★ ★				10cm	5cm	sun or part shade	trouble-free	13
Corydalis cheilanthifolia	★ ★	★ ★	★ ★	★ ★	45cm	45cm	sun, well-drained soil	trouble-free	13
Corylopsis pauciflora	★ ★	★ ★	★ ★		1.5m	2m	sun, moist soil	trouble-free	26
Corylus avellana 'Tortuosa'	★ ★	★ ★	★ ★		2.5m	2.5m	sun or shade, any soil	trouble-free	192
Cosmos atrosanguineus		★ ★	★ ★ ★		75cm	40cm	sun, well-drained soil	rather tender	119
Cosmos bipinnatus 'Sonata Carmine'		★ ★	★ ★ ★		60cm	40cm	sun, well-drained soil	trouble-free	119
Cotinus coggygria		★ ★ ★	★ ★		3m	3m	sun, well-drained soil	trouble-free	163
Cotoneaster conspicuus 'Decorus'	★ ★	★ ★	★ ★	★ ★	1.5m	2m	sun or shade, any soil	trouble-free	164
Cotoneaster frigidus 'Cornubia'	★ ★	★ ★	★ ★	★ ★	5m	5m	sun or shade, any soil	trouble-free	164
Cotoneaster horizontalis	★ ★	★ ★	★ ★		1m	1m	sun or shade, any soil	trouble-free	164
Crataegus laevigata 'Rosea Flore Pleno'	★ ★	★ ★	★ ★		5m	5m	sun or shade, any soil	trouble-free	26
Crinum x powellii		★ ★	★ ★ ★		1.2m	1m	sun, moist soil	rather tender	137
Crocosmia 'Lucifer'		★ ★	★ ★ ★		1m	30cm	sun, any soil	trouble-free	137
Crocus speciosus	★ ★ ★		★ ★		15cmm	5cm	sun, well-drained soil	trouble-free	179
Crocus tommasinianus	★ ★ ★ ★				15cm	5cm	sun, well-drained soil	trouble-free	43
Crocus vernus 'Remembrance'	★ ★ ★				15cm	5cm	sun, well-drained soil	trouble-free	43
Cyclamen coum	★ ★ ★ ★			★ ★	5cm	15cm	sun or shade, any soil	trouble-free	214
Cyclamen hederifolium	★ ★ ★		★ ★ ★	★ ★	5cm	20cm	sun or shade, any soil	trouble-free	179
Cytisus x praecox 'Warminster'	★ ★	★ ★	★ ★	★ ★	1.2m	1.2m	sun, well-drained soil	trouble-free	26
Dahlia 'Bishop of Llandaff'		★ ★ ★	★ ★ ★		1.2m	1m	sun, fertile, moist soil	slugs and earwigs	138
Daphne bholua	★ ★	★ ★	★ ★	★ ★ ★	1.5m	1m	sun, well-drained soil	aphids, virus	27
Daphne mezereum	★ ★	★ ★	★ ★		1.2m	1m	sun, well-drained soil	aphids, virus	27
Delphinium 'Magic Fountains'		★ ★ ★	★ ★		80cm	60cm	sun, well-drained soil	slugs, powdery mildew	61
Deschampsia caespitosa 'Goldhange'		★ ★ ★	★ ★		1.2m	1m	sun, well-drained soil	trouble-free	145
Deutzia 'Mont Rose'		★ ★ ★	★ ★		1.2m	1.2m	sun or shade, any soil	trouble-free	98
Dianthus	★ ★	★ ★ ★	★ ★	★ ★	45cm	30cm	sun, well-drained soil	trouble-free	61

★ in flower ★ in flower with leaf ★ in leaf

Plant	Spring	Summer	Autumn	Winter	Height	Spread	Cultivation	Pests/Disease	Page
Diascia 'Lilac Belle'	★ ★	★ ★ ★	★ ★ ★		40cm	40cm	sun, well-drained soil	trouble-free	61
Dicentra 'Pearl Drops'	★ ★ ★	★ ★ ★	★ ★ ★		30cm	45cm	sun or shade, moist soil	trouble-free	62
Dicentra spectabilis	★ ★ ★	★ ★ ★	★ ★		60cm	60cm	sun or shade, moist soil	trouble-free	62
Dierama pulcherrimum	★ ★ ★ ★	★ ★ ★ ★	★ ★ ★	★	1.5m	1m	sun, well-drained soil	slow to establish	62
Digitalis purpurea	★ ★ ★	★ ★ ★ ★	★ ★ ★	★ ★	1.5m	30cm	sun or shade, seeds freely	trouble-free	63
Doronicum orientale 'Magnificum'	★ ★ ★	★ ★ ★	★ ★ ★		50cm	50cm	sun or shade, moist soil	powdery mildew	13
Dryopteris erythrosora	★ ★ ★	★ ★ ★	★ ★ ★	★ ★	60cm	45cm	sun or part shade	trouble-free	63
Eccremocarpus scaber	★ ★ ★	★ ★ ★	★ ★		3m	2m	sun, fertile soil	trouble-free, aphids	132
Echinacea purpurea	★ ★ ★	★ ★ ★	★ ★		90cm	60cm	sun, well-drained soil	trouble-free	145
Echinops ritro	★ ★ ★	★ ★ ★	★ ★		90cm	60cm	sun, well-drained soil	powdery mildew	63
Elaeagnus x ebbingei	★ ★ ★	★ ★ ★	★ ★ ★	★ ★	3m	2m	sun or part shade	coral spot	193
Ensete ventricosum	★ ★ ★	★ ★ ★	★ ★ ★	★ ★	2m	2m	sun, shelter from wind	not hardy	120
Epimedium grandiflorum 'Snow Queen'	★ ★ ★	★ ★ ★	★ ★		20cm	30cm	sun or shade, moist soil	trouble-free	14
Epimedium x perralchicum 'Frohnleiten'	★ ★ ★	★ ★ ★	★ ★		40cm	60cm	sun or shade, any soil	trouble-free	14
Eremurus 'Cleopatra'	★ ★ ★	★ ★			1.5m	30cm	sun, moist, fertile soil	slugs and snails	138
Erica arborea 'Albert's Gold'	★ ★ ★	★ ★ ★	★ ★ ★	★ ★	2m	80cm	sun, well-drained soil	trouble-free	98
Erica carnea	★ ★ ★	★ ★ ★	★ ★ ★	★ ★	30cm	50cm	sun, well-drained soil	trouble-free	194
Erica cinerea 'Hookestone White'	★ ★ ★	★ ★ ★	★ ★ ★	★ ★	30cm	50cm	sun, acid soil	trouble-free	99
Erica darleyensis	★ ★ ★	★ ★ ★	★ ★ ★	★ ★	30cm	50cm	sun, well-drained soil	trouble-free	194
Erica vagans 'Mrs D F Maxwell'	★ ★ ★	★ ★ ★	★ ★ ★	★ ★	40cm	50cm	sun, acid soil	trouble-free	99
Eryngium	★ ★ ★	★ ★ ★	★ ★		90cm	60cm	sun, well-drained soil	trouble-free	64
Erysimum 'Bowles' Mauve'	★ ★ ★	★ ★ ★	★ ★ ★	★ ★	60cm	60cm	sun, well-drained soil	short-lived	27
Erysimum cheiri 'Fair Lady Mixed'	★ ★ ★	★		★ ★ ★ ★	40cm	40cm	sun, well-drained soil	clubroot	38
Erythronium 'Pagoda'	★ ★ ★				30cm	10cm	sun or shade, moist soil	trouble-free	44
Escallonia laevis 'Gold Brian'	★ ★ ★	★ ★ ★	★ ★ ★	★ ★	1.5m	1.5m	sun or light shade	trouble-free	99
Eucalyptus pauciflora subsp. *niphophila*	★ ★ ★	★ ★ ★	★ ★ ★	★ ★	6m	5m	sun, well-drained soil	trouble-free	164
Eucryphia x nymansensis 'Nymansay'	★ ★ ★	★ ★ ★	★ ★ ★	★ ★	3m	1m	sun, acid soil, shelter	trouble-free	164
Euonymus alatus	★ ★ ★	★ ★ ★	★ ★		2m	3m	sun, well-drained soil	trouble-free	165
Euonymus europaeus 'Red Cascade'	★ ★ ★	★ ★ ★	★ ★		2m	3m	sun, well-drained soil	aphids	165

★ in flower   ★ in flower with leaf   ★ in leaf

Plant	Spring	Summer	Autumn	Winter	Height	Spread	Cultivation	Pests/Disease	Page
Euonymus fortunei	★ ★ ★	★ ★ ★	★ ★ ★	★ ★ ★	1.2m	1.2m	sun, well-drained soil	trouble-free	26
Eupatorium purpureum subsp. maculatum	★ ★ ★	★ ★ ★ ★	★		2m	1m	sun, fertile, moist soil	slugs and snails	146
Eupatorium rugosum 'Chocolate'	★ ★ ★	★ ★ ★ ★	★		1.5m	80cm	sun, fertile, moist soil	slugs and snails	145
Euphorbia amygdaloides var. robbiae	★ ★ ★	★ ★ ★	★ ★ ★	★ ★ ★	60cm	1m	sun or shade, any soil	aphids	28
Euphorbia characias subsp. wulfenii	★ ★ ★	★ ★ ★	★ ★ ★	★ ★ ★	1.2m	1m	sun, well-drained soil	trouble-free	28
Euphorbia dulcis 'Chameleon'	★ ★	★ ★ ★ ★	★ ★		45cm	60cm	sun, fertile, moist soil	trouble-free	64
Euphorbia griffithii 'Dixter'	★ ★	★ ★ ★	★ ★		1m	1m	sun, fertile, moist soil	trouble-free	64
Euphorbia polychroma	★ ★ ★	★ ★ ★	★ ★		1.2m	1m	sun, any soil	trouble-free	15
Exochorda x macrantha 'The Bride'	★ ★ ★	★ ★ ★	★ ★		3m	3m	sun, any soil	trouble-free	28
Fatsia japonica	★ ★ ★	★ ★ ★	★ ★ ★	★ ★ ★	3m	4m	sun or shade, shelter	frost kills shoots	194
Festuca glauca	★ ★ ★	★ ★ ★	★ ★ ★	★ ★ ★	25cm	25cm	sun, well-drained soil	trouble-free	65
Filipendula ulmaria 'Aurea'	★ ★ ★	★ ★ ★	★ ★		75cm	40cm	sun, moist soil	powdery mildew	65
Forsythia 'Courtalyn'	★ ★ ★	★ ★ ★	★ ★		2m	1m	sun, well-drained soil	trouble-free	29
Fritillaria imperialis 'Maxima Lutea'	★ ★ ★				1m	30cm	sun, fertile, moist soil	lily beetle	44
Fuchsia magellanica	★ ★ ★	★ ★ ★	★ ★ ★		2m	1m	sun, any soil	trouble-free	100
Gaillardia 'Kobold'	★ ★	★ ★ ★ ★	★ ★ ★		30cm	30cm	sun, well-drained soil	trouble-free	65
Galanthus nivalis	★ ★ ★				15cm	10cm	sun or shade, any soil	trouble-free	214
Garrya elliptica	★ ★ ★	★ ★ ★	★ ★ ★	★ ★ ★	3m	2m	sun or shade, shelter	trouble-free	211
Gaultheria mucronata	★ ★ ★	★ ★ ★	★ ★ ★	★ ★ ★	80cm	1m	sun or shade, acid soil	trouble-free	195
Gaultheria shallon	★ ★ ★	★ ★ ★	★ ★ ★	★ ★ ★	90cm	1.5m	sun or shade, acid soil	trouble-free	195
Gaura lindheimeri	★ ★ ★	★ ★ ★ ★	★ ★		70cm	80cm	sun, well-drained soil	rot in winter	146
Gazania 'Daybreak Series'	★ ★ ★	★ ★ ★ ★	★ ★		20cm	30cm	sun, well-drained soil	aphids	120
Genista aetnensis	★ ★ ★	★ ★ ★	★ ★		5m	5m	sun, well-drained soil	trouble-free	100
Genista tinctoria 'Royal Gold'	★ ★ ★	★ ★ ★	★ ★		60cm	1m	sun, well-drained soil	trouble-free	101
Gentiana sino-ornata	★ ★ ★	★ ★ ★	★ ★		10cm	30cm	sun, moist, acid soil	aphids	146
Geranium endressii	★ ★ ★	★ ★ ★ ★	★ ★		45cm	60cm	sun or shade, any soil	trouble-free	66
Geranium macrorrhizum	★ ★ ★	★ ★ ★	★ ★ ★	★ ★ ★	30cm	60cm	sun or shade, any soil	trouble-free	66
Geranium x oxonianum 'Spring Fling'	★ ★ ★	★ ★ ★ ★	★ ★		45cm	60cm	sun or shade, any soil	trouble-free	66
Geranium 'Rozanne'	★ ★ ★	★ ★ ★ ★	★ ★		45cm	60cm	sun or shade, any soil	trouble-free	67

★ in flower ★ in flower with leaf ★ in leaf

Plant	Spring	Summer	Autumn	Winter	Height	Spread	Cultivation	Pests/Disease	Page
Geum 'Lady Strathedon'	★ ★ ★	★ ★ ★	★ ★ ★		45cm	60cm	sun or shade, any soil	trouble-free	67
Gladiolus callianthus	★ ★	★ ★ ★	★ ★		90m	20cm	sun, well-drained soil	trouble-free	138
Gladiolus communis subsp. byzantinus	★ ★	★ ★ ★	★		90m	20cm	sun, well-drained soil	trouble-free	139
Gypsophila elegans	★ ★ ★	★ ★			60cm	30cm	sun or shade, any soil	trouble-free	67
Hakonechloa macra 'Aureola'	★ ★ ★	★ ★ ★	★ ★		30m	40cm	sun or shade, moist soil	trouble-free	68
Hamamelis x intermedia	★ ★ ★	★ ★ ★	★ ★	★ ★	2m	3m	light shade, moist soil	coral spot	195
Hamamelis vernalis	★ ★ ★	★ ★ ★	★ ★	★ ★	2m	2m	light shade, moist soil	coral spot	196
Hebe x franciscana 'Variegata'	★ ★ ★	★ ★ ★	★ ★ ★	★ ★	90cm	1m	sun, well-drained soil	trouble-free	101
Hebe pinguifolia 'Pagei'	★ ★ ★	★ ★ ★	★ ★ ★	★ ★	30cm	80cm	sun, well-drained soil	trouble-free	102
Hebe 'Pink Paradise'	★ ★ ★	★ ★ ★	★ ★ ★	★ ★	30cm	60cm	sun, well-drained soil	trouble-free	101
Hedera canariensis 'Gloire de Marengo'	★ ★ ★	★ ★ ★	★ ★ ★	★ ★	5m	4m	sun or shade, shelter	hard frosts	212
Hedera colchica	★ ★ ★	★ ★ ★	★ ★ ★	★ ★	5m	4m	sun or shade, any soil	trouble-free	212
Hedera helix	★ ★ ★	★ ★ ★	★ ★ ★	★ ★	5m	4m	sun or shade, any soil	trouble-free	213
Hedychium gardnerianum	★ ★	★ ★ ★	★ ★		1.5m	1m	sun, moist rich soil	damaged by frost	147
Helenium 'Moerheim Beauty'	★ ★ ★	★ ★ ★	★ ★		90cm	60cm	sun, well-drained soil	trouble-free	147
Helianthemum 'Fire Dragon'	★ ★ ★	★ ★ ★	★ ★ ★	★	30cm	60cm	sun, well-drained soil	trouble-free	102
Helianthus multiflorus	★ ★ ★	★ ★ ★	★		2m	1m	sun, well-drained soil	trouble-free	148
Helianthus salicifolius	★ ★ ★	★ ★ ★	★ ★		3m	2m	sun, well-drained soil	trouble-free	148
Helichrysum petiolare 'Variegatum'		★ ★ ★	★ ★		60cm	80cm	sun, well-drained soil	trouble-free	120
Helleborus argutifolius	★ ★ ★	★ ★ ★	★ ★ ★	★ ★ ★	90cm	50cm	sun, well-drained soil	aphids	183
Helleborus foetidus	★ ★ ★	★ ★ ★	★ ★ ★	★ ★ ★	60cm	60cm	sun or shade, any soil	aphids	183
Helleborus hybridus	★ ★ ★	★ ★ ★	★ ★ ★	★ ★ ★	50cm	50cm	sun or shade, any soil	aphids	182
Helleborus x nigercors	★ ★ ★	★ ★ ★	★ ★ ★	★ ★ ★	40cm	50cm	sun or shade, any soil	aphids	183
Hemerocallis 'Pink Damask'	★ ★ ★	★ ★ ★	★ ★		80cm	70cm	sun, well-drained soil	trouble-free	68
Heptacodium miconioides	★ ★ ★	★ ★ ★	★ ★		3m	3m	sun, well-drained soil	trouble-free	166
Heuchera 'Chocolate Ruffles'	★ ★ ★	★ ★ ★	★ ★ ★	★ ★	50cm	40cm	sun or shade, any soil	aphids	68
Hibiscus syriacus	★ ★ ★	★ ★ ★	★ ★		2.5m	2m	sun, well-drained soil	trouble-free	166
Hippophae rhamnoides	★ ★ ★	★ ★ ★	★ ★		4m	2m	sun, well-drained soil	trouble-free	196
Hosta	★ ★ ★	★ ★ ★	★ ★		60cm	60cm	sun or shade, moist soil	slugs and snails	69

★ in flower   ★ in flower with leaf   ★ in leaf

Plant	Spring	Summer	Autumn	Winter	Height	Spread	Cultivation	Pests/Disease	Page
Humulus lupulus 'Aureus'	★ ★ ★	★ ★ ★	★ ★ ★		3m	3m	sun, well-drained soil	trouble-free	132
Hyacinth 'Blue Jacket'	★ ★ ★				25cm	10cm	sun, well-drained soil	trouble-free	44
Hydrangea 'General Vicomtesse de Vibraye'	★ ★ ★	★ ★	★ ★ ★		2m	22m	sun, moist soil	trouble-free	167
Hydrangea paniculata 'Grandiflora'	★ ★ ★	★ ★	★ ★ ★		2m	22m	sun, well-drained soil	trouble-free	167
Hydrangea quercifolia	★ ★ ★	★ ★	★ ★ ★		1.2m	1.5m	sun, well-drained soil	trouble-free	167
Hypericum 'Hidcote'	★ ★ ★	★ ★	★ ★ ★		1.5m	1.5m	sun, well-drained soil	trouble-free	102
Ilex x altaclerensis 'Lawsoniana'	★ ★ ★	★ ★ ★	★ ★ ★	★ ★ ★	4m	3m	sun or shade, any soil	leaf miner	196
Ilex aquifolium	★ ★ ★	★ ★ ★	★ ★ ★	★ ★ ★	4m	3m	sun or shade, any soil	leaf miner	197
Ilex crenata 'Golden Gem'	★ ★ ★	★ ★ ★	★ ★ ★	★ ★ ★	1m	1.5m	sun or shade, any soil	trouble-free	197
Indigofera amblyantha	★ ★ ★	★ ★	★ ★ ★		2m	22m	sun, well-drained soil	trouble-free	149
Ipheion uniflorum 'Froyle Mill'	★ ★ ★			★	15cm	15cm	sun, well-drained soil	trouble-free	45
Iris – bearded	★ ★ ★	★ ★ ★	★ ★ ★	★ ★ ★	30-90cm	40cm	sun, well-drained soil	leaf spot	70
Iris foetidissima	★ ★ ★	★ ★ ★	★ ★ ★	★ ★ ★	70cm	40cm	shade, any soil	leaf spot	184
Iris – Pacific Coast	★ ★ ★	★ ★ ★	★ ★ ★	★ ★ ★	40cm	40cm	sun, well-drained soil	trouble-free	70
Iris – Siberian	★ ★ ★	★ ★	★ ★ ★		80cm	50cm	sun or shade, moist soil	trouble-free	70
Iris unguicularis	★ ★ ★	★ ★ ★	★ ★ ★	★ ★ ★	50cm	50cm	sun, dry soil	trouble-free	184
Itea ilicifolia	★ ★ ★	★ ★ ★	★ ★ ★	★ ★ ★	3m	2m	sun or shade, any soil	trouble-free	132
Jasminum nudiflorum	★ ★ ★	★ ★ ★	★ ★ ★	★ ★ ★	2m	2m	sun or shade, any soil	trouble-free	213
Jasminum officinale 'Fiona Sunrise'	★ ★ ★	★ ★ ★	★ ★		4m	2.5m	sun, well-drained soil	trouble-free	133
Juniperus chinensis x pfitzeriana 'Aurea'	★ ★ ★	★ ★ ★	★ ★ ★	★ ★ ★	90cm	2m	sun, well-drained soil	trouble-free	198
Juniperus squamata 'Blue Carpet'	★ ★ ★	★ ★ ★	★ ★ ★	★ ★ ★	40cm	1m	sun, well-drained soil	trouble-free	198
Kalmia latifollia 'Pink Charm'	★ ★ ★	★ ★ ★	★ ★ ★	★ ★ ★	1.5m	1m	sun, acid soil	trouble-free	103
Kerria japonica 'Pleniflora'	★ ★ ★	★ ★ ★	★ ★		2m	1m	sun or shade, any soil	trouble-free	29
Knautia macedonica	★ ★ ★	★ ★ ★	★ ★		80cm	50cm	sun, well-drained soil	trouble-free	71
Kniphofia 'Bressingham Comet'	★ ★ ★	★ ★ ★	★ ★		45cm	30cm	sun, well-drained soil	trouble-free	71
Kolkwitzia amabilis 'Pink Cloud'	★ ★ ★	★ ★ ★	★		3m	33m	sun, well-drained soil	trouble-free	103
Laburnum x watereri 'Vossii'	★ ★ ★	★ ★ ★	★		6m	4m	sun, well-drained soil	trouble-free	104
Lamium maculatum 'White Nancy'	★ ★ ★	★ ★ ★	★ ★ ★	★ ★ ★	15cm	45cm	sun or shade, moist soil	trouble-free	15
Lamium galeobdolon 'Hermann's Pride'	★ ★ ★	★ ★ ★	★ ★ ★	★ ★ ★	15cm	45cm	sun or shade, moist soil	trouble-free	15

★ in flower ★ in flower with leaf ★ in leaf

Plant	Spring	Summer	Autumn	Winter	Height	Spread	Cultivation	Pests/Disease	Page
Lamium orvala	★ ★ ★ ★ ★ ★ ★ ★				60cm	45cm	sun or shade, moist soil	trouble-free	16
Lathyrus latifolius	★ ★ ★ ★ ★ ★ ★ ★				2m	1.5m	sun, well-drained soil	trouble-free	133
Lathyrus odoratus	★ ★ ★ ★ ★ ★ ★				2m	1.5m	sun, fertile, moist soil	powdery mildew	134
Lathyrus vernus 'Alboroseus'	★ ★ ★ ★ ★ ★ ★				40cm	40cm	sun, well-drained soil	trouble-free	16
Laurus nobilis	★ ★ ★ ★ ★ ★ ★ ★ ★ ★ ★ ★				5m	3m	sun, well-drained soil	bay sucker, scale	104
Lavendula angustifolia 'Sawyers'	★ ★ ★ ★ ★ ★ ★ ★ ★ ★ ★				70cm	70cm	sun, well-drained soil	frog hopper	104
Lavendula stoechas	★ ★ ★ ★ ★ ★ ★ ★ ★ ★ ★				60cm	50cm	sun, well-drained soil	frog hopper	105
Lavatera x clementii 'Bredon Springs'	★ ★ ★ ★ ★ ★ ★ ★				2m	2m	sun, well-drained soil	trouble-free	105
Lavatera trimestris 'Silver Cup'	★ ★ ★ ★ ★ ★ ★ ★				80cm	40cm	sun, well-drained soil	trouble-free	121
Leucanthemum x superbum	★ ★ ★ ★ ★ ★ ★				60cm	80cm	sun, fertile, moist soil	trouble-free	72
Leucojeum vernum	★ ★ ★ ★				20cm	10cm	sun or shade, moist soil	trouble-free	45
Leptospermum scoparium 'Red Damask'	★ ★ ★ ★ ★ ★ ★ ★ ★ ★ ★				2m	2m	sun, well-drained soil	trouble-free	106
Leycesteria formosa	★ ★ ★ ★ ★ ★ ★ ★				2m	2m	sun or shade, most soil	trouble-free	106
Liatris spicata	★ ★ ★ ★ ★ ★ ★ ★				90cm	40cm	sun, well-drained soil	trouble-free	72
Ligularia dentata 'Britt-Marie Crawford'	★ ★ ★ ★ ★ ★ ★ ★				1m	1m	sun, moist soil	slugs and snails	72
Ligustrum lucidum 'Excelsum Superbum'	★ ★ ★ ★ ★ ★ ★ ★ ★ ★ ★				5m	3m	sun, well-drained soil	trouble-free	168
Ligustrum ovalifolium	★ ★ ★ ★ ★ ★ ★ ★ ★ ★ ★				2m	1.5m	sun, well-drained soil	trouble-free	198
Lilium 'African Queen'	★ ★ ★ ★ ★ ★ ★				1.5m	30cm	sun, fertile, moist soil	lily beetle	140
Lilium 'Casa Blanca'	★ ★ ★ ★ ★ ★ ★				1.5m	30cm	sun, fertile, moist soil	lily beetle	140
Lilium 'Grand Cru'	★ ★ ★ ★ ★ ★ ★				1m	30cm	sun, fertile, moist soil	lily beetle	139
Linaria maroccana 'Fairy Bouquet'	★ ★ ★ ★ ★				30cm	15cm	sun, well-drained soil	trouble-free	121
Liquidambar styraciflua	★ ★ ★ ★ ★ ★ ★ ★				20m	10m	sun, well-drained soil	trouble-free	168
Liriope muscari 'John Burch'	★ ★ ★ ★ ★ ★ ★ ★ ★ ★ ★				30cm	40m	sun or shade, any soil	trouble-free	149
Lobelia erinus 'Crystal Palace'	★ ★ ★ ★ ★ ★ ★				15cm	15cm	sun, well-drained soil	trouble-free	121
Lobelia siphilitica	★ ★ ★ ★ ★ ★ ★				70cm	30cm	sun, fertile, moist soil	trouble-free	73
Lonicera japonica 'Hall's Prolific'	★ ★ ★ ★ ★ ★ ★ ★ ★ ★ ★				3m	2m	sun, well-drained soil	trouble-free	134
Lonicera nitida	★ ★ ★ ★ ★ ★ ★ ★ ★ ★ ★				1.5m	1.5m	sun or shade, any soil	trouble-free	199
Lonicera pileata 'Silver Lining'	★ ★ ★ ★ ★ ★ ★ ★ ★ ★ ★				1m	1.5m	sun or shade, any soil	trouble-free	200
Lonicera purpusii	★ ★ ★ ★ ★ ★ ★ ★				1m	1.5m	sun or shade, any soil	trouble-free	199

★ in flower   ★ in flower with leaf   ★ in leaf

Profiled plants

Plant	Spring	Summer	Autumn	Winter	Height	Spread	Cultivation	Pests/Disease	Page
Lunaria annua 'Variegata'	★ ★ ★	★ ★ ★		★ ★ ★ ★	70cm	45cm	sun or shade, any soil	clubroot	122
Lupinus arboreus	★ ★ ★	★ ★ ★	★ ★ ★	★ ★ ★	2m	2m	sun, well-drained soil	lupin aphid	73
Lupin – Gallery 'The Page'	★ ★ ★	★ ★ ★	★ ★ ★		90cm	60cm	sun, well-drained soil	lupin aphid	73
Luzula sylvatica 'Aurea'	★ ★ ★	★ ★ ★	★ ★ ★	★ ★ ★	30cm	40cm	sun or shade, any soil	trouble-free	184
Lychnis chalcedonica	★ ★ ★	★ ★ ★	★ ★ ★		90cm	60cm	sun, well-drained soil	trouble-free	74
Lychnis coronaria	★ ★ ★	★ ★ ★	★ ★ ★	★ ★ ★	80cm	60cm	sun, well-drained soil	trouble-free	74
Lysimachia ciliata 'Fire Cracker'	★ ★ ★	★ ★ ★	★ ★ ★		80cm	60cm	sun, well-drained soil	trouble-free	75
Lysimachia nummularia 'Aurea'	★ ★ ★	★ ★ ★	★ ★ ★		10cm	60cm	sun/shade, moist soil	trouble-free	75
Lysimachia punctata 'Alexander'	★ ★ ★	★ ★ ★	★ ★ ★		80cm	60cm	sun, well-drained soil	trouble-free	74
Lythrum salicaria	★ ★ ★	★ ★ ★	★ ★ ★		80cm	60cm	sun, moist soil	trouble-free	75
Macleaya microcarpa 'Kelway's Coral Plume'	★ ★ ★	★ ★ ★	★ ★ ★		2m	1m	sun, well-drained soil	invasive	76
Malva moschata forma *alba*	★ ★ ★	★ ★ ★	★ ★ ★		70cm	50cm	sun, well-drained soil	trouble-free	76
Magnolia grandiflora	★ ★ ★	★ ★ ★	★ ★ ★	★ ★ ★	7m	5m	sun, well-drained soil	trouble-free	106
Magnolia stellata	★ ★ ★	★ ★ ★	★ ★ ★		2m	2m	sun/shade, moist soil	trouble-free	29
Magnolia x soulangeana	★ ★ ★	★ ★ ★	★ ★ ★		5m	4m	sun, moist, neutral soil	trouble-free	30
Magnolia 'Iolanthe'	★ ★ ★	★ ★ ★	★ ★ ★		5m	4m	sun, moist, neutral soil	trouble-free	30
Magnolia aquifolium	★ ★ ★	★ ★ ★	★ ★ ★	★ ★ ★	1m	1m	sun or shade, any soil	powdery mildew	201
Mahonia x media 'Charity'	★ ★ ★	★ ★ ★	★ ★ ★	★ ★ ★	2.5m	2m	sun or shade, any soil	trouble-free	200
Mahonia x wagneri	★ ★ ★	★ ★ ★	★ ★ ★	★ ★ ★	1m	1m	sun or shade, any soil	trouble-free	201
Malus 'Evereste'	★ ★ ★	★ ★ ★	★ ★ ★		5m	4m	sun, well-drained soil	trouble-free	169
Malus tschonoskii	★ ★ ★	★ ★ ★	★ ★ ★		5m	2m	sun, well-drained soil	trouble-free	169
Matteuccia struthiopteris	★ ★ ★	★ ★ ★	★ ★ ★		1m	70cm	sun/shade, moist soil	trouble-free	76
Meconopsis betonicifolia	★ ★ ★	★ ★ ★	★ ★ ★		1m	70cm	sun/shade, moist soil	trouble-free	77
Meconopsis cambrica	★ ★ ★	★ ★ ★	★ ★ ★		50cm	40cm	sun or shade, any soil	trouble-free	77
Melianthus major	★ ★ ★	★ ★ ★	★ ★ ★	★ ★ ★	2m	1m	sun, well-drained soil	frost-tender	149
Mentha suaveolens 'Variegata'	★ ★ ★	★ ★ ★	★ ★ ★		50cm	50cm	sun/shade, moist soil	trouble-free	77
Mimilus cardinalis	★ ★ ★	★ ★ ★	★ ★ ★		60cm	50cm	sun/shade, moist soil	trouble-free	78
Mirabilis jalapa	★ ★ ★	★ ★ ★	★ ★ ★		60cm	60cm	sun, well-drained soil	trouble-free	78
Miscanthus sinensis 'Cosmopolitan'	★ ★ ★	★ ★ ★	★ ★ ★	★	2m	1m	sun, moist soil	trouble-free	150

★ in flower ★ in flower with leaf ★ in leaf

Plant	Spring	Summer	Autumn	Winter	Height	Spread	Cultivation	Pests/Disease	Page
Monarda 'Beauty of Cobham'	★ ★ ★	★ ★ ★	★ ★		90cm	50cm	sun, fertile, moist soil	powdery mildew	78
Muscari 'Valerie Finnis'	★ ★ ★	★			15cm	10cm	sun, moist soil	trouble-free	45
Myosotis 'Blue Ball'	★ ★ ★		★ ★	★ ★ ★	20cm	20m	sun or shade, any soil	powdery mildew	38
Myrtus communis	★ ★ ★ ★	★ ★ ★	★ ★	★ ★	2m	1.5m	sun, well-drained soil	trouble-free	107
Nandina domestica	★ ★ ★ ★	★ ★ ★	★ ★	★ ★	2m	1.5m	sun, moist soil	trouble-free	169
Narcissus 'Ice Follies'	★ ★ ★				45cm	20cm	sun, well-drained soil	trouble-free	46
Narcissus dwarf 'Pipit'	★ ★ ★				30cm	10cm	sun, well-drained soil	trouble-free	46
Nemesia 'Blue Lagoon'	★ ★ ★	★ ★ ★	★ ★		30cm	20cm	sun, fertile, moist soil	trouble-free	122
Nepeta 'Six Hills Giant'	★ ★ ★	★ ★ ★	★		90cm	60cm	sun, well-drained soil	trouble-free	79
Nerine bowdenii	★ ★ ★		★ ★	★	45cm	10cm	sun, well-drained soil	trouble-free	180
Nerium oleander 'Petite Pink'	★ ★ ★ ★	★ ★ ★	★ ★	★	2m	1.5m	sun, well-drained soil	red spider mite	122
Nicotiana x sanderae	★ ★ ★	★ ★ ★	★ ★		50cm	30cm	sun, fertile, moist soil	mildew	123
Nicotiana sylvestris	★ ★ ★ ★	★ ★ ★	★		1.5m	50cm	sun, fertile, moist soil	trouble-free	123
Nigella damascena 'Persian Jewel'	★ ★ ★	★ ★			40cm	30cm	sun, well-drained soil	trouble-free	123
Oenothera fruticosa 'Fyverkeri'	★ ★ ★	★ ★ ★	★ ★		70cm	40cm	sun, well-drained soil	trouble-free	79
Oenothera speciosa 'Siskyou'	★ ★ ★	★ ★ ★	★ ★		30cm	40cm	sun, well-drained soil	trouble-free	79
Olearia macrodonta	★ ★ ★ ★	★ ★	★ ★	★ ★	3m	1.5m	sun, well-drained soil	trouble-free	107
Omphalodes cappadocica 'Starry Eyes'	★ ★ ★	★ ★ ★	★ ★		20cm	40cm	sun or shade, moist soil	trouble-free	16
Ophiopogon planiscapus 'Nigrescens'	★ ★ ★ ★	★ ★ ★	★ ★	★ ★	15cm	25cm	sun or shade, moist soil	trouble-free	185
Origanum laevigatum	★ ★ ★	★ ★ ★	★ ★		50cm	40cm	sun, well-drained soil	trouble-free	150
Origanum vulgare	★ ★ ★ ★	★ ★ ★	★		30cm	40cm	sun, well-drained soil	trouble-free	150
Osmanthus heterophyllus	★ ★ ★ ★	★ ★ ★	★ ★	★ ★	3m	2m	sun or shade, any soil	trouble-free	201
Osteospermum	★ ★ ★	★ ★ ★	★ ★		25–40cm	40cm	sun, well-drained soil	trouble-free	124
Paeonia 'Bowl of Beauty'	★ ★ ★	★ ★ ★	★ ★		80cm	45cm	sun, well-drained soil	peony blight	80
Paeonia lutea var. ludlowii	★ ★ ★	★ ★ ★	★ ★		2m	1m	sun, well-drained soil	trouble-free	108
Paeonia rockii	★ ★ ★	★ ★ ★	★ ★		1m	1m	sun, well-drained soil	trouble-free	108
Papaver commutatum	★ ★ ★	★ ★			80cm	30cm	sun, well-drained soil	trouble-free	125
Papaver nudicaule	★ ★ ★	★ ★ ★	★		60cm	20cm	sun, well-drained soil	trouble-free	81
Papaver orientale 'Patty's Plum'	★ ★ ★	★ ★ ★	★		60cm	60cm	sun, well-drained soil	trouble-free	80

★ in flower ★ in flower with leaf ★ in leaf

Profiled plants

Plant	Spring	Summer	Autumn	Winter	Height	Spread	Cultivation	Pests/Disease	Page
Papaver rhoeas 'Angels' Choir'	★ ★ ★ ★ ★ ★				70cm	30cm	sun, well-drained soil	trouble-free	124
Papaver somniferum var. *paeoniflorum*	★ ★ ★ ★ ★ ★				1m	30cm	sun, well-drained soil	trouble-free	124
Parottia persica	★ ★ ★ ★ ★ ★ ★ ★ ★ ★		★		3m	5m	sun, moist, acid soil	trouble-free	170
Parthenocissus henryana	★ ★ ★ ★ ★ ★ ★ ★ ★				8m	5m	sun or shade, any soil	trouble-free	177
Passiflora caerulea	★ ★ ★ ★ ★ ★ ★ ★ ★				5m	3m	sun, well-drained soil	trouble-free	134
Paulownia tomentosa	★ ★ ★ ★ ★ ★ ★ ★				10m	8m	sun, well-drained soil	frost kills flowers	30
Pelargonium crispum 'Variegatum'	★ ★ ★ ★ ★ ★ ★ ★ ★ ★ ★ ★				60cm	30cm	sun, well-drained soil	trouble-free	126
Pelargonium 'Frank Headley'	★ ★ ★ ★ ★ ★ ★ ★ ★ ★ ★ ★				60cm	30cm	sun, well-drained soil	trouble-free	125
Pelargonium 'Sensation'	★ ★ ★ ★ ★ ★ ★ ★ ★ ★ ★ ★				40cm	30cm	sun, well-drained soil	trouble-free	126
Pennisetum alopecuroides	★ ★ ★ ★ ★ ★ ★ ★ ★				60cm	60cm	sun, well-drained soil	slightly tender	151
Pennisetum setaceum 'Rubrum'	★ ★ ★ ★ ★ ★ ★ ★ ★				90cm	80cm	sun, well-drained soil	tender	151
Penstemon 'Pershore Pink Necklace'	★ ★ ★ ★ ★ ★ ★ ★ ★ ★ ★ ★				60cm	40cm	sun, well-drained soil	trouble-free	81
Perilla frutescens var. *crispa*	★ ★ ★ ★ ★ ★ ★				60cm	30cm	sun, well-drained soil	slightly tender	126
Perovskia atriplicifolia 'Blue Spire'	★ ★ ★ ★ ★ ★ ★ ★ ★				90cm	80cm	sun, well-drained soil	trouble-free	170
Persicaria affinis	★ ★ ★ ★ ★ ★ ★ ★				25cm	80cm	sun, well-drained soil	trouble-free	151
Persicaria campanulata	★ ★ ★ ★ ★ ★ ★ ★				80cm	80cm	sun or shade, any soil	trouble-free	152
Petunia 'Million Bells Terracotta'	★ ★ ★ ★ ★ ★ ★				20cm	20cm	sun, well-drained soil	trouble-free	127
Petunia 'Surfinia Series'	★ ★ ★ ★ ★ ★ ★				20cm	60cm	sun, well-drained soil	trouble-free	127
Phalaris arundinacea var. *Picta*	★ ★ ★ ★ ★ ★ ★ ★ ★				90cm	60cm	sun, well-drained soil	trouble-free	81
Philadelphus 'Belle Etoile'	★ ★ ★ ★ ★ ★ ★ ★ ★				1.2m	2m	sun or shade, any soil	trouble-free	108
Philadelphus coronarius 'Aureus'	★ ★ ★ ★ ★ ★ ★ ★ ★				2m	2m	sun or shade, any soil	trouble-free	109
Philadelphus microphyllus	★ ★ ★ ★ ★ ★ ★ ★ ★				1m	1.2m	sun, well-drained soil	trouble-free	109
Phlomis fruticosa	★ ★ ★ ★ ★ ★ ★ ★ ★ ★ ★ ★				1m	1m	sun, well-drained soil	trouble-free	110
Phlox paniculata 'Harlequin'	★ ★ ★ ★ ★ ★ ★ ★ ★				1m	60cm	sun, well-drained soil	eelworm, mildew	82
Phormium 'Yellow Wave'	★ ★ ★ ★ ★ ★ ★ ★ ★ ★ ★ ★				1.5m	2m	sun, well-drained soil	trouble-free	185
Photinia x fraseri 'Red Robin'	★ ★ ★ ★ ★ ★ ★ ★ ★ ★ ★ ★				3m	2m	sun or shade, any soil	trouble-free	31
Phygelius rectus 'Moonraker'	★ ★ ★ ★ ★ ★ ★ ★ ★				1m	80cm	sun, well-drained soil	trouble-free	152
Phyllostachys aurea	★ ★ ★ ★ ★ ★ ★ ★ ★ ★ ★ ★				3m	2m	sun/shade, moist soil	trouble-free	202
Physalis alkekengi	★ ★ ★ ★ ★ ★ ★ ★ ★				80cm	1m	sun, well-drained soil	invasive	153

★ in flower   ★ in flower with leaf   ★ in leaf

Plant	Spring	Summer	Autumn	Winter	Height	Spread	Cultivation	Pests/Disease	Page
Physocarpus opulifolius 'Diabolo'	★ ★ ★ ★ ★ ★ ★ ★				3m	2m	sun, well-drained soil	trouble-free	110
Physostegia virginiana 'Summer Snow'	★ ★ ★ ★ ★ ★ ★ ★				60cm	60cm	sun or shade, any soil	trouble-free	82
Picea breweriana	★ ★ ★ ★ ★ ★ ★ ★ ★ ★ ★ ★				10m	5m	sun, acid, moist soil	aphids	203
Picea glauca var. *albertiana*	★ ★ ★ ★ ★ ★ ★ ★ ★ ★ ★ ★				2m	1m	sun, acid or neutral soil	aphids	203
Picea oungens	★ ★ ★ ★ ★ ★ ★ ★ ★ ★ ★ ★				10m	5m	sun, acid or neutral soil	aphids	202
Pieris japonica 'Debutante'	★ ★ ★ ★ ★ ★ ★ ★ ★ ★ ★ ★				1m	1m	sun, acid, moist soil	trouble-free	31
Pinus mugo	★ ★ ★ ★ ★ ★ ★ ★ ★ ★ ★ ★				2m	2m	sun, well-drained soil	aphids, adelgids	203
Pinus sylvestris Aureus Group	★ ★ ★ ★ ★ ★ ★ ★ ★ ★ ★ ★				60m	4m	sun, well-drained soil	aphids, adelgids	204
Pinus wallichiana	★ ★ ★ ★ ★ ★ ★ ★ ★ ★ ★ ★				30m	5m	sun, well-drained soil	aphids, adelgids	204
Pittosporum tenuifolium	★ ★ ★ ★ ★ ★ ★ ★ ★ ★ ★ ★				30m	2m	sun, well-drained soil	trouble-free	204
Platycodon grandiflorum	★ ★ ★ ★ ★ ★ ★ ★				60cm	30cm	sun, well-drained soil	trouble-free	83
Pleioblastus viridistriatus	★ ★ ★ ★ ★ ★ ★ ★ ★ ★ ★ ★				1.2m	1m	sun, well-drained soil	invasive	83
Plumbago auriculata	★ ★ ★ ★ ★ ★ ★ ★				2m	1m	sun, well-drained soil	trouble-free	127
Polemonium caeruleum	★ ★ ★ ★ ★ ★ ★ ★				60cm	30cm	sun or shade, any soil	trouble-free	84
Polyanthus (primula)	★ ★ ★ ★ ★ ★ ★ ★				20cm	20cm	sun or shade, any soil	vine weevil	39
Polygonatum x hybridum	★ ★ ★ ★ ★ ★ ★ ★				60cm	40cm	sun or shade, any soil	sawfly	84
Polystichum aculeatum	★ ★ ★ ★ ★ ★ ★ ★ ★ ★ ★ ★				60cm	80cm	sun or shade, any soil	trouble-free	186
Poncirus trifoliata	★ ★ ★ ★ ★ ★ ★ ★				4m	4m	sun, well-drained soil	trouble-free	32
Potentilla 'Abbotswood'	★ ★ ★ ★ ★ ★ ★ ★				1m	1m	sun, well-drained soil	trouble-free	111
Potentilla 'William Rollison'	★ ★ ★ ★ ★ ★ ★ ★				40cm	60cm	sun or shade, any soil	sawfly	84
Primula denticulata	★ ★ ★ ★ ★ ★ ★ ★				30cm	20cm	sun/shade, moist soil	vine weevil	17
Primula florindae	★ ★ ★ ★ ★ ★ ★ ★				70cm	30cm	sun/shade, moist soil	vine weevil	17
Primula veris	★ ★ ★ ★ ★ ★ ★ ★				30cm	20cm	sun or shade, any soil	vine weevil	17
Primula vulgaris	★ ★ ★ ★ ★ ★ ★ ★				15cm	15cm	sun/shade, moist soil	vine weevil	18
Prunella grandiflora 'Pagoda'	★ ★ ★ ★ ★ ★ ★ ★				20cm	60cm	sun or shade, any soil	vine weevil	85
Prunus cerasifera 'Nigra'	★ ★ ★ ★ ★ ★ ★ ★				8m	6m	sun, any soil	trouble-free	32
Prunus 'Kanzan'	★ ★ ★ ★ ★ ★ ★ ★				8m	8m	sun, any soil	shot hole	33
Prunus 'Kursar'	★ ★ ★ ★ ★ ★ ★ ★				6m	4m	sun, any soil	trouble-free	32
Prunus laurocerasus	★ ★ ★ ★ ★ ★ ★ ★ ★ ★ ★ ★				5m	4m	sun/shade, not chalk	trouble-free	206

★ in flower ★ in flower with leaf ★ in leaf

Plant	Spring	Summer	Autumn	Winter	Height	Spread	Cultivation	Pests/Disease	Page
Pseudopanax lessonii 'Gold Splash'					3m	2m	sun, well-drained soil	trouble-free	206
Pulmonaria 'Occupol' (Opal)					25cm	30cm	sun/shade, moist soil	powdery mildew	18
Pulmonaria rubra					20cm	30cm	sun/shade, moist soil	powdery mildew	18
Pulmonaria angustifolia					25cm	30cm	sun/shade, moist soil	powdery mildew	19
Pulsatilla vulgaris					25cm	30cm	sun, well-drained soil	powdery mildew	19
Pyracantha 'Saphyr'					3m	2m	sun/shade, any soil	trouble-free	171
Ranunculus aconitifolius					60cm	45cm	sun/shade, moist soil	trouble-free	85
Ranunculus ficaria var. *aurantiacus*					10cm	10cm	sun/shade, any soil	invasive	47
Rehmannia elata					90cm	40cm	sun, well-drained soil	trouble-free	153
Rhododendron 'Pink Pearl'					3m	3m	sun/shade, acid soil	bud blast	33
Rhododendron 'Percy Wiseman'					1m	1m	sun/shade, acid soil	bud blast	34
Rhododendron – Japanese azalea					1.2m	1.2m	sun/shade, acid soil	leafy gall	34
Rhododendron – deciduous azalea					1.2m	1.2m	sun/shade, acid soil	trouble-free	34
Rhodohypoxis baurii					10cm	10cm	sun, moist, acid soil	trouble-free	85
Rhus typhina 'Dissecta'					4m	4m	sun, well-drained soil	suckers freely	171
Ribes x *gordonianum*					2m	2m	sun/shade, any soil	trouble-free	35
Ribes sanguineum 'Brocklebankii'					1m	1m	sun/shade, any soil	trouble-free	35
Ricinus communis 'Carmencita'					1.8m	1m	sun, well-drained soil	poisonous	128
Robinia pseudoacacia 'Frisia'					10m	5m	sun, well-drained soil	trouble-free	111
Rodgersia pinnata 'Superba'					1.2m	70cm	sun/shade, moist soil	trouble-free	86
Romneya coulteri					1.2m	1m	sun, well-drained soil	invasive	86
Rosa glauca					2m	2m	sun, any soil	aphids	112
Rosa rugosa					2m	2m	sun, any soil	aphids	172
Rosa 'Albertine'					3m	3m	sun, any soil	aphids, black spot	135
Rosa 'Geranium'					2.5m	2m	sun, any soil	aphids	172
Rosa 'Golden Wings'					1m	80cm	sun, any soil	aphids, black spot	112
Rosa 'Madame Gregoire Stachelin'					3m	3m	sun, any soil	aphids, black spot	135
Rosmarinus officinalis					1.2m	1m	sun, well-drained soil	trouble-free	35
Rubus cockburnianus					2m	2m	sun/shade, any soil	trouble-free	207

★ in flower   ★ in flower with leaf   ★ in leaf

Plant	Spring	Summer	Autumn	Winter	Height	Spread	Cultivation	Pests/Disease	Page
Rudbeckia fulgida var. *sullivantii*	☆ ☆ ☆ ☆	★ ★ ★	★ ★		80cm	70cm	sun, well-drained soil	trouble-free	153
Rudbeckia 'Herbstsonne'	☆ ☆ ☆ ☆	☆ ★	★ ★		2m	1m	sun, well-drained soil	trouble-free	154
Ruscus aculeatus	☆ ☆ ★ ☆	☆ ☆ ☆	☆ ☆	☆ ☆	1m	60cm	sun/shade, any soil	trouble-free	186
Salix alba var. *vitellina*	☆ ☆ ☆ ☆	☆ ☆ ☆	☆ ☆		15m	6m	sun, moist or wet soil	sawfly	207
Salix 'Erythroflexuosa'	☆ ☆ ☆ ☆	☆ ☆ ☆	☆ ☆		5m	5m	sun, moist or wet soil	sawfly	207
Salvia guaranitica	☆ ☆ ☆ ☆	☆ ☆ ★	★ ★		2m	1m	sun, well-drained soil	trouble-free/frost	154
Salvia patens	☆ ☆ ☆ ★	★ ★ ★	★		60cm	40cm	sun, well-drained soil	trouble-free/frost	154
Salvia uliginosa	☆ ☆ ☆ ☆	☆ ☆ ★	★		2m	1m	sun, moist soil	trouble-free	155
Sambucus nigra 'Black Beauty'	☆ ☆ ☆ ★	☆ ☆ ☆	☆		5m	4m	sun, any soil	trouble-free	114
Sambucus racemosa 'Sutherland Gold'	☆ ☆ ★ ☆	☆ ☆ ☆	☆		3m	3m	sun/shade, any soil	trouble-free	114
Santolina chamaecyparissus	☆ ☆ ☆ ★	★ ☆ ☆	☆ ☆	☆ ☆	50cm	50cm	sun, well-drained soil	trouble-free	114
Sarcococca hookeriana var. *digyna*	☆ ☆ ☆ ☆	☆ ☆ ☆	☆ ☆	★ ★	1.5m	1.2m	sun or shade, moist soil	trouble-free	208
Saxifraga x *urbium*	☆ ☆ ★ ☆	☆ ☆ ☆	☆ ☆	☆ ☆	30cm	60cm	sun/shade, any soil	trouble-free	19
Scabiosa atropurpurea 'Chilli Sauce'	☆ ☆ ☆ ★	★ ★ ★	★		80cm	30cm	sun, well-drained soil	short-lived	87
Scabiosa 'Butterfly Blue'	☆ ☆ ★ ★	★ ★ ☆	☆		40cm	40cm	sun, well-drained soil	mildew	87
Scilla sibirica	☆ ★ ☆				30cm	60cm	sun/shade, any soil	trouble-free	47
Schizostylis coccinea 'Jennifer'	☆ ☆ ☆ ☆	☆ ★ ★	★ ★	☆ ☆	60cm	40cm	sun, moist soil	trouble-free	155
Sedum 'Herbstfreude'	☆ ☆ ☆ ☆	☆ ☆ ★	★ ★		60cm	60cm	sun, well-drained soil	vine weevil	155
Sedum spathulifolium	☆ ☆ ★ ★	☆ ☆ ☆	☆ ☆	☆ ☆	10cm	60cm	sun, well-drained soil	vine weevil	87
Sempervivum arachnoideum	☆ ☆ ★ ★	★ ☆ ☆	☆ ☆	☆ ☆	15cm	40cm	sun, well-drained soil	vine weevil	186
Senecio cineraria 'Silver Dust'	☆ ☆ ☆ ★	★ ★ ☆	☆ ☆	☆ ☆	30cm	30cm	sun, well-drained soil	trouble-free	88
Senecio viravira	☆ ☆ ☆ ★	★ ★ ☆	☆ ☆	☆ ☆	1m	60cm	sun, well-drained soil	trouble-free	88
Sidalcea 'Elsie Heugh'	☆ ☆ ★ ★	☆ ★ ☆	☆		80cm	40cm	sun, well-drained soil	trouble-free	88
Sisyrinchium striatum 'Aunt May'	☆ ☆ ★ ★	★ ☆ ☆	☆ ☆	☆ ☆	50cm	30cm	sun, well-drained soil	trouble-free	89
Skimmia japonica 'Rubella'	★ ★ ☆ ☆	☆ ☆ ☆	☆ ☆	☆ ☆	1.2m	1.5m	sun/shade, acid soil	trouble-free	208
Solanum crispum	☆ ☆ ☆ ★	★ ★ ★	☆		4m	3m	sun, well-drained soil	trouble-free	136
Solidago 'Goldenmosa'	☆ ☆ ☆ ☆	☆ ★ ★	★ ☆		70cm	40cm	sun, well-drained soil	mildew	155
Sorbus cashmeriana	☆ ☆ ★ ☆	☆ ☆ ☆	☆		7m	6m	sun, fertile soil	trouble-free	173
Sorbus hupehensis	☆ ☆ ★ ☆	☆ ☆ ☆	☆		7m	6m	sun, fertile soil	trouble-free	172

★ in flower   ★ in flower with leaf   ☆ in leaf

Plant	Height	Spread	Cultivation	Pests/Disease	Page
Sorbus 'Joseph Rock'	8m	5m	sun, fertile soil	fireblight	172
Spartium junceum	3m	2m	sun, well-drained soil	trouble-free	115
Spiraea japonica 'Goldflame'	75cm	75cm	sun, any soil	trouble-free	115
Spiraea prunifolia	1.5m	1.5m	sun, any soil	trouble-free	36
Stachys macrantha 'Superba'	50cm	40cm	sun, well-drained soil	trouble-free	89
Stachyrus praecox	3m	2m	sun, well-drained soil	trouble-free	115
Sternbergia lutea	15cm	10cm	sun, well-drained soil	trouble-free	180
Stipa arundinacea	75cm	75cm	sun, any soil	trouble-free	156
Stipa gigantea	2m	1m	sun, well-drained soil	trouble-free	156
Stipa tenuissima	60cm	30cm	sun, well-drained soil	trouble-free	157
Stokesia laevis	60cm	45cm	sun, well-drained soil	slugs and snails	89
Strobilanthes attenuata	1.2m	80cm	sun, well-drained soil	trouble-free	89
Symphytum 'Goldsmith'	30cm	30cm	sun, moist, fertile soil	trouble-free	90
Syringa 'Charles Joly'	5m	4m	sun, well-drained soil	trouble-free	37
Tagetes 'Lemon Gem'	30cm	30cm	sun, well-drained soil	trouble-free	128
Tamarix tetranda	3m	3m	sun, well-drained soil	trouble-free	37
Taxus baccata 'Fastigiata'	8m	2m	sun/shade, any soil	trouble-free	156
Teucrium fruticans	1m	1.5m	sun, well-drained soil	trouble-free	115
Teucrium scorodonia 'Crispum'	40cm	60cm	sun/shade, any soil	trouble-free	116
Thalictrum delavayi 'Hewitt's Double'	1.5m	3m	sun, well-drained soil	slugs and snails	90
Thymus pulegeoides	20cm	40cm	sun, well-drained soil	trouble-free	116
Tolmeia menziesii 'Taff's Gold'	50cm	40cm	sun/shade, any soil	trouble-free	20
Trachelospermum jasminoides	8m	4m	sun, well-drained soil	trouble-free	177
Trachycarpus fortunei	8m	2m	sun, well-drained soil	trouble-free	209
Tradescantia 'Concorde Grape'	45cm	60cm	sun, well-drained soil	trouble-free	91
Tricyrtis formosana	80cm	40cm	sun/shade, moist soil	trouble-free	157
Trillium grandiflorum	40cm	50cm	sun/shade, moist soil	slugs and snails	20
Trollius x cultorum 'Orange Globe'	60cm	40cm	sun/shade, moist soil	mildew	91
Tropaeolum majus 'Alaska'	20cm	20cm	sun, well-drained soil	caterpillars, aphids	129

★ in flower   ★ in flower with leaf   ★ in leaf

Plant	Spring	Summer	Autumn	Winter	Height	Spread	Cultivation	Pests/Disease	Page
Tropaeolum peregrinum	☆☆	★★★	★★★		1.5m	1.5m	sun, well-drained soil	caterpillars, aphids	129
Tulipa 'Apeldoorn'	☆☆★	☆			50cm	10cm	sun, well-drained soil	tulip fire	48
Tulipa tarda	☆★★	☆			10cm	15cm	sun, well-drained soil	trouble-free	48
Uncinia egmontiana	☆☆☆★	☆☆☆	☆☆☆	☆	30cm	30cm	sun, well-drained soil	trouble-free	158
Verbascum bombyciferum	☆☆★	★☆☆	☆☆☆	☆	2m	60cm	sun, well-drained soil	mullein moth	91
Verbascum 'Helen Johnson'	☆☆★	★★☆	☆☆☆	☆	80cm	40cm	sun, well-drained soil	mullein moth	92
Verbena bonariensis	☆☆	★★★	★★		1.5m	60cm	sun, well-drained soil	trouble-free	130
Verbena 'Quartz Burgundy'	☆☆	★★★	★★		25cm	40cm	sun, well-drained soil	mildew	130
Vernonia crinata	☆☆	☆☆☆	★★★		2m	60cm	sun, moist soil	slugs and snails	158
Veronica spicata 'Silver Carpet'	☆☆★	★★★	★☆		30cm	40cm	sun, well-drained soil	mildew	92
Veronicastrum virginicum	☆☆☆	★★★	☆☆		1.5m	50cm	sun, well-drained soil	mildew	158
Viburnum x burkwoodii	☆★★	☆☆☆	☆☆☆	☆☆	2m	2m	sun, well-drained soil	trouble-free	37
Viburnum davidii	☆☆★	☆☆☆	☆☆☆	☆☆	1m	1.5m	sun/shade, any soil	trouble-free	210
Viburnum rhytidophyllum	☆☆★	☆☆☆	☆☆☆	☆☆	3m	3m	sun/shade, any soil	trouble-free	210
Viburnum tinus	★☆☆	☆☆☆	☆☆★	★★	2m	2m	sun/shade, any soil	viburnum beetle	209
Vinca minor 'Illumination'	☆★★	☆☆☆	☆☆☆	☆☆	25cm	60cm	sun/shade, any soil	trouble-free	20
Vinca major 'Maculata'	☆★★	☆☆☆	☆☆☆	☆☆	45cm	1m	sun/shade, any soil	trouble-free	21
Vinca difformis 'Jenny Pim'	★★★	☆☆☆	☆☆☆	☆★	45cm	60cm	sun/shade, any soil	trouble-free	21
Viola	☆★★	★☆☆	★★☆	☆☆	15cm	20cm	sun/shade, any soil	mildew/aphids	39
Vitis vinifera 'Purpurea'	☆☆★	☆★☆	★★		2.5m	2.5m	sun, well-drained soil	mildew	178
Weigela 'Briant Rubidor'	☆☆★	★★☆	☆☆		1.5m	1.5m	sun, well-drained soil	trouble-free	116
Wisteria sinensis 'Prolific'	☆☆★	★☆☆	☆☆		6m	6m	sun, well-drained soil	trouble-free	40
Yucca filamentosa 'Bright Edge'	☆☆☆★	★★★	☆☆☆	☆	80cm	50cm	sun, well-drained soil	trouble-free	174
Yucca flaccida 'Ivory'	☆☆☆★	★★★	☆☆☆	☆	60cm	60cm	sun, well-drained soil	trouble-free	174
Yucca gloriosa	☆☆☆★	★★★	☆☆☆	☆	1.5m	1.5m	sun, well-drained soil	trouble-free	175
Zantedeschia aethiopica	☆★★	★☆☆	☆☆		1m	70cm	sun, moist soil	trouble-free	92
Zauschneria californica 'Garrettii'	☆☆☆	☆☆★	★★		45cm	60cm	sun, well-drained soil	trouble-free	175
Zinnia 'Dreamland Red'	☆☆☆	★★★	★☆		30cm	30cm	sun, well-drained soil	trouble-free	130

★ in flower   ★ in flower with leaf   ☆ in leaf

Planting notes

A garden is constantly evolving and each year is different. Use the space on these pages to note down when plants are looking their best, which combinations have worked and which have not, and new plants you would like to try out.

Spring

Plants grow and flower rapidly in spring. Every week the garden looks different.